D1570771

JOE JACKSON

JOE JACKSON

A BIOGRAPHY

KELLY BOYER SAGERT

BASEBALL'S ALL-TIME GREATEST HITTERS

GREENWOOD PRESS
WESTPORT, CONNECTICUT • LONDON

Library of Congress Cataloging-in-Publication Data

Sagert, Kelly Boyer.
    Joe Jackson : a biography / Kelly Boyer Sagert.
        p. cm.—(Baseball's all-time greatest hitters)
    Includes bibliographical references and index.
    ISBN 0–313–32961–3 (alk. paper)
    1. Jackson, Joe, 1888–1951. 2. Baseball players—United States—Biography. I. Title.
II. Series.
    GV865.J29S34   2004
    796.357'092—dc22   2004048555
    [B]

British Library Cataloguing in Publication Data is available.

Library of Congress Catalog Card Number: 2004048555
ISBN: 0–313–32961–3

First published in 2004

Greenwood Press, 88 Post Road West, Westport, CT 06881
An imprint of Greenwood Publishing Group, Inc.
www.greenwood.com

Printed in the United States of America

The paper used in this book complies with the
Permanent Paper Standard issued by the National
Information Standards Organization (Z39.48–1984).

10 9 8 7 6 5 4 3 2 1

To my father, Tom, who took me to my first Cleveland Indians game in 1971—and who took me to many, many more, after that. To my husband, Don, for his patience and understanding. To my son, Ryan, whose artistry with the written word amazes me, and to my son, Adam, whose love of colors inspires me.

CONTENTS

Contents

SERIES FOREWORD

The volumes in Greenwood's "Baseball's All-Time Greatest Hitters" series present the life stories of the players who, through their abilities to hit for average, for power, or for both, most helped their teams at the plate. Much thought was given to the players selected for inclusion in this series. In some cases, the selection of certain players was a given. **Ty Cobb**, **Rogers Hornsby**, and **Joe Jackson** hold the three highest career averages in baseball history: .367, .358, and .356, respectively. **Babe Ruth**, who single-handedly brought the sport out of its "dead ball" era and transformed baseball into a home-run hitters game, hit 714 home runs (a record that stood until 1974) while also hitting .342 over his career. **Lou Gehrig**, now known primarily as the man whose consecutive-games record Cal Ripken Jr. broke in 1995, hit .340 and knocked in more than 100 runs eleven seasons in a row, totaling 1,995 before his career was cut short by ALS. **Ted Williams**, the last man in either league to hit .400 or better in a season (.406 in 1941), is widely regarded as possibly the best hitter ever, a man whose fanatical dedication raised hitting to the level of both science and art.

Two players set career records that, for many, define the art of hitting. **Hank Aaron** set career records for home runs (755) and RBIs (2,297). He also maintained a .305 career average over twenty-three seasons, a remarkable feat for someone primarily known as a home-run hitter. **Pete Rose** had ten seasons with 200 or more hits and won three batting titles on his way to establishing his famous record of 4,256 career hits. Some critics have claimed that both players' records rest more on longevity than excellence. To that I would say there is something to be said about longevity and, in both cases, the player's excellence was the reason why he had the opportunity to keep playing, to keep tallying hits for his team. A base hit is the mark of a successful plate appearance; a home run is the apex of an at-bat. Accordingly, we could hardly have a series titled "Baseball's All-Time Greatest Hitters" without including the two men who set the career records in these categories.

Joe DiMaggio holds another famous mark: fifty-six consecutive games in which he obtained a base hit. Many have called this baseball's most unbreakable record. (The player who most closely approached that mark was Pete Rose, who hit safely in forty-four consecutive games in 1978.) In his thirteen seasons, DiMaggio hit .325 with 361 home runs and 1,537 RBIs. This means he *averaged* 28 home runs and 118 RBIs per season. MVPs have been awarded to sluggers in various years with lesser stats than what DiMaggio achieved in an "average" season.

Because **Stan Musial** played his entire career with the Cardinals in St. Louis—once considered the western frontier of the baseball world in the days before baseball came to California—he did not receive the press of a DiMaggio. But Musial complied a career average of .331, with 3,630 hits (ranking fourth all time) and 1,951 RBIs (fifth all time). His hitting prowess was so respected around the league that Brooklyn Dodgers fans once dubbed him "The Man," a nickname he still carries today.

Willie Mays was a player who made his fame in New York City and then helped usher baseball into the modern era when he moved with the Giants to San Francisco. Mays did everything well and with flair. His over-the-shoulder catch in the 1954 World Series was perhaps his most famous moment, but his hitting was how Mays most tormented his opponents. Over twenty-two seasons the "Say Hey Kid" hit .302 and belted 660 home runs.

Only four players have reached the 600-home-run milestone: Mays, Aaron, Ruth, and **Barry Bonds**, who achieved that feat in 2002. Bonds, the only active player included in this series, broke the single-season home-run record when he smashed 73 for the San Francisco Giants in 2001. In the 2002 National League Championship Series, St. Louis Cardinals pitchers were so leery of pitching to him that they walked him ten times in twenty-one plate appearances. In the World Series, the Anaheim Angels walked him thirteen times in thirty appearances. He finished the Series with a .471 batting average, an on-base percentage of .700, and a slugging percentage of 1.294.

As with most rankings, this series omits some great names. Jimmie Foxx, Tris Speaker, and Tony Gwynn would have battled for a hypothetical thirteenth volume. And it should be noted that this series focuses on players and their performance within Major League Baseball; otherwise, sluggers such as Josh Gibson from the Negro Leagues and Japan's Sadaharu Oh would have merited consideration.

There are names such as Cap Anson, Ed Delahanty, and Billy Hamilton who appear high up on the list of career batting average. However, a number of these players played during the late 1800s, when the rules of baseball were drastically different. For example, pitchers were not allowed to throw overhand until 1883, and foul balls weren't counted as strikes until 1901 (1903 in the American League). Such players as Anson and company undeniably were the stars of their day, but baseball has evolved greatly since then, into a game in which hitters must now cope with night games, relief pitchers, and split-fingered fastballs.

Ultimately, a list of the "greatest" anything is somewhat subjective, but Greenwood offers these players as twelve of the finest examples of hitters throughout history. Each volume focuses primarily on the playing career of the subject: his early years in school, his years in semi-pro and/or minor league baseball, his entrance into the majors, and his ascension to the status of a legendary hitter. But even with the greatest of players, baseball is only part of the story, so the player's life before and after baseball is given significant consideration. And because no one can exist in a vacuum, the authors often take care to recreate the cultural and historical contexts of the time—an approach that is especially relevant to the multidisciplinary ways in which sports are studied today.

Batter up.

ROB KIRKPATRICK
GREENWOOD PUBLISHING

ACKNOWLEDGMENTS

Many thanks to the librarians at the Lorain Public Library. As always, I appreciate your patience, your knowledge, your resources and, perhaps most important, your support.

I would also like to thank Gene Carney, the "Notes from the Shadows of Cooperstown" columnist, for his willingness to help me analyze and dissect some of the most confounding aspects of the Black Sox Scandal, as well as Mike Nola, creator and keeper of "Shoeless Joe Jackson's Virtual Hall of Fame" flame, for his endlessly helpful supply of knowledge and relevant resources.

I thank Tom Perry, author of *Textile League Baseball*, for his explanation of mill town baseball and Tom Simon, chair of the Society for American Baseball Research's Deadball Era Committee, for his elucidation of the dead ball era. Many thanks, too, to the National Baseball Hall of Fame and Museum, and the Cleveland Public Library, for their assistance in photo selection.

Finally, my gratitude to Clay Reynolds, Professor of Literary Studies at the University of Texas at Dallas and fellow baseball fan, for his honest assessments, clear and concise editing suggestions, and encouragement through the rough spots.

Clichés are sometimes true, and this one is—I couldn't have done it without you!

CHRONOLOGY

1888 Born Joseph Jefferson Wofford Jackson in Pickens County, South Carolina, on July 16.

1894 Moves to Brandon Mill, South Carolina, where he begins working at the cotton mill at the age of 6.

1901 Begins, at the age of 13, to play on the Brandon Mill men's baseball team, where he hits and handles a ball as well as—or perhaps even better than—the adults in the league.

1908 Earns the nickname of "Shoeless Joe" after playing a game in his stocking feet, due to blisters raised from a pair of new spikes.

1908 The Philadelphia Athletics, managed by Connie Mack, acquire Jackson. His performance is sporadic, leading some to believe that Jackson is not big league material.

1910 Philadelphia trades Jackson to the Cleveland Indians.

1911 Jackson posts a rookie record .408 batting average and gains the attention and admiration of fellow major leaguers, managers, and fans.

1915 Cleveland trades Jackson to the Chicago White Sox.

1917 Jackson bats .307 in the World Series, helping his team beat the New York Giants.

1918   Jackson spends several months working at a shipyard in Delaware to support the war effort.

1919   Jackson plays in the 1919 World Series against the Cincinnati Reds, amid rumors of a game-fixing scheme in collusion with gamblers. He bats .375, setting a World Series record for number of hits (12) and plays errorless ball, although the White Sox lose the series.

1920   Jackson testifies about the fix of the 1919 World Series in front of a Chicago Grand Jury and is subsequently suspended from his team. This action gives rise to the poignant "Say It Ain't So, Joe" myth.

1921   Jackson is acquitted on charges of conspiracy, but is nevertheless banned from professional baseball for life by the first Commissioner of Baseball, Judge Kenesaw Mountain Landis.

1922   Jackson begins playing "outlaw ball" around the country.

1924   Sues Chicago White Sox owner Charles Comiskey for back pay, but ends up briefly jailed for perjury.

1942   Tells his side of the 1919 World Series scandal in a newspaper article published by Carter "Scoop" Latimer.

1949   Again tells his story, this time in Furman Bisher's article, "This Is the Truth."

1951   Jackson is inducted into the Cleveland Baseball Hall of Fame, and invited to appear on a national television show, "Toast of the Town," on December 16.

1951   Dies after a heart attack on December 5 and is buried in Woodlawn Memorial Park.

1969   Jackson is inducted into the South Carolina Athletic Hall of Fame.

1980   Jackson is inducted into the Ohio Baseball Hall of Fame.

1995   Jackson is inducted into the Pennsylvania Baseball Sports Hall of Fame.

1998   Hall-of-Famers Ted Williams and Bob Feller petition for Jackson's reinstatement into professional baseball and induction into the National Baseball Hall of Fame and Museum.

2001   Jackson's bat, Black Betsy, is sold for $577,610, nearly double the price of any other bat sold before mid-2004.

2004   Former Cincinnati Reds player, Pete Rose, who had long denied charges of betting on baseball that had gotten him banned from the sport, confesses his guilt in hopes that this admission would qualify him for Hall of Fame status. How this confession will affect Jackson's potential induction remains uncertain.

INTRODUCTION

Baseball lives in a realm halfway between religious metaphor—with its themes of redemption, conversion, faith and doubt—and superstition.
—John Spaulding[1]

We tend to label baseball players as either saints or sinners, and nowhere can this myth-making phenomenon—with faith and doubt, sin and redemption serving as its backdrop—be better illustrated than with the extraordinary story of "Shoeless" Joe Jackson. Born to illiterate sharecropper parents in 1888, Jackson appeared destined for a hardscrabble, hand-to-mouth existence of poverty and grueling manual labor. Nothing in his early life belied that presumption. After his family moved to Brandon Mill, South Carolina, when Joe was only six, he began working in the cotton mill, foregoing school entirely. Life-sapping textile dust and deafening din surrounded him, and his days were filled with drudgery, broken only by the weekly game of baseball played on a dirt field near the mill. It was there, on the diamond, that family, friends, and coworkers began to glimpse a special talent in young Joe Jackson—the ability to hit and handle a baseball as well as, or perhaps even better than, adult ballplayers throughout the greater Greenville region.

Invited to join the Brandon Mill men's baseball team at the age of thirteen, Jackson spent several glorious seasons of sun-filled Saturdays on the ballfield as his batting prowess prompted admiring spectators to cheer and toss him coins—and impelled baseball managers of rival mill towns to lure him away to play for their teams. From all accounts, Jackson would have been content to remain in South Carolina, working in the mill during the week and playing Saturday ball. However, his exceptional skill caught the attention of scouts who roamed the region in search of unusual talent. They brought his name to the now-legendary major league manager, Connie Mack; in 1908, Jackson was unwillingly separated from the predictable rhythm of his former lifestyle when he was acquired by Mack's Philadelphia Athletics.

Jackson, a man born to the type of rural existence where men plowed fields with mules and women cooked meals and washed clothes over wood fires, where horses served as transportation and electric lights and indoor plumbing were unheard of, suddenly found himself surrounded by air filled with auto exhaust fumes and a cacophony of immigrant languages, in a city where hastily ordered meals were eaten at greasy spoon restaurants. Unable to read or write, he was thrust into a fast-paced world that was increasingly relying upon the written word as communication. He was a stranger in a strange land, a confused youth without any real support or guiding mentor, lonely for his encouraging bride, Katie Jackson. He couldn't even read Katie's letters without assistance, and he wasn't sure whom to trust to read them.

He also faced the difficulties inherent in being a gifted young ballplayer from the south in the presence of veteran players from northern states. The bitter bloodbath of the Civil War still existed in the living memory of many people, and anti-southern prejudices combined with the natural fear that he might replace them on the A's roster caused his teammates to shun him. Extremely talented but unable to adjust to life in the teeming city, Jackson appeared to stumble and fall more than once, succumbing to the sociological and psychological pressures surrounding him. Jackson was twice sent down to minor league ballclubs and three times he even abandoned his ambitions and fled back to Greenville.

Even so, Jackson finally passed through this trial by fire to confirm his true calling as a major league ballplayer. In 1910, he was traded to Cleveland, where he began to establish his reputation as a player whose deeds would far exceed anyone's expectations. He soon surpassed the accomplishments of any other rookie, before or since. During the 1910 season, Jackson batted .408, becoming the only rookie to ever bat .400 or above. Two years after being traded to the Chicago White Sox, he contributed to that club's 1917 World Series title. Managers, sportswriters, fans, and fellow baseball players alike took note of and paid tribute to this unlikely star. The life story of Shoeless Joe Jackson appeared ready to be included in the annals of a hero's journey. But then, Jackson's career, along with his promise and potential, was derailed by the most familiar of temptations—easy money.

In September 1919, Jackson was offered a cash payoff to assist other players in ensuring a White Sox loss to Cincinnati in the upcoming World Series. The offer came from a teammate who was in collusion with gamblers. According to Eliot Asinof, best known for his book *Eight Men Out*, "Seductive operators with flashy styles, sharp men who knew the best places in town, they would offer the visiting players something to do, bathe them in flattery, speak the right language, always with a full measure of respect."[2] These gamblers intended to place bets on the "fixed" Series, sure of their chances to win easy money.

Although the gamblers' overtures to the players could be slick and smooth, the game-fixing scheme itself was far from polished. Dubbed the "Black Sox Scandal" by the popular press, writer John Lardner labeled it "the biggest, sloppiest, crudest fix of a sporting event that ever was known to man. It was a makeshift job, compounded in equal parts of bluff and welsh and cold gall, with no contributor or agent-contributor knowing what the man next to him was up to, and very seldom bothering to find out."[3]

Joe Jackson's precise role in the confusing swirl of events surrounding the "Black Sox" affair remains a source of controversial debate, but after a close examination of the facts that can be verified, it's possible to determine with some confidence what he did or did not do and why, as well as place the scandal into the context of Jackson's overall life. The best that can be offered, though, is hindsight. Because the actual motives and personal feelings of the principals involved can never be determined, there will always be speculation over the deeper facts of the matter.

In 1920, as suspicions of game-fixing rose, Jackson, along with seven of his teammates, was suspended from his team. Because there was no Illinois law prohibiting the intentional loss of a game, even if money was exchanged as part of the deal, he was cleared of charges of conspiracy. The newly appointed commissioner of baseball, Judge Kenesaw Mountain Landis, nevertheless banned Jackson and his accused cohorts from Organized Baseball for life.

For a while after his banishment, Jackson lived an almost underworld existence, playing baseball outside the reach of the major leagues, often under a false name. Because he was publicly disgraced, Jackson's legendary reputation no longer appeared entirely credible. At best, he was a fallen hero.

However, in classical terms, a fallen hero can be redeemed if it is shown that he was tempted but overcame the urge to succumb; or that he fell to temptation but then actively and purposefully redeemed himself. Both arguments have been made in regards to Jackson's role in the "Black Sox" scandal.

Some recent Jackson supporters claim that he never really fell to the temptation to throw any games. They claim that he was an innocent victim of evil forces at work in Chicago in 1919. Close assessment of the known facts suggests that such an explanation is too simple; surely the issue of his role, no matter if it was minor or something more substantial, was more complicated than that. But does that preclude the possibility of his redemption?

It is possible to perceive Jackson as redeeming himself and his reputation during his post–major league years; even though professional baseball had banished him forever, he never abandoned the sport that he loved. Humiliated by Commissioner Landis' ban, prohibited from competing in the professional arena, and unable to participate in the sport at the level of his abilities, he continued to play "outlaw ball" in towns and cities throughout many parts of the country, and in Greenville until well into his forties. Later in life, he also concentrated on mentoring young ballplayers.

In a way, Jackson was expiated when he served as baseball's sacrificial lamb. Corruption in baseball had been rampant during the nineteenth and early-twentieth centuries; yet no ballplayer had ever been singled out for public shame to the degree that Joe Jackson suffered. The outcry to "clean up" baseball had never been louder than in 1920; and since the "Black Sox" affair, no baseball scandal has come close to that level of notoriety. It is entirely possible that, when lesser ballplayers saw that even the great Shoeless Joe could be brought to his knees by his association with gamblers—no matter what the degree of his connection—then the same could surely happen to them. It seems likely that this discouraged more than one ballplayer, whether raw rookie or hardened veteran, from becoming involved in game fixing. Therefore, because Jackson was, in a sense, sacrificed for the good of the game even though his actual role in the scandal cannot be determined with certainty, it is fair to say that he was also an essential ingredient of the game's rebirth.

Who, then, was Joe Jackson? After stripping away the hype and romantic recreations of his persona, and upon examination of the powerful and conflicting forces at work during the game-fixing and resulting scandal, it seems ludicrous to label him as either a villain or a hero. Heroes are, or should be, more concerned with larger issues than themselves; although a hero's actions may seem unconventional or ambiguous, heroic motivation must be beneficial, and it is doubtful that Jackson, who was neither educated nor capable of sophisticated intellectual interpretation, would have related to these subtleties. He did not focus on outside issues or his influence on those events; instead, Jackson simply lived his life as best he knew how, from one day to the next.

Jackson was also a gifted man who found himself confronted by overwhelming forces that ultimately destroyed him, at least insofar as professional baseball was concerned. In that sense, he resembles less the classic, mythological archetype of a hero, and more closely resembles the "naturalistic" hero of modernist thought so popular in Jackson's own time, the hopelessly struggling individual, doomed to defeat by an array of adversaries he can never overcome.

In the final analysis, Joe Jackson was neither villain nor hero, saint nor sinner. Instead, Shoeless Joe Jackson was a talented and generous man, a loving husband and a good friend, and an outstanding ballplayer who contributed much to the game, but he was also a flawed person needing the forgiveness that is increasingly being offered to him today. He was a stalwart human being who faced challenges and overcame most of them, just not the one that ultimately defined him in history. He stared down fears and accomplished goals and had many successes. He lived an extraordinary existence and, as such, his life should be celebrated.

NOTES

1. John D. Spalding, "Undoing Baseball's Original Sin," belief.net; see http://www.belief.net/story/134/story_13405_1.html.

2. Eliot Asinof, *Bleeding Between the Lines* (New York: Holt, Rinehart, and Winston, 1979), 100.

3. John Lardner, "Remember the Black Sox?" *Saturday Evening Post*, April 30, 1938, 14–15, 85; see http://www.baseball1.com/carney/index.php?storyid=172.

Joe Jackson in about 1918 when he was with the Chicago White Sox. *Cleveland Public Library*.

MILLTOWN BOY

Such sport as this brightens a man up, and improves him, both in mind and body.

—Captain Frank Pigeon, pitcher, 1856[1]

Joe Jackson hated being called a "lint head" almost as much as the millwork that gave him the nickname. He'd been sweeping the dusty floors of Brandon Mill since he was six and had spent countless hours dragging bags of cotton across the floor. Now that he was older, he'd also begun to lift and haul awkward rolls of cotton, loading them onto transportation carts. Besides the increased physical labor and the derogatory nickname, he also suffered from the hot, humid air in the mill. The rooms stank and the looms shuddered and roared with a deafening din. What Joe longed to do, rather than slog through gritty millwork, was to sneak outside into the sunshine, where he could enjoy a refreshing game of baseball.

Born on July 16, 1888[2] to George Elmore and Martha Ann (nee Jenkinson) Jackson, Joseph Jefferson Wofford Jackson was the oldest of eight children, six of them boys. He was born in the "upcountry" of South Carolina, located in Pickens County at the northwest corner of the state, nestled along the edge of the Blue Ridge Mountains.

Joe wasn't born into a mill family. In 1888, his father was toiling as a sharecropper on a rundown plantation well past its glory. During the 1880s, South Carolina still suffered from the economic ravages of the Civil War and the effects of Reconstruction policies that followed the war. As a result of this economic and political upheaval, many stately plantations splintered into smaller farms, with the average size of a carved-up farm being ninety acres.[3]

Smaller farms might seem easier to manage than plantations, but the cultural, economic and political changes after the Civil War necessitated the creation of a sharecropping system, whereby tenant farmers paid their rent and purchased farming implements with a percentage of the profits they gained from their crops, principally tobacco, cotton, and sugar cane; because the farms were more manageable in size than the sprawling plantations from which they were subdivided, landowners no longer needed a large labor force to manage their crops. Therefore, a tenant farmer such as George would work the land, employing no one but his own family.

Although George could support his growing family with the crops that he grew, along with supplementary income derived from working in a nearby sawmill, and although the Jackson family owned a cow, a few pigs and chickens, and one or two horses, the family's situation wasn't ideal or particularly stable.[4] Their landlord was cantankerous, known as an "eccentric old fire-eater" who longed to quarrel with others.[5] Besides that, sharecroppers were always at the mercy of the weather, and the Jacksons were no exception.

George, a "wiry type of South Carolina backwoodsmen"[6] who drank whiskey and chewed tobacco, was also a restless soul, with one foot always across the next threshold. Therefore, the dual challenges of alternating floods and droughts and the misery of the disagreeable landowner gave George the excuse he needed to leave sharecropping behind forever. Choosing the work of a mill hand, he worked briefly at a textile mill in nearby Pelzer. At textile mills, workers and machines transformed raw cotton into usable cloth.

At that time, the town of Pelzer already boasted three mills, with 1,600 looms and 52,000 spindles. The location was ideal for millwork because of its proximity to both the Saluda River and the Southern Railway. The water powered the mill and the railway could bring in supplies and ship out the final product: cotton cloth.[7]

George Jackson had just escaped from a hardscrabble existence and a fractious landlord, and must have wondered what fate awaited him in Pelzer. The transition from farm work to mill work must have been difficult as well. "First-generation millhands had to adjust from the rhythm of life on the farm, where they worked for themselves and according to the pace of the seasons, to the rhythm of the factory, where they worked for someone else's profit and synchronized their labor to the steady and quick pace of machines."[8]

Mill owners ranged from greedy opportunists who cared little for workers and much for profits, to those who saw themselves as protectors of the working class and provided some benefits to their workers. The owners of the Pelzer mills were among the best and, as one indication of their progressive thinking, these mills contained the first-ever incandescent lighting, which greatly reduced the threat of fire associated with the old-fashioned kerosene lanterns. The very first automatic looms were also installed in a Pelzer mill and, in 1895, the company installed the first electric power in a mill town, extending service to workers' homes.[9]

The Pelzer mill owners built a school in 1882, and added two more over the next seventeen years. Their employees signed a contract stating, "all children, members of my family, between the ages of five and twelve years, shall enter the school maintained by said company at Pelzer, and shall attend every school day during the school session, unless prevented by sickness or other unavoidable causes."[10] At the age of twelve, those children were required to begin working at the mill.

Mill owners eventually added a library containing 5,000 books, subscriptions to twenty-five different magazines and newspapers, and a comfortable, well-lit reading room.[11] For reasons unknown, George uprooted his young family again, moving them twelve miles to Brandon Mill, located at the western brim of the city of Greenville, in Greenville County. Here, the emphasis on education didn't exist.

George's actions may seem irregular, but his transition from sharecropper to mill worker wasn't uncommon during this era, and actually echoed a growing trend towards urbanization. Before the Civil War, the economy of the southern states of the country had been almost exclusively agrarian. Shortly before the Civil War began, though, in 1860, three small mills sprouted in the Greenville area. Between 1870 and 1880, the population of Greenville doubled as people left their more rural surroundings in search of employment, and significant construction of new mills in the region began to occur around 1895, right about the time that George Jackson and his family moved to Brandon Mill.[12] The fast-moving Reedy River powered the mills; the breakup of plantations provided ready chunks of land for mills and poverty-stricken farmers from the Blue Ridge Mountain region presented a ready-made workforce willing to labor for low but reliable wages.

The town of Brandon Mill, with a population of 13,000 in 1895,[13] was named after a large, five-story textile factory in town. George found steady employment as tender of the engine for about one dollar per day, and the family moved into a company-owned house. A typical mill house contained two to four rooms; rent charged was fifty cents per room per month; as typical for the era, the family began working at the mill together.[14] "In this way, mills attracted a core of mature workers at low cost along with younger, even cheaper laborers who could perform simple tasks and move in and out of the mills in response to market fluctuations."[15]

This thriving mill employed over 800 people and, common for its day, Brandon Mill operated on one giant engine, using Reedy River as its source of power. If that engine broke down, owners sent everyone home without pay, so George's job was important, both personally and to the mill workforce as a whole.[16] A typical day started at 4:15 A.M., when the factory whistle blew; workers reported to work at 6:00 A.M. and didn't leave until twelve hours later, Monday through Friday. Saturdays, they generally worked from 6:00 A.M. until noon[17]; George worked nearly seventy-hour weeks to ensure that the mill ran smoothly.

Mill employees and their families faced significant challenges, but so did the owners. Because millwork was dangerous and tedious, the hours long and the pay low, owners struggled to keep a quality workforce. Mills were dirty and loud, and workers often developed lung disease from breathing in too much lint. They also could become deaf from the din. Besides those factors, some workers left the mills for factory work in the north; others sought railroad jobs further west.

To counteract the problems of high turnover and a transient work force, owners created minicommunities for their employees, complete with houses, stores, and churches. Community stores might offer items ranging from furniture to livestock, food to musical instruments, all available on credit, taken out against future wages. This helped mill families establish themselves, but also kept them beholden to the mill, to which they now owed a debt.[18]

While owners clearly had self-serving motivations in the creation of mill communities, benefits of a stable lifestyle were significant to workers, as well. Many of them had grown up in rural areas and were new to the relatively urban environment, so a ready-made town helped their transition.

The Jackson family, in any case, had few options and George's job at the mill provided them with necessities of life. Little is known about Joe's mother, Martha, but she is described as a "stout and no-nonsense" woman who pulled her dark hair back into a tight knot and served as the anchor of her family. She was also fiercely protective of her children; some say that Joe, who was born when she was twenty-four, was her favorite. People praised her cooking, particularly her hot biscuits and homemade apple jelly, but she refused to cook on Sundays. The family was not known to be churchgoers, but they considered themselves Baptists and followed a tenet of not working on the Sabbath. This meant that Saturdays were doubly busy for Martha, because she needed to cook meals for both Saturday and Sunday.[19]

Joe may have been Martha's favorite child, but his facial features resembled those of his father, who was thirty-two when he was born. George may have been slightly shorter than Joe when his son reached full height, but both men had exceptionally long arms. While people would sometimes comment on the size of Joe's hands, they seldom missed noticing the length of his arms.[20]

By the time Joe was six, he was performing chores at the mill, rather than attending school. This was common practice in the mill towns of the era—Pelzer mills, with their schooling requirement, an extraordinary exception—and no one questioned this decision. When early reformers did begin criticizing this practice, one mill owner "proudly cited a gentlemen's agreement" that limited children, ages ten and under, from working more than a sixty-six-hour workweek.[21]

There was no state education agency in South Carolina when Joe was six (the State Board of Education was founded the following year, in 1895) and there were no child labor laws in South Carolina until 1903.[22] Besides that, Greenville County during that era was a "county of corn whiskey and ignorance. If a man learned to read or write, he was looked on as a freak."[23] Far more importantly, though, the Jackson family needed Joe's income. He supplemented family coffers by twenty-five to fifty cents per day, cash that might mean the difference between having or not having enough food to eat.

Whereas society accepted that children performed millwork, serious dangers lurked. No safety devices covered the fast-moving belts that helped power the mill. Joe's younger brother, Dave, broke his right arm at least five times when he became caught up in a conveyor. Once, the belt dragged Dave up towards the ceiling and, when he crashed to the floor, he broke both an arm and a leg.[24]

Joe's worst childhood experience, though, wasn't related to millwork. At the age of ten, he contracted measles and became paralyzed for two months. Joe lay in bed, knees tightly pulled up to his chest, as Martha nursed him back to health. She fed him, soothed him and placed hot towels soaked in boiled water over his legs.[25] While paralysis was not a typical symptom of the illness and was otherwise inexplicable, he recovered and returned to both millwork and baseball, a sport good-naturedly nicknamed "cow pasture ball" because of the former farm boys who played the game at the mills and the fact that the diamond was carved out of ground where cattle frequently grazed.[26]

The game of baseball played an important role in Brandon Mill and surrounding communities, a role more significant than merely providing entertainment for the workers and a chance to blow off steam during idle times. Mill owners encouraged social events for their families to further entice them to remain at their jobs, and the organized and competitive baseball games on Saturday afternoons proved the most popular events.

Spectators could buy Coca-Cola for a nickel and baseball players served as local heroes. Neighbors visited at the games and youth courted; surely the stars of the game drew special attention from the girls, as well. As author Thomas

Perry put it, "They became the mill's boys of summer, whose exploits on rough fields of baked clay waxed legendary when passed from father to son."[27]

Because of the high status accorded baseball players, men competed fiercely for spots on mill teams. There were, however, also economic reasons to want to earn a spot on the roster. Grown men still earned only one dollar per day for millwork (they would get a twenty-five-cent raise in 1905), but mill owners often gave baseball players a bonus of $2.50 for each game that they played.[28] Even if owners couldn't pay the bonus, players usually benefited from cash tossed in a hat that was passed around the stands. Owners also assigned players less difficult tasks at the mill, another significant advantage in such a dangerous work environment.

Joe loved to play baseball after mill shifts ended or whenever he could get a break from his drudgery. Teams generally consisted of grown men, but fellow workers quickly realized how talented the young Joe Jackson was. His long arms gave him a distinct throwing and catching advantage that was combined with an apparently natural playing ability.

Therefore, by age thirteen, he joined the Brandon Mill baseball team at a time when, by fortunate coincidence, mill town baseball was reaching a high point in its history and people in Brandon Mill flocked to the games. "The villagers," hypothesizes author Donald Gropman, "perhaps hungering for the sense of identity with place and familiarity of local heroes, both of which they'd left behind in the hills and hollows of the uplands, adopted their new mill teams with an immediate loyalty."[29]

Perry points out that, "Mill employees came out to enjoy the game, to get away from tedious jobs in the midst of roaring machinery, to bask in the sunshine, to visit with neighbors and catch up on the latest village gossip."[30]

Far more than a distraction, the games afforded fans an opportunity to develop pride in their communities. The textile industry in South Carolina provided the perfect environment for baseball, as well. Mills were scattered along the Reedy River, connected by a railway known as the Belt Line; this created ready competition and allowed easy transportation to rival fields for both players and fans who, without the railway, might take half a day to travel by horse and wagon.[31]

Competition among mill teams was natural, and soon became fierce as fans became adamant supporters of their home teams. Rivalries became so intense that, at times, mill workers didn't travel to other mill towns, for fear of a bad reception. The games themselves could collapse into brawls fueled by liberal consumption of corn liquor, so much so that the editor of the Piedmont *Bridge* "chose to admonish the village players and fans for such disagreeable tendencies, noting that gambling, brawling, cursing and loud mouth bragging became contemptible habits easily acquired when the wrong kinds of people were involved in the game."[32]

This possibly contributed to a growing concern among local ministers about the sport's popularity, but there were other worrisome issues, as well, including casual gambling. The *Greenville News* cheerfully reported that people bet "goodly sums of money" on the games, which was taken as a sign that the popularity of the sport was growing.[33]

The Lutheran Reverend W. L. Seabrook in Newberry was one who expressed anxiety over this side form of entertainment. Commenting that, while baseball was a good game, there was reason for concern over the taint of money entering the sport, Seabrook especially feared the betting that accompanied the game.[34]

Despite such comments, by 1907, only one cotton mill was without a ball-park and August Kohn noted that, "base ball fever extends from the mill president to the janitor, and the community that did not have its bunch of fans was indeed a rarity."[35] The ball field in Greenville rested between the mill and rows of mill houses; bare dirt defined the bumpy infield and a dump served as the outer edge of center field.[36] Rain could cause "infields (to become) quagmires and outfields veritable marshlands."[37] Nevertheless, this location provided prime entertainment in a town without theater or any other wholesome activities to distract people from the harshness of their lives.

Joe attempted the positions of both catcher and pitcher, but neither suited him. When he served as pitcher, he hit a man on the forearm, breaking a bone, and then no one on the Brandon Mill team would hit against Joe. While playing the position of catcher—which he disliked—a ball hit his mask, bending it and scarring his forehead. Always protective of her favorite son, Martha banned him from the position located behind home plate. Joe settled then on the position of outfielder, where he found his permanent position on the diamond.[38]

Jackson was, without question, a multitalented player. He fielded so well that, in later years, people called his two-dollar glove the "place where triples die." He was an extraordinary hitter and his home runs quickly became legendary. Known as "Saturday Specials," Jackson could hit home runs both inside and outside the park. While inside-the-park homers are rare today, the opposite was true at the turn of the century, and fans were in awe of the balls that left the confines of the park. Jackson also earned a reputation for hitting "blue darters," line drives so powerful that people claimed to see a trail of blue flame shooting out from behind the ball.

Joe's arms had developed incredible strength, probably from lifting heavy cotton in the mill. Using this strength, Joe loved to perform a "show-out," especially if he had just caught the last out of the game. During a show-out, Jackson would catch the ball and then, from the deepest point of the outfield, throw the ball hard enough to zip past home plate. Fans hollered in delight.

One local fan, Charlie Ferguson, knew of Joe's preference for dark bats and made him a special one. Using a four by four beam from the north side of a tree, Ferguson crafted a thirty-six-inch long bat that weighed forty-eight ounces. (Contemporary bats weight between only thirty-three and thirty-six ounces.) Although the bat was white in color, Ferguson darkened it with tobacco juice to please Joe. Please him it did. Joe nicknamed the bat "Black Betsy," rubbing it with sweet oil and wrapping it in clean cotton whenever it wasn't in use.[39]

By the time that Joe was fifteen, fans were comparing him to James Champlin "Champ" Osteen, a former mill team shortstop.[40] Osteen had been the first local star, and rumors circulated that Osteen had earned more playing mill town ball than the governor of South Carolina did "doing whatever it was politicians did."[41] Osteen was picked up by the major leagues in 1903 and he played with three different teams.

Joe, meanwhile, continued to dazzle local crowds with his "Saturday Special" home runs and, whenever he hit one, his brothers would pass around a hat, collecting money that fans offered up as tributes. It wasn't unusual for the Jackson family to garner an additional twenty-five dollars—nearly a month's salary for a typical mill worker—for just one of Joe's amazing swings of his bat.

Joe Jackson soon outgrew the Brandon Mill baseball team. While still a teenager, he surpassed the skill levels of most adult men; in 1907, a rival team, Victor Mills in nearby Greer, offered Jackson a better deal and he began playing with them. About the same time, a semiprofessional league headed up by former collegiate star Lawrence "Lollie" Gray started up in Greenville. This team, dubbed the "Near Leaguers" because they were as close to major league as a player could get without actually participating on one of its teams, consisted mostly of men from local colleges. Gray kept hearing stories about an amazing mill team player and, even though he assumed them exaggerations, he eventually came to watch Joe play. Gray was so impressed that he literally couldn't wait until the end of the game to invite Jackson to join his team. He introduced himself between innings and sealed the deal before the bats had cooled.[42]

Thus, Joe found himself in the enviable position of alternating among local teams, playing for whomever could pay him the most. Fortunately, opportunities abounded. "Baseball," writes Gropman, "was more than a private fever in the blood of many young men; it was in the air of the new century."[43] Jackson already seemed to be a player designated for stardom and nobody begrudged Jackson his team-alternating strategy, as it had already become a tradition for mill teams to attempt to lure away better players from rival teams.

By 1907, Jackson clearly served as the region's star player. During that year, he also reported to a game without realizing how much it would determine the direction of the rest of his life. He played against Thomas Carl Stouch, a second baseman who had played one year of major league baseball with the Louisville Colonels in 1898. Stouch admits that, when he first met Jackson, all he saw was a tall and skinny kid. When Jackson hit the ball, though, Stouch described the hit as a "shell out of a Krupp mortar." Stouch asked his pitcher if he'd uncovered any of Jackson's weaknesses; the pitcher replied, ruefully, "No, but he discovered mine all right."[44]

Stouch's team lost to Jackson's team five games in a row and it couldn't have escaped Stouch's attention that Jackson's name was appearing on major league scouting reports. In 1908, Stouch became the player-manager of the semipro Greenville Spinners of the Class D Carolina Association. He then approached Jackson, asking him to play for his team.

Before agreeing, Jackson calculated that, between his mill wages and baseball pay, he was bringing in forty-five dollars per month. He asked Stouch for sixty-five dollars, to which the manager replied, "Joe, if you promise to leave corn whiskey alone and stick to your business, I will pay you seventy-five dollars a month." In response, Jackson promised to "play my head off."[45]

He kept his promise, although initial game scenarios sound comical to modern ears. On Opening Day, 1908, fans could drive an automobile, buggy, or carriage up to the left-field foul line for fifty cents, or they could pay a quarter to sit in the grandstands.[46] To add to the ceremonies, the mayor of Greenville, His Honor G. Heywood Mahon, headed to the pitcher's mound to toss the first pitch. Unfortunately, he aimed so badly that it whizzed past the catcher and landed against the backstop. Nevertheless, Joe hit two doubles and a triple, and made a dazzling catch that raised fans to their feet; Greenville won 14–1.[47]

Play continued to be haphazard. At times, the crowd of people watching the game determined the shape of the outfield by the swell of their enthusiasm and, more than once, Joe showed his lack of formal training when he attempted to steal a base already occupied by a teammate.

Fans delighted in their hometown hero's performances, though. They'd shout, "Give 'em Black Betsy!" whenever he came to bat, and they continued to bathe him in coins after spectacular hits. One extraordinary home run earned $29.75; Stouch tossed in his own quarter to make it an even $30.00. Even the *Greenville News* joined in the camaraderie, suggesting that spectators, "Watch the fielders get back this afternoon when . . . Jackson come(s) to bat. Laugh at them."[48]

Some outfielders on opposing teams, certain that Joe would hit a home run against them, would back up so far that it became almost ludicrous. This led to the following baseball chant:

When Jackson steps up to the plate
To hit the horsehide ball
The Fielders get so far away
They really look quite small.[49]

As Joe's plaudits grew, so did George Jackson's dissatisfaction with his mill job. Therefore, using money earned by Joe's baseball playing, George opened a butcher shop. While George remained gainfully employed, Joe clearly became the family's main breadwinner. By the end of 1908, Joe was being given a five-dollar bonus for every home run and he ended the season at .350, the best batting average in the league.[50]

Ironically, during that successful season, Joe Jackson, who disliked the nickname of "lint head," earned another nickname, one that he also hated: "Shoeless" Joe. While many stories exist to explain the nickname, they differ in detail but match in spirit. Joe had gotten a new pair of spikes, the legend goes, and he hadn't broken them in properly; his feet blistered in protest. So, either in mid-game or before the following game, depending upon whose rendering is accurate, Jackson told Stouch that he couldn't play; Stouch, of course, wasn't going to allow two sore feet to get in the way of another potential win, this time against a team dubbed the Anderson Electricians, so Jackson ended up playing in his stocking feet. Nobody noticed at first, but then a fan of the opposing team shouted, just as Jackson was sliding into third base, "You shoeless bastard, you!" (Other versions substitute "son-of-a-bitch" or "son-of-a-gun" for the word "bastard.")

No matter the specifics, Jackson hated the nickname, thinking that it highlighted his reputation as a barefoot illiterate. As he later explained, "I never played the outfield barefoot and that was the only day I ever played in my stockinged feet, but it [the nickname] stuck with me."[51]

Perhaps the reason that the nickname stuck is that a newspaper reporter—Carter "Scoop" Latimer—repeated this offbeat happening in the *Greenville News*, thus allowing the story to spread and transform itself into baseball legend. Moreover, it's likely that, because Latimer was reporting to an early-twentieth-century Bible Belt audience, he cleaned up the phrasing originally shouted to Jackson.

Jackson may have been unfortunate in receiving a nickname that he despised, but he was lucky to be playing baseball when the sport was truly becoming the national pastime, a part of the country's public consciousness. Songs about baseball abounded, including "Take Me Out to the Ballgame,"[52] and workweeks were shortening, providing more leisure time; urbanization was ideal for a sport that required teams with larger rosters.[53] Hundreds of semipro teams were traveling around the southern states, and improvements in newspaper printing allowed the spread of baseball reporting to increase the excitement about the sport. "Wherever a game was played, it was the right and respectable place to be," writes Perry, "cheering on the local boys and getting in some good natured ragging of the opponents."[54]

Anyone dropping by Greenville in that era could also listen to someone announcing baseball results that arrived by telegraph wire, an activity known as attending a "baseball matinee" in this preradio, prenewsreel era.[55] Although baseball reporting was a fine reason to come into town, Jackson had another reason to go to Greenville. He often visited Harrison's Drugstore to chat with the brown-haired, blue-eyed, and younger Katie Wynn. Even though they were five years apart in age, Joe and Katie enjoyed the chance to share "dope and limes," which were really Coca-Colas with a squirt of lime juice.[56]

Courtship progressed and Joe and Katie married on July 19, 1908, when Joe was 20 years old and Katie was 15. A wedding picture shows Joe wearing a hat, bow tie, and light-colored suit, while Katie sported a high-collared blouse beneath her own full-length suit, along with a large, full-brimmed hat topped by a dramatic white feather. She is wearing dark gloves and her purse is petite.

Again, the newspaper shared the news. "Joe Jackson," the *Greenville News* reported, "made the greatest home run of his career on Sunday. The home run was made on Cupid's diamond and the victory was a fair young lady."[57]

The next day, Joe returned to center field and fans cheered their congratulations. In return, he got two hits and made one of the "prettiest catches of this season."[58] Just four weeks after his wedding, though, Joe's life was altered forever. Manager Stouch had just sold Jackson's contract to a major league team, one led by the now-legendary Connie Mack.

Shoeless Joe Jackson, it seemed, was heading to Philadelphia.

NOTES

1. Albert G. Spalding, *Base Ball: America's National Game 1839–1915*, ed. Samm Coombs and Bob West (San Francisco: Halo Books, 1991), 42.

2. Jackson's death certificate lists his year of birth as 1889, but his tombstone reads 1888. Other sources use 1887. Birth certificates were not required in South Carolina at the time Jackson was born; the family Bible, where births were often recorded, was lost in a fire. The most common year used is 1888.

3. Richland School District Two of Columbia, South Carolina, provides an overview of Reconstruction and the Rural South at the following Web site: http://www.rich land2.k12.sc.us/rce/reconstr.htm.

4. Donald Gropman, *Say It Ain't So, Joe! The True Story of Shoeless Joe Jackson*, rev. 2nd ed. (New York: Citadel Press Kensington Publishing Corp., 2001), 16.

5. Eliot Asinof, *Eight Men Out: The Black Sox and the 1919 World Series* (New York: Henry Holt and Company, 1963), 54.

6. David L. Fleitz, *Shoeless: The Life and Times of Joe Jackson* (Jefferson, NC: McFarland and Company, 2001), 8.

7. Thomas K. Perry, *Textile League Baseball: South Carolina's Mill Teams, 1880–1955* (Jefferson, NC: McFarland and Company, 1993), 2.

8. Jacquelyn Dowd Hall, et al., *Like a Family: The Making of a Southern Cotton Mill World* (Chapel Hill: University of North Carolina Press, 1987). The book's Web site includes information about farm-to-mill transition: http://www.ibiblio.org/sohp/laf/overview.html.

9. Perry, *Textile League Baseball*, 1–2.

10. Ibid., 2–3.

11. Ibid., 3.

12. Judith Bainbridge, "How Textiles Became King in the Piedmont," Greenvilleonline.com, October 29, 2000.

13. Harvey Frommer, *Shoeless Joe and Ragtime Baseball* (Lanham, MD: Taylor Trade Publishing, 1992), 6.

14. Gropman, *Say It Ain't So, Joe!*, 6.

15. Hall, *Like a Family*, 52.

16. Fleitz, *Shoeless*, 7.

17. Perry, *Textile League Baseball*, 1.

18. Gropman, *Say It Ain't So, Joe!*, 5–6.

19. Frommer, *Shoeless Joe and Ragtime Baseball*, 6.

20. Fleitz, *Shoeless*, 8–9.

21. Gropman, *Say It Ain't So, Joe!*, 17–18.

22. See http://www.richland2.k12.sc.us/rce/reconstr.htm.

23. Asinof, *Eight Men Out*, 54.

24. Fleitz, *Shoeless*, 9.

25. Gropman, *Say It Ain't So, Joe!*, 18–19.

26. Perry, *Textile League Baseball*, 6.

27. Ibid., 5–6.

28. Fleitz, *Shoeless*, 8–9.

29. Gropman, *Say It Ain't So, Joe!*, 7.

30. Perry, *Textile League Baseball*, 40.

31. Ibid., 21.

32. Ibid., 11, 34.

33. Gropman, *Say It Ain't So, Joe!*, 25.

34. Perry, *Textile League Baseball*, 11.

35. Ibid., 10–11.

36. Gropman, *Say It Ain't So, Joe!*, 8.

37. Perry, *Textile League Baseball*, 22.

38. Fleitz, *Shoeless*, 10.
39. Frommer, *Shoeless Joe and Ragtime Baseball*, 8.
40. Fleitz, *Shoeless*, 10.
41. Perry, *Textile League Baseball*, 12.
42. Gropman, *Say It Ain't So, Joe!*, 23–24.
43. Ibid., 24.
44. Asinof, *Eight Men Out*, 55.
45. Fleitz, *Shoeless*, 12–13.
46. Frommer, *Shoeless Joe and Ragtime Baseball*, 12.
47. Gropman, *Say It Ain't So, Joe!*, 29.
48. Fleitz, *Shoeless*, 15.
49. Gropman, *Say It Ain't So, Joe!*, 36.
50. Fleitz, *Shoeless*, 16.
51. Ibid., 17.
52. Frommer, *Shoeless Joe and Ragtime Baseball*, 4–5.
53. See Library of Congress http://memory.loc.gov/ammem/ndlpedu/index.html.
54. Perry, *Textile League Baseball*, 39.
55. Gropman, *Say It Ain't So, Joe!*, 31.
56. Frommer, *Shoeless Joe and Ragtime Baseball*, 7.
57. Gropman, *Say It Ain't So, Joe!*, 37.
58. Ibid., 38.

Jackson with the White Sox. *National Baseball Hall of Fame Library, Cooperstown, N.Y.*

CITY OF BROTHERLY LOVE

His sole object in life for two mortal hours is to gain victory for the home team.
—Albert G. Spalding[1]

Philadelphia, Pennsylvania must have sounded mighty big to "Shoeless" Joe Jackson of Greenville, South Carolina fame. Jackson was accustomed to playing in front of a few hundred people, many of whom he knew, and all of whom probably knew—or knew of—him. A huge crowd of fans, in Jackson's estimation, generally measured no more than a thousand strong. He was used to being the hometown hero, the wonder boy of the mill towns located along the fast flowing Reedy River. When Jackson thought of a city, he pictured Greenville. Now he was expected to move to Philadelphia, a city with a population of over one and a half million people.

In 1908, the year that Jackson was to start major league play, people were immigrating to the United States in record numbers. Overall, from 1870 until 1920, nearly 25,000,000 immigrants moved to America, with most of them settling in the urban areas of the northern states. Philadelphia proper had started as a planned city laid out as an organized checkerboard; but as immigrants continued to flood the city, Philadelphia grew wildly, resulting in chaos. Its population had nearly tripled since 1860, and had grown by nearly twenty percent since 1900. From 1908 to 1914, officials recorded approximately 6,800,000 arrivals to the United States, which signaled congestion and confusion at about the time that the native southerner Jackson was to arrive in the northern state of Pennsylvania.[2]

By contrast, few immigrants—possibly as small as two percent of the total—had settled in the rural areas of the south, so the demographic changes seen elsewhere had not entered Jackson's world.[3] Accustomed to quieter times and more familiar faces, Jackson was also used to being surrounded by fellow Southerners. During the entire 1908 major league season, though, there were fewer than one dozen players from the South, and that trend was not changing any time soon.[4]

These factors didn't bode well for a smooth transition for Jackson. Other factors stacked against him included his heavy southern drawl and his manner of speaking in colloquialisms, the fact that he could not read or write, and a nickname that implied that he was a barefooted rube. Jackson was headed into a world where derogatory southern stereotypes were often believed to be actual, and it was unlikely that his gangly physical form and general immaturity would serve as an effective rebuttal.

When it became time for him to go to Philadelphia, Jackson insisted upon playing one final game at home. At the time, the request probably didn't seem unusual. Mill team loyalties were strong, so strong that the former mill team star, Champ Osteen, would ask for a break from major league play during the Fourth of July holiday in order to return home for baseball festivities. During Jackson's farewell game on Greer's mill team, he hit the longest home run ever witnessed on that ball field and its distance grew with every person who described that hit.[5]

It was a stunning farewell. Still, there were dilemmas. His manager, Tom Stouch, waited patiently to witness Jackson's departure, assuming that every ballplayer's dream was to play in the major leagues and believing that, after playing in the big Greer game, Jackson would happily leave for Philadelphia. When he chatted with Jackson, though, the player's response wasn't reassuring. "I hardly know," the young star said, "how I'd like it in those big northern cities."[6]

To assist in the transition and ease his fears, Stouch accompanied Jackson on his train ride to Philadelphia; but when Stouch awoke the following morning, he couldn't find the ballplayer. He searched for him, fruitlessly, and he arrived in Philadelphia without the prize player in tow. When Stouch spoke to Connie Mack, the manager of the Philadelphia Athletics, he learned that Mack had received the following telegram from his newest rookie: "Am unable to come to Philadelphia at this time. Joe Jackson."[7]

This cryptic message initially puzzled both Mack and Stouch, but the explanation proved simple. After traveling as far as Charlotte, North Carolina, Jackson changed his mind about playing in the major leagues; he left the northbound train, bought a return ticket, and slipped back home to the security and comfort of his southern family life.

Mack wasn't pleased. He had been anxious to see Jackson—a man described in the *Sporting News* as the "Southern whirlwind who is to be Ty Cobb's rival of the future"[8]—play, so much that the *Philadelphia Evening Times* had written that, "All you have to do to raise a smile from Connie Mack is to mention Jackson's name."[9] This new "hide and seek game," as some reporters had dubbed Jackson's change of heart, made news around the country, and Mack resolved that something must be done.

Accordingly, Mack sent Ralph Orlando "Socks" Seybold, the Athletics center fielder, to fetch Joe and allay his fears. "Go down to Greenville," Mack ordered Seybold, "and get this fellow's brothers and sisters and his whole family to come back with you if necessary. See that he doesn't give you the slip on the way."[10]

Seybold, known as the "steadiest and most serviceable of players,"[11] did persuade Jackson to give professional baseball another try; on August 25, 1908, Jackson once again headed back to Philadelphia. This time, he arrived without a problem, and Seybold took him directly to the ballpark where the Athletics played against the Cleveland Naps, a team that would be renamed the Indians in 1915. Once Jackson arrived at the ballpark in Philadelphia, it seemed that he had overcome his case of the jitters. On the second pitch Jackson ever faced in major league ball, he hit a single that drove in a run, racking up the first of his 1,774 major league hits and the first of 785 RBIs.[12]

During that game, Mack was "immensely pleased" to witness Jackson's "splendid fielding," most likely referring to an over the shoulder catch and an incredible throw from center field. "Evidently," Mack was quoted as saying, "Jackson is strong in all respects, without a weakness, and will make a great player for us." The *Evening Times* echoed this sentiment, calling Jackson the "find of the season."[13]

In the midst of this high-level praise, though, Jackson's rising career almost took another reversal. When he returned that evening to gather his bags from the train station, he heard an employee calling out the destinations of the outgoing trains. When he heard "Greenville," he attempted, once again, to purchase a ticket. This time, though, the alert staff of the Philadelphia Athletics stopped him.[14]

If Jackson had succeeded in his late-night flight, he would have let down fans and sports writers alike. Their interest in the southern rookie was strong, especially since the Athletics were slated to challenge the first-place Detroit Tigers. Newspapers touted Shoeless Joe as "General Jackson" and "Stonewall," and speculated on the results of a matchup between Jackson and Cobb, the twenty-one-year-old Georgian who was the top hitter in the American League.

For Jackson, who was already intimidated by the crowded northern city and unfamiliar, unfriendly faces, this increased the pressure. He once again slipped out of Philadelphia and headed back home to Greenville. Newspaper reporters who'd recently praised Jackson became brutal, accusing Jackson of cowardice, saying that he was afraid to face the powerful Ty Cobb. When contacted for a response, Jackson claimed that he had returned to Greenville because Katie was ill and an uncle was dying. When she was questioned, his protective mother, Martha, protested, "I don't see how anyone could criticize Joe for doing what any man with any self-respect could not help doing." When people challenged her son's courage, she added, "Joe is game and always has been game."[15]

Jackson's teammates, probably fearful that the talented rookie might bump one of them off the roster, wouldn't have minded if Jackson stayed away for good. From the very start, they mocked Jackson's inability to read or write, and carried out mean-spirited pranks. For example, they convinced him that finger bowls in restaurants were for drinking purposes and laughed uproariously at his naiveté. Unable to decipher restaurant menus, Jackson always ordered ham and eggs for breakfast, figuring that all restaurants served those food items; for dinner, he'd intently study the menu and then order whatever he'd overheard someone else request, and this further convinced Jackson's teammates that this southerner was a fool.

Mack, however, wanted Jackson to return, in part because of the $900 invested in this young man, and in part because of his talent and potential value to the Athletics. Mack may have also sympathized with Shoeless Joe Jackson because of his own rough childhood. Born in 1862 in East Brookfield, Massachusetts, Cornelius Alexander McGillicuddy was the oldest son of Irish immigrants Mike and Mary McGillicuddy. When Connie was born, the Civil War raged and Mike was serving in the Union Army. When he returned home, Mike worked in factories and mills.[16] Perhaps the common mill experience sparked a bit of empathy in Mack[17] and allowed him to sympathize with the gangly and uncertain Joe Jackson, whose family struggled at the mill by Greenville, South Carolina, and whose younger brother was maimed by the experience.

Mack, described as a "complex personality, a blend of patience and impetuosity, kindness and stubbornness, tightfistedness and generosity,"[18] once again sent for Jackson. Already regarded as one of baseball's toughest and smartest owners, Mack was a man who usually found a way to get what he wanted and what his team needed. He also exercised, in this instance, more than a modicum of patience.

This time, Mack's assistant, Sam Kennedy, traveled south to retrieve his raw star in the making. When Kennedy's pleas didn't suffice, Mack sent Jackson's former manager, Tom Stouch, as a backup. Although Joe apparently displayed reluctance, he did return to Philadelphia on September 7, 1908.

In his first game back, though, he went 0 for 5 at the plate; during the next three games, he didn't do much better. On this low note, Jackson headed back home to Greenville; this time, Mack finally lost patience. He suspended Jackson from professional baseball for the remainder of the 1908 season; it seemed possible, if not likely, that "Shoeless" Joe Jackson's major league career had ended in dismal failure.[19]

If so, it wasn't because of a lack of talent or athletic ability. Rather, Jackson struggled with the foreign atmosphere and unkind barbs. This treatment—by teammates, fans and newspaper reporters—was definitely rougher than what was typical; but this entire age of baseball, dubbed the "dead ball era" (1901–1919), was rough, still struggling to define itself. Box scores were something new, and rules were undergoing dynamic changes while standardization of every element was being debated. The games themselves bristled with fierce edges, unpolished atmospheres and rough-and-tumble action. According to author Jules Tygiel, "During these decades immigrant (primarily Irish and German) and working-class Americans predominated in the major leagues, bringing with them a more contentious manner of play than that which had characterized the earlier years of the game."[20] The stands were often filled with raucous fans, who sometimes brought their own musical instruments and formed bands to play between innings. Gamblers set up wagering booths, and pickpockets, prostitutes, and con men worked the crowds.

Although some factors favored the offense—bumpy playing fields that caused unpredictable bounces, and fielders' mitts that were nowhere near as sophisticated as today's webbed hand coverings—the equipment and rules of the dead ball era gave pitchers enormous advantages.

Generally, the same ball, made of tightly wrapped yarn covered by cowhide, was used for an entire game, or until it completely wore out. If a ball landed in the stands, spectators were expected to toss it back into play. The quality of stitching was never uniform, causing many balls to have a loose, spongy covering. Balls also became misshapen before too many innings were played, making them harder to hit. Pitchers could legally darken the ball with tobacco juice, which impeded the sphere's visibility, and scuffling and scraping the ball was not only legal, it was anticipated.[21] The custom of infielders snapping the ball among themselves during warm-ups and in between innings may have originated during this time, a practice that gave each of the infielders an opportunity to intentionally deface the ball.

Dead-ball games offered other special advantages to the pitcher. The relative softness of the ball made it difficult to hit long distances, so few batters were power hitters; besides that, the fields were generally larger and over-the-fence homers were rare. During the entire dead ball era, no hitter ever achieved a thirty-home-run season and, during thirteen of those years, the home-run champion boasted only single digit accomplishments. In 1902, for example, Tommy Leach won with only six.[22] Ballparks were not lighted, either, and games often lasted until twilight. As daylight faded, artificially darkened balls were very difficult to see.

The days of the dead ball were also the days of "little ball," when singles were the bread and butter of a team's offense, and extra-base hits were not necessarily expected from the offense. Doubles, triples, and home runs were sensational and appreciated by fans, but it was the hitter who consistently put the ball in play and beat out grounders who earned high status on his team. Because of this, the bunt served as a far more important tool than in later eras, as did the stolen base. Because rules dictated that strike zones loomed larger in the dead ball era, some batters also relied upon getting hit by pitches, hoping that their baggy and woolen uniforms would make random and painless contact with the ball. That way, they earned safe passage to first base through a "walk."

Umpires' voices could pierce through the sounds of the fans' cheers and taunts in the smaller grandstands of dead-ball days, which gave the games a more immediate feel. The status of baseball players during those games differed significantly from their twenty-first-century counterparts, as well. Dead ball era players weren't considered the stuff of high society and often enjoyed no better status than burlesque players on the vaudeville circuit. They often traveled in dingy train coaches and stayed in second-class hotels. If someone ate "baseball steak," that meant that they'd just eaten meat of lesser quality.[23]

Although all dead ball era players faced these same challenges, to some degree, Jackson faced an additional dilemma: he simply was not fitting in with the Philadelphia Athletics team, a group of grown men who were both professional and comparatively well educated. Because of this disparity in education, experience, and maturity, Jackson was excluded from the camaraderie that partially made up for the lack of status and luxury, and this made his rookie experience less bearable than it might be for most other players. Besides that, Jackson's all-too-regular escapes from Philadelphia had put his major league future in jeopardy.

After his rookie season ended in disgrace, Jackson spent the winter in Greenville where he worked with his father, George, in the butcher shop that Joe helped finance. Jackson also talked to his mother, whose advice he valued, and it's possible that her encouragement gave him the courage to return to Philadelphia in the spring of 1909, when he learned that he still had a valid contract to fulfill with the Philadelphia Athletics. He would, it seemed, be given one more chance to prove his worth.[24]

Mack was attempting to transform his older team into one with younger potential and stronger hitting power. During the spring of 1909, Mack divided his team into two components during practices: the Regulars, who were the older members of the team, and the Yannigans, who were the rookies, which included Jackson. The southern slugger batted an impressive .350 during the spring and the Yannigans consistently beat the Regulars; still, Jackson was soon back in the minor leagues, this time in Savannah, Georgia.

One now-legendary anecdote claims that Joe had requested to go back to Savannah after seeing empty milk cans being loaded on a train. The cans were coded with red, which meant that they were returning to the south, and Jackson is supposed to have asked Mack to tie one of those labels on him, and send him somewhere else.[25]

Whether or not Jackson said those words, he was often homesick; and doubtless, his arrival in Savannah to play minor league ball in the South Atlantic League (also referred to as the "Sally League") pleased him. Katie joined him and he was happier back in the South, traveling throughout Georgia, South Carolina, and North Carolina. During his first month in this league, he batted .450 and even pitched a little. During one three-inning outing, he struck out two batters and gave up only one hit.

Jackson also enjoyed playing for Bobby Gilks, which added to his contentment. Gilks, a Cincinnati, Ohio native who had played for a major league team, the Cleveland Spiders, encouraged Jackson. "You're just as fast (as Cobb)," Gilks told him, "and you can field and hit just as well. He's got a lot of nerve and that's all you need to show him up."[26]

Besides the support of Katie and Bobby, Jackson was also receiving fan support, some of whom were even calling Jackson the "Ty Cobb of the Sally League."[27] Unfortunately, the team in Savannah performed poorly overall and the owner fired Gilks. Jackson's batting average slid after that and so did his behavior. He began to miss practice, and he even left the field during a game with teammate Ed Luzon, to eat peanuts in the stand. Two different people went to fetch Jackson and Luzon, but they both ended up eating peanuts as well. For his role in this disobedience, the umpire fined Jackson fifty dollars.[28]

Overall, Jackson was displaying a disturbing pattern of immaturity and disregard for consequences. Jackson was still young, though, and in a 1912 interview, he said the following: "Like most young fellows, when they get into the big leagues, I thought I knew as much as any of the oldsters, and not only that, but I had made up my mind that I'd do as I pleased, regardless of what anyone said. I know now that I was wrong, but I don't suppose that excuses my conduct any."[29]

Even as Jackson demonstrated his lack of experience and maturity, and even though his average dipped after management fired Gilks, he remained the league leader, batting .358 in 118 games. Jackson also stole thirty-two bases and threw out twenty-five runners from the outfield. His playing so impressed sportswriters that they chose him for the all-star game of the Sally League, with one writer saying that, "Jackson is a sensation in all departments of the great American game and that's saying a whole lot."[30]

Because of Jackson's prowess on the minor league team, Mack recalled him to the major leagues. Successful in spite of himself, Jackson found himself on a train, heading to Philadelphia once again. Arriving on September 4, 1909, he was greeted with the sight of Philadelphia's new ballpark, the first concrete and steel baseball stadium in the country. Shibe Stadium seated 20,500 fans and provided standing-room viewing, as well.

When Jackson returned, the Athletics were desperately trying to catch up to the Detroit Tigers, who were in first place, four games ahead of Philadelphia; because of the importance of these games, Mack benched the mercurial Jackson after just one game, until after the Tigers clinched the American League title. When he did return to play, his performance was lackluster.[31]

This revived comments made earlier in the newspapers, stating that Jackson simply couldn't survive in major league's more competitive and hectic atmosphere. "Big league life," according to the *Washington Post*, "just wasn't to the young man's liking. The tall buildings, and big crowds, and the clanging of the electric cars had the effect of making Joe long for that noiseless quiet life at home."[32] The *Detroit Free Press* also tossed in this comment: "Joseph is some ball player, but he shies at the cars."[33]

Connie Mack concurred with those assessments. "He was the town hero on his mill team," Mack was quoted as saying, "and thoroughly satisfied with his lot. He was the center of attraction at the village store in the evening and the whole town rang with his exploits. The trouble was that Jackson didn't want to come to the major leagues."[34]

It was obvious that, at a minimum, Jackson didn't want to play professional ball, at least not in Philadelphia; but the situation, in Mack's mind, was far more complex. Although the manager had finally lost patience with Jackson, Mack also realized that if he sold Jackson's contract to another major league team, Jackson's hitting and fielding skills might someday come back to haunt the Athletics.

Mack's solution was to send Jackson back to the minor leagues in March 1910, this time to the New Orleans Pelicans of the Southern League. New Orleans was a city containing people of even more diverse nationalities and cultures than Philadelphia, but the atmosphere differed from the big East Coast city. For one thing, people were more congenial. Fans, even Philly fans, sometimes taunted Jackson, but they supported him in New Orleans. Sportswriters ran hot and cold up north, but newspapers in New Orleans praised Jackson, with the *New Orleans Times Picayune* calling him a "star of the first magnitude."[35]

Jackson formed friendships in that league, as well, especially with Joe Phillips of the Mobile Sea Gulls. Phillips introduced Jackson to the vaudeville circuit in New Orleans, suggesting that Jackson could someday travel that circuit and earn extra cash. Jackson renewed his friendship with former mill-town star, Scotty Barr, also from Greenville, and that improved his spirits. Jackson seemed to outgrow some of his immaturity, as well, and he began practicing strength routines and eye exercises, knowing that his power and keen vision were prime assets.

The New Orleans Pelicans boasted one of baseball's newer improvements, an electric scoreboard, and Jackson's hitting caused the board to work overtime as he batted over .500 during his first fifteen games with the team. His reputation was, without a doubt, growing. When the Pelicans played the Sea Gulls, the opposing first baseman advised the pitcher to simply give Jackson an intentional walk. The pitcher refused, saying that, "He looks just like the rest of them to me."

On the first pitch, Jackson drove in two runs, winning the game. The captain of the Sea Gulls "scolded his pitcher, heated words led to a fight, and in addition to losing the game, the pitcher took a drubbing behind the clubhouse."[36]

When writers chose the all-star team for the Southern League in 1910, Jackson surfaced on every person's list. Therefore, whether Shoeless Joe liked it or not, he was major league material and that's where he was headed. During the next trip to the majors, though, he would not be working with Mack. Instead, his new boss would be Charles Somers, owner of the Cleveland Naps.

According to Mack's recollection, "Jackson was a rather difficult man to handle." Mack added that, although it was true that Jackson's Philadelphia teammates did not like or appreciate him, that was not why Mack negotiated a trade. Instead, "things were going none too well for Charlie Somers in Cleveland," Mack explained, "and I was anxious to do him a good turn in appreciation for the way he had helped us out in Philadelphia."[37]

Mack was referring to events that culminated in the formation of the American League itself. In 1900, the National League had dropped the four least profitable teams from its roster and the newly formed American League moved into three of those locales: Cleveland, Washington, and Baltimore. At the same time,

American League organizers promoted two minor league teams—in Detroit and Milwaukee—to major league status, and they also directly competed with the National League by organizing teams in Chicago, Boston, and Philadelphia.[38]

Mack longed to be a "magnate," the pompous name given to baseball team owners of the era, but he could only invest $5,000 to $10,000 in the newly formed Philadelphia Athletics. Cleveland coal dealer Somers, though, underwrote four teams (Cleveland, Chicago, Boston, and Philadelphia) and he agreed that Mack should serve as the Athletics manager. Ben Shibe, the "mechanical genius of baseball" who perfected standardized baseballs, also invested money in the newly formed Philadelphia team and, through a series of negotiations, the management of the Athletics team was a go for Mack. Somers, in turn, decided to manage the team in Cleveland.[39]

Although it's likely that Mack wanted to trade Jackson to Somers because it was advantageous for him, it was also true that Mack hadn't forgotten Somers' generosity from a decade ago. He also knew that, when Somers' Cleveland team had played against Jackson in New Orleans during spring training, Somers longed for Jackson's bat in his line-up. This trade, then, was Mack's chance to repay the favor from 1900 and potentially gain an advantage for the Athletics team.

Somers and Mack needed to go through a series of machinations to get around the waiver restrictions of the day. First, Mack traded infielder Morrie Rath to Cleveland for Bristol Robotham "Bris" Lord; he was an outstanding outfielder, and his ability to spot line drives was so extraordinary that fans bestowed upon him the nickname of "Human Eyeball." Mack also received an undisclosed amount of cash; this money was forwarded to the New Orleans Pelicans in exchange for Joe Jackson. Although the ballet of trade was tricky, in the end, each manager was satisfied with the transaction. So Lord headed to Philadelphia while Jackson left behind the City of Brotherly Love, Savannah, and New Orleans, traveling with Katie to their new home in Cleveland.[40]

NOTES

1. Spalding, *Base Ball: America's National Game 1839–1915*, 7.
2. Philadelphia statistics are provided by the U.S. Department of the Interior; see http://mcmcweb.er.usgs.gov/phil. For information about national immigration patterns, see also the University of Colorado's Web site: http://web.uccs.edu/~history/fall2000websites/hist153/immigrants.htm.
3. See http://www.bergen.org/AAST/Projects/Immigration/destination.html#1830-1890.
4. Fleitz, *Shoeless*, 24.
5. Gropman, *Say It Ain't So, Joe!*, 43.

6. Fleitz, *Shoeless*, 20.

7. Ibid., 21.

8. Gropman, *Say It Ain't So, Joe!*, 44.

9. Ibid.

10. Fleitz, *Shoeless*, 21.

11. This description of Seybold can be found at his profile located at http://www.baseballlibrary.com. Seybold hit 16 home runs in 1904, an American League record until George Herman "Babe" Ruth broke it in 1919 with 29.

12. Frommer, *Shoeless Joe and Ragtime Baseball*, 19.

13. Fleitz, *Shoeless*, 22.

14. Ibid., 22–23.

15. Ibid., 23.

16. Jules Tygiel, *Past Time: Baseball as History* (Oxford: Oxford University Press, 2000), 37.

17. Connie Mack worked as the foreman of a local shoe factory, a quirky job for a man destined to bring Shoeless Joe Jackson to the major leagues.

18. This description of Mack can be found at his profile located at http://www.baselllibrary.com.

19. Fleitz, *Shoeless*, 24, 26–28.

20. Tygiel, *Past Time*, 40.

21. Frommer, *Shoeless Joe and Ragtime Baseball*, 17–18.

22. Home run records can be found at the National Baseball Hall of Fame and Museum Web site at http://www.baseballhalloffame.org.

23. Frommer, *Shoeless Joe and Ragtime Baseball*, 18.

24. Gropman, *Say It Ain't So, Joe!*, 55–56.

25. Ibid., 57.

26. Fleitz, *Shoeless*, 29–30.

27. Ibid., 30.

28. Ibid., 30.

29. Ibid., 33.

30. Gropman, *Say It Ain't So, Joe!*, 64.

31. Fleitz, *Shoeless*, 30–32.

32. Ibid., 27.

33. Ibid., 28.

34. Ibid., 28.

35. Gropman, *Say It Ain't So, Joe!*, 68.

36. Ibid., 73.

37. Frommer, *Shoeless Joe and Ragtime Baseball*, 28.

38. Tygiel, *Past Time*, 49.

39. Ibid., 49.

40. Fleitz, *Shoeless*, 36.

TRADED TO CLEVELAND, 1910–1911

The game of baseball is a clean, straight game, and it summons to its presence everybody who enjoys clean, straight athletics.
  —William H. Taft, first president to throw out an Opening Day
pitch, April 14, 1910[1]

Joe and Katie Jackson arrived in their new home in Cleveland, Ohio on September 15, 1910, leaving New Orleans only after ensuring that the Pelicans had clinched the division title. Team management in Cleveland worried when Jackson was late in arriving, assuming that he'd conjured up yet another disappearing act; but in fact, he had merely missed a train connection in Cincinnati.

Between the confirmation of the trade from the Philadelphia Athletics—Jackson had been "on loan" to the minor league team in New Orleans—and the time of Jackson's arrival in Cleveland, local newspapers published numerous accounts about the South Carolina ballplayer; the day after he arrived, one headline read, "Southern Star is to Play Today."[2] Fans, eager to glimpse the exciting addition to their team, cheered him at batting practice and hushed whenever he came to the plate during the game. Katie was nervous, she later confessed, but "Black Betsy's song had calmed her nerves."[3]

Debuting with the Cleveland Naps on Friday, September 16, Jackson rapped a single and snagged an impressive center field catch. "Joe Jackson," proclaimed the *Plain Dealer*, "looks good."[4] Although he had one only hit in four at bats that first game, he struck one ball so hard that it knocked the second baseman's glove cleanly from his hand. Jackson also attempted to steal second without spiking the baseman and, the following day, the Cleveland paper noted that "Jackson showed that he was not a dirty ball player."[5]

Possibly spurred on by opening day success, Jackson tagged a two-run homer the following day, probably one of the longest balls hit by anyone that year. The power of that hit, just like many other legendary Jackson home runs from mill town days, grew with every retelling. Jackson's performance impressed fans and they welcomed his presence. Jackson, who had demonstrated a pattern of playing well whenever he felt comfortable in his surroundings, adjusted quickly to Cleveland.[6]

The city that greeted Jackson, though, also presented him with contradictions. Although it differed significantly from Brandon Mill and Greenville, those locations shared some similarities with the urban and industrialized Cleveland, similarities which may have allowed Jackson to feel at ease in his new environment. Greenville rested along the Reedy River and Cleveland boasted the Cuyahoga River; although Cleveland didn't have cotton mills located along the banks of its waterfront, the northern Ohio economy did rely upon often-grimy steel mills located upon its river banks, and about a quarter of Cleveland's workers toiled in the super-heated foundries.[7]

Cleveland, having experienced a significant immigration influx over the past few decades, also resembled Philadelphia. In 1860, the entire Cleveland population was 43,000. Just thirty years later, it grew more than six times that size and became the tenth largest city in the country, with a population of 261,000.[8] The city was bursting its seams and would more than double its size during the next twenty years. By the time that Joe and Katie Jackson arrived in Ohio in 1910, Cleveland was America's sixth largest city, with a population of 560,000.[9]

By this time, Jackson's new home also had a significant history of professional baseball. Cleveland was one of the earliest cities to field a professional team and, in December 1870, stockholders of a local baseball association "resolved to organize the very best baseball team that could be secured."[10] Their team, dubbed the Forest Citys because of Cleveland's many trees,[11] lasted only until 1872 because of financial difficulties; but by 1887, Cleveland developed a professional baseball team under the ownership of Frank Dehaas Robison and his brother, Stanley, a duo who also owned Cleveland's horse-drawn trolley system. For two years, the Robison team participated in the American Association, then they joined the modern-day National League in 1889. That year, fans nicknamed the team the "Spiders" because of several exceptionally thin players.[12]

In 1890, the Robison brothers signed a young man who lived on a local farm: Denton True "Cy" Young. Giddy because of early success that season, in large part because of Young's ability, the Spiders ended up in second place in 1892 and were one of only two baseball teams that made money that year. They enjoyed good seasons in 1895 and 1896, as well.[13]

The Spiders played in a ballpark built by the Robisons, and the brothers, never the sort to miss financial opportunity, placed League Park along one of their own streetcar lines. The park contained one level of wooden stands and fans often arrived early to watch batting practice and enjoy a picnic lunch.

Although the Spiders enjoyed a brief period of success, Frank Robison, frustrated by poor ticket sales, sold off many quality players after the 1898 season.[14] In 1899, the Cleveland Spiders fared so badly that they were the league joke and people jeeringly nicknamed them "the Misfits." Finishing their season at 20–134, it came as no surprise that, when the National League decided to eliminate four teams from professional baseball, they chose to banish the Spiders.

In retrospect, their timing was ideal because it coincided with the formation of the rival American League led by Byron Bancroft "Ban" Johnson. Charles Somers agreed to invest in an American League team in Cleveland, so the home of the former Forest Citys and the former Spiders became the home of the all-new Cleveland Blues, renamed the Bronchos in 1902. By 1903, the team became known as the Naps, in honor of star player Napoleon Lajoie.[15] Largely because of Lajoie's skill, the Naps finished in second place in 1908; however, most of the rest of the Cleveland Naps—pitchers Cy Young and Addie Joss, infielder Bill Bradley and outfielder Elmer Flick—were either at the end of their careers or suffering from injuries. Therefore, Jackson was joining a team that needed to rebuild its potential, and fans had high hopes that the skillful Lajoie-Jackson combination would create the necessary excitement.[16]

When Jackson arrived in Cleveland in 1910, he found double-decker seating in League Park, a luxury that owners had added in 1909. This addition increased fan capacity to 21,000, although game attendance at League Park in that era averaged only about 4,000.[17] Box seats also became available and, as a fire safety precaution, Cleveland converted its stadium to steel and concrete to replace the traditional wooden frame.[18]

Euclid Avenue served as the main street connecting downtown Cleveland with League Park. Many newly rich, including oil magnate John D. Rockefeller, built their homes on Euclid Avenue and it soon became known as "Millionaires Row." In 1910, the avenue boasted 250 mansions—ranging from Gothic villas to Victorian manors—a far cry from what Jackson knew in South Carolina. Samuel Mather's house, built in 1907, cost $3 million and contained two-and-a-half acres of formal gardens, squash courts, an eight-car garage and forty-three rooms.

Just a few miles away from Millionaires Row stood League Park, and Jackson, along with almost everyone else, probably puzzled over its quirky contours.

Later described as "a house of insanity, a place where baseball was contorted to fit into the most illogical dimensions ever conceived,"[19] the odd shape of right field resulted because the owners of two houses and a saloon wouldn't sell out to ballpark owners. The right-field barrier—a forty-foot-high fence composed of concrete, steel beams, and chicken wire—stood only 290 feet from home plate.

Fans who couldn't afford a ticket positioned themselves on the street outside right field because, if they turned in a ball that cleared the fence, they earned an admission ticket at no cost; this policy presumably prevented the home run balls from shattering the windows of the residences located near the fence. Balls would also become entangled in the wiry construct or take unpredictable bounces. This unique feature inspired right-handed batters to change their stance, to take advantage of the short distance required for a home run; left-handed batters, such as Jackson, loved the advantage this offered them.

The layout of the rest of the outfield also served Jackson well. He handled the wildly careening balls that hit the oddly constructed right-field fence with such skill that fans eventually called him the "outfielding billiardist." The deepest part of center field was 460 feet. Not even Joe Jackson in his prime could throw that far, but then again, nobody was hitting that far, either. Even so, Jackson's powerful arm served as a marvelous defensive tool and he saved a lot of extra bases when opposing hitters found the power alleys. Jackson could have excelled in any ballpark, but the structure of League Park might have served as an impetus to even greater glory.[20]

Besides the advantages of the physical layout, Jackson quickly discovered other things that he liked about Cleveland, including another kindred spirit in Lajoie. Although Lajoie was French Canadian and although he grew up on the East Coast, the big slugger worked in textile mills as a youth, and such commonality may have helped bond the two players.[21] Unlike the players on the Philadelphia Athletics team, who had taunted Jackson, Lajoie—already an established star who did not fear being displaced or overshadowed by the new player—welcomed the rookie to the Cleveland team. He and his wife socialized with Jackson and his wife, Katie, at restaurants, the movies, theaters, and amusement parks. Moreover, Lajoie stayed in touch with Jackson in their later years of life, when feelings of respect continued to be mutual. On Jackson's 54th birthday, for example, he and Lajoie granted an interview to the *Greenville News* where Jackson shared nostalgic anecdotes about Lajoie's play; in turn, Lajoie suggested that Jackson could have been the greatest hitter ever, had he played in the "lively ball era" when more hitter-friendly baseballs were in use. Although Jackson modestly disputed that claim, he always appreciated how Lajoie had welcomed him to Cleveland.

When Jackson arrived in Cleveland in 1910, local newspapers also treated him well, splashing hyperbolic nicknames about Jackson in their pages, including "Champion Batter of Dixie," "Southern Star," and the "Caroline Crashsmith."[22] Other nicknames included "Carolina Confection" and "Candy Kid from Carolina."[23]

Jackson also appreciated that other southerners played on the Cleveland Naps team, and that many of the northerners, after playing in New Orleans, were familiar with southern culture. Additionally, several Cleveland Naps were not adverse to imbibing alcoholic beverages, and this made Joe's taste for corn whiskey fit right in.[24] (He was known to wash down animal crackers at bedtime with a glass of corn whiskey.) As Jackson matured, he also realized the necessity of hard work in professional-level baseball, or as he put it in an interview, he discovered that it was time to "cut out my kiddish ways" and "attend strictly to my knitting."[25]

In Cleveland, Jackson made other friends, including roommate "Brother" George Stovall, the rough and tumble team captain of the Naps who once, in a fit of anger, smashed a chair over Lajoie's head. The incident occurred in a hotel lobby, which could have been embarrassing for Lajoie because it occurred in public, but Lajoie forgave Stovall and the two continued in an amicable relationship.[26]

Other friends included fellow ballplayers, Vean Gregg and Specs Harkness, men who dubbed themselves the "Ancient Order of Retired Insects" with the motto of "Bugs once, but not now." "Bugs," in their parlance, were eccentrics who didn't follow the rules of common sense.[27] Jackson was appointed President of the Bug Club.

Through a combination of maturity and a friendlier community, and with Katie at his side, Joe Jackson finally found his rhythm. After rapping a sharp single in his first game in a Cleveland uniform and a home run in the second game, the team then traveled to Philadelphia, where Jackson faced taunting crowds and the derision of his former teammates, the first place Athletics. Jackson, apparently undeterred, pounded out a powerful triple and appeared confident.

"Jackson," commented former teammate Topsy Hartsel after that game, "does not look like the same player he was with us. He has improved 1,000 percent."[28]

Shoeless Joe Jackson played twenty games with the Cleveland Naps to finish out the 1910 season. At times, his batting average hovered around .400, and he completed the season with a batting average of .387, finishing with the highest batting average in both of the major leagues. Only a lack of games played prevented Jackson from capturing the batting title from Ty Cobb's .385 average that season. Fans, players, and sports writers alike all took notice, with owner Charlie Somers telling him, "You're the greatest natural hitter I ever saw."[29]

As a side note, controversy raged that year over whether Cobb or Jackson's teammate, Nap Lajoie, should have won the batting title; accuracy was especially vital that year because the Chalmers automobile company had promised a new car to the winner. The controversy started when, with only two games left in the regular season, Cobb sat out a game; Cobb was holding a slight edge in the batting average contest and, by sitting out a game, he was forcing Lajoie to get eight hits in a double-header to secure the batting title.

Lajoie got his eight hits that day, but seven of them were suspect, writes Harvey Frommer, or "more than suspect . . . Jack O'Connor . . . bribed and bullied the official scorer, offering a forty-dollar new suit of clothes as a barter for bunts scored as hits."[30] After the game ended, sportswriter Hugh Fullerton reversed a decision he had made as a scorer, which originally ruled one of Cobb's hits an error. This meant that Cobb's final batting average for 1911 was .3850687, while Lajoie's was .3840947.[31]

The Chalmers automobile company avoided involvement in the dispute by awarding a car to both players. To avoid such controversies in the future, the company determined that a group of sportswriters would choose the winner in upcoming seasons, and from that decision came the Most Valuable Player Award of today.[32]

In October 1910, after the regular season ended, the Cleveland Naps challenged the Cincinnati Reds to an "All-Ohio Championship." Although the Reds beat the Naps, four games to three, Jackson received an additional payment of $171.30 for his series participation, in which he batted .357.

When the season ended, Joe returned to Greenville to winter in glory, taking Black Betsy with him. "Bats," Jackson explained, "don't like to freeze no more than me."[33] Back in Greenville, he enjoyed the "laid-back style of life, to old overalls and home cooking"[34] and he spent the winter months helping George in the butcher shop and sharing baseball chitchat with old friends. These friends "delighted in hearing all the fabulous stories of the big city, the tales of the sounds of the tin lizzies chugging up and down the streets and avenues, the clanging trolleys with their posters featuring baseball personalities."[35] More importantly, though, they reveled in the exploits of their hometown hero, Joe Jackson.

In 1911, Jackson didn't hesitate to return to major league ball. Indeed, he left early and reported to New Orleans in February so that he could get in an extra week of practice before reporting to the Naps spring training camp in Louisiana. While in New Orleans, nearly three thousand fans came to see him play, and reporters said that he was the most popular player in the city's history.[36]

When he reported to training camp, Jackson announced that he, rather than Lajoie or Cobb, the "Georgia Peach," would win the 1911 batting championship. Jackson and Cobb grew up less than 100 miles from one another, but did not meet until both were in the major leagues. As their teams played one another, the two developed a friendship, a rarity for the temperamental Cobb. When hearing of his friend's boast for the batting championship, Cobb responded that he wished Jackson a season of .400 ball, adding that he intended to hit a point or two higher than that.[37] Lajoie's response to Jackson's claim was to laugh and say, "More power to you, old boy."

Because Jackson arrived in Cleveland during the latter part of the 1910 season, many Cleveland sportswriters didn't have a chance to spend adequate time with him that year. To make up for that lapse, they followed Jackson intently during the spring of 1911. Jackson wore stylish clothes that season, including a variety of expensive shoes. Besides that, he "sported a double-breasted suit and a jaunty felt porkpie hat" and the writers dubbed him the team's "Beau Brummell," after an eighteenth-century Englishman who introduced long trousers and high fashion for men.[38]

Newspaper headlines in southern states praised Jackson, while the *Sporting News* claimed that Jackson was "endowed with all the eccentricities that possess many Southerners."[39] Although this did indicate a fairly typical "Yankee" bias that many southern players experienced when they traveled north, Jackson did display genuinely odd habits and superstitions. For example, he traveled with a pet parrot who screeched, "You're out!" He would also collect hairpins, the rustier the better, and he stored them in his pockets. Sometimes, his pockets would literally bulge with rusty hairpins; when his batting seemed to slump, he threw them away and starting collecting them all over again.

To please her husband, Katie always sat in the same spot in the stands, ostensibly to bring him luck, but she always left at the seventh inning to prepare her husband a quality, home-cooked meal. This pattern was apparently important to Jackson, and he and Katie referred to this ritual as "the hunch."

Jackson had other superstitions, as well. Whenever he wasn't pleased with his batting, he'd ditch his collection of bats and begin a new one, believing that bats contained a limited number of hits ("Black Betsy" was apparently exempt from this rule). Jackson also named his bats. He had, of course, "Black Betsy," which traveled everywhere with him. Other bat names included "Ol' Ginril," "Caroliny," and "Dixie." Once, when in a particularly bad slump, he shoved the end of one bat into tar; shortly afterwards, the dry spell ended. After that, he wanted all the tops of his bats to be black.[40]

An obsession with bats wasn't unique to Jackson, of course. Players shaved, honed, and heated their bats. Ty Cobb picked his own wood and shaped the bats with a steer's bone. Cap Anson hung bats like hams in the cellar and one player named Perring collected pieces of the hickory wood that had formed the scaffolding in the Ohio State Penitentiary. When the scaffold was dismantled in 1880, Perring took the wood and fashioned it into a bat that lasted for two decades.[41]

Although other players also had odd superstitions and personal quirks, people seemed to focus more intently on Jackson's, perhaps because his lack of education made the superstitions more obvious, or perhaps because that made Jackson an easier target. Naps owner, Charlie Somers, as Connie Mack had done before him, encouraged schooling for Jackson, but Jackson once again declined. "I ain't afraid," Jackson replied, "to tell the world that it don't take school stuff to help a fella play ball."[42]

Jackson seemed comfortable with this philosophy, but it alienated Hugh Fullerton, a prominent sportswriter of the day. "A man who can't read or write," Fullerton pronounced, "simply can't expect to meet the requirements of big-league baseball as it is played today."[43] Although Jackson may not have cared about such attitudes, Fullerton's opinions would later have far reaching effects on Jackson's life.

Even during this disconcerting debate over his lack of education, and even though some sportswriters still called Jackson a coward because of the times he'd fled Philadelphia, Jackson's bats offered his most eloquent response. His average never dipped below .360 in 1911. After seventeen games into the season, Jackson was batting .408 and, on April 21, he hit a home run over the forty-foot fence in League Park, only the second time that had ever happened.[44] Sportswriter Ring Lardner wondered "which was more dangerous—to ride in a St. Louis taxi cab or play the outfield or infield against Mr. Jackson, because you are bound to get killed sooner or later, either way."[45]

Jackson was consistent at the plate and rarely changed his batting stance to adjust to the pitcher. One notable exception was when Walter "Big Train" Johnson, one of baseball's all-time fastballers, was on the mound. Against Johnson, Jackson shortened his swing, and this adjustment allowed him to hit nearly .500 against this extraordinary pitcher, who many contemporary analysts believe threw the ball harder and faster than any hurler who ever took the mound. Johnson's opinion of Joe Jackson can be summarized in just one statement. "Jackson didn't seem to have a weakness."[46]

Like his fellow southerner, Cobb, Jackson had incredible speed. He could reach first base in 4.2 seconds.[47] Such fleetness of foot allowed Jackson to cover large expanses in the outfield, as well, and when he threw out Jimmy Austin, one of the fastest runners in the league, Jackson impressed many onlookers. Some players and fans continued to taunt Jackson, calling him "Professor" and other sarcastic names, but Jackson ignored them now. He answered all catcalls with his speed and his bat.

On May 7, Jackson hit an impressive inside-the-park home run, the first of his four career grand slams, and on May 14, he participated in a milestone game in the Naps history: the first Sunday game for a professional baseball team in Cleveland was played.

From the perspective of fans, many of whom were factory workers working six days a week, a ban on Sunday games prevented them from watching their favorite sport, so they were thrilled to have the blue law repealed. From the perspective of owners, having Sunday play was a lucrative financial move. Therefore, on May 14, fifteen thousand people[48] attended this game, while ticket messages warned fans against "boisterous rooting." The Naps won, 16–3.[49] That was only the beginning, though, for from that point on, Jackson's hitting streak continued. From July 11 through August 26, he reached base by a hit in thirty-six of thirty-seven games, including a twenty-eight-game stretch.[50] His batting average rose again to .405, while fans shouted, "Give 'em Black Betsy!" and "Give 'em Dixie!" Over the course of those thirty-seven exceptional games during July and August, Jackson's average was .462. During twelve of these games, his average reached .509; an editorial cartoon of the day shows an infielder ducking when Jackson came to bat.[51]

Unable to pitch effectively against Jackson, pitchers started throwing *at* him; Jackson was pegged or beaned eight times during the 1911 season (this increased to twelve times in 1912) and "only his superior reflexes" kept him from being hit more frequently. He simply refused to back away from the ball. "I never pulled away from the plate," he said in a 1942 interview, "as long as I was in baseball."[52]

He was rapidly earning the respect of players—including the pitchers—throughout professional baseball. Pitcher Ernie Shore described Jackson's batting this way. "Everything he hit was really blessed. He could break bones with his shots. Blindfold me and I could still tell you when Joe hit the ball. It had a special crack."[53] Author Donald Gropman recalls his father's description: "you didn't have to know anything at all about baseball to see that Joe Jackson was someone special. There was a beauty in him, even in the way he walked. . . . He walked like a big cat . . . sure and graceful in his every move."[54]

On September 1, Jackson's average stood at .400, and he ended his first complete major league season with an extraordinary batting average of .408. Cobb, however, was true to his prediction about his own performance; he batted .420, once again earning the batting title. Still, Jackson's was a remarkable batting average, particularly for a more-or-less rookie player. It wound up as standing as the sixth highest single-season average in the twentieth century, the highest for a rookie player,[55] and the highest ever in Cleveland baseball history. He also received the fourth number of votes for the Chalmers Most Valuable Player award.[56]

In an era when statistics were fairly new to the game and people were just becoming excited about the "game of numbers," Jackson stood out and gave fans something to talk about. He racked up incredible accomplishments on the field and at the plate, but he couldn't quite escape the shadow of the Georgia Peach. Jackson tagged two hundred and thirty-three hits in 1911, the second most hits of that season. He boasted thirty-two outfield assists, along with forty-five doubles, 337 total bases, 126 runs scored, and a slugging percentage of .590. Jackson led the league in on-base percentage (.468), but Cobb surpassed him in every other hitting category. The sometimes rancorous and almost always competitive Cobb was generous in his commentary, saying that, "Joe is a grand ball player, and one who will get better and better."[57]

Later in his life, however, Cobb published his autobiography, where he included an anecdote saying that he had psychologically tricked Jackson into losing the batting title in 1911. Calling Jackson "a friendly, simple and gullible sort of fellow,"[58] Cobb claimed that he'd refused to speak to Jackson during this batting title race and, because of this bullying tactic, Jackson's batting average sank.

Such deliberate snubbing may have played a role in Jackson's performance, but a review of the batting averages does not support Cobb's claim. At no point was Jackson in close contention for the title; nor did his average significantly sink at any point of the season. Jackson's explanation of the batting title race was much simpler and more direct: "A story you now hear from time to time that Ty bulldozed me by getting my goat in a conceived plan to ignore me in Cleveland in that important final series is just a lot of hooey. Ty was able to beat me out because he got more hits than I did."[59]

Although the two sluggers remembered the 1911 batting title race differently, both players were creating terrific excitement on the baseball diamond. And, by the end of the 1911 season, Jackson was no longer an up-and-coming rookie. Instead, "Shoeless" Joe was now a bona fide major league baseball star.

NOTES

1. See http://web.bryant.edu/~history/h365/baseball/Presidents.htm.
2. Gropman, *Say It Ain't So, Joe!*, 85.
3. Ibid., 85.
4. Fleitz, *Shoeless*, 41.
5. Gropman, *Say It Ain't So, Joe!*, 86.
6. Ibid., 87.
7. For the Cleveland timeline, see http://tiger.chuh.cleveland-heights.k12.oh.us/TRG/Timeline.html.

8. See http://physics.bu.edu/~redner/projects/population/cities/Cleveland.html.

9. See http://ech.cwru.edu/timeline.html.

10. See the Encyclopedia of Cleveland History, maintained by Case Western Reserve University, at http://ech.cwru.edu/ech-cgi/.

11. Frommer, *Shoeless Joe and Ragtime Baseball*, 29.

12. Encyclopedia of Cleveland History, http://ech.cwru.edu/ech-cgi/.

13. Ibid.

14. Ibid.

15. Fleitz, *Shoeless*, 39.

16. Ibid., 40.

17. See http://www.baseball-reference.com/teams/CLE/attend.shtml.

18. Encyclopedia of Cleveland History, http://ech.cwru.edu/ech-cgi/.

19. See http://www.sportingnews.com/baseball/ballparks/league.html.

20. Frommer, *Shoeless Joe and Ragtime Baseball*, 36; for another description of the park, see http://www.ballparksofbaseball.com/past/LeaguePark.htm.

21. Fleitz, *Shoeless*, 39.

22. Frommer, *Shoeless Joe and Ragtime Baseball*, 29.

23. Gropman, *Say It Ain't So, Joe!*, 74, 77.

24. Fleitz, *Shoeless*, 41.

25. Ibid., 35.

26. Ibid., 40.

27. Ibid., 48.

28. Ibid., 41.

29. Frommer, *Shoeless Joe and Ragtime Baseball*, 32.

30. Ibid., 31.

31. Ibid., 31.

32. Fleitz, *Shoeless*, 43.

33. Ibid., 43.

34. Frommer, *Shoeless Joe and Ragtime Baseball*, 33.

35. Ibid.

36. Gropman, *Say It Ain't So, Joe!*, 96.

37. Fleitz, *Shoeless*, 46–47.

38. Ibid., 47.

39. Ibid., 47.

40. Frommer, *Shoeless Joe and Ragtime Baseball*, 40.

41. Ibid., 39–40.

42. Gropman, *Say It Ain't So, Joe!*, 101.

43. Ibid., 97.

44. Fleitz, *Shoeless*, 50.

45. Gropman, *Say It Ain't So, Joe!*, 106.

46. Ibid., 104.

47. Fleitz, *Shoeless*, 48.

48. Frommer, *Shoeless Joe and Ragtime Baseball*, 36.

49. Fleitz, *Shoeless*, 52.

50. Ibid.

51. Gropman, *Say It Ain't So, Joe!*, 103, 105–106.

52. Fleitz, *Shoeless*, 52.

53. See http://www.shoelessjoejackson.com/about/quotes.html.

54. Gropman, *Say It Ain't So, Joe!*, xxiii.

55. Fleitz, *Shoeless*, 57.

56. Ibid., 57; for more information about Jackson and his standings, see http://www.baseball-reference.com/j/jacksjo01.shtml.

57. Ibid., 57.

58. Gropman, *Say It Ain't So, Joe!*, 109.

59. Ibid., 110–114.

CLEVELAND NAPS, 1912–1914

Joe Jackson Made Good Against Fearful Odds. Ballplayers Thought He Had a Yellow Streak and Did Everything on Earth to Make It Crop Out, But the South Carolina Kid Stood Fast and Fairly Set the American League Ablaze.
—Umpire Billy Evans, creating a title for one of his newspaper articles[1]

When Joe Jackson reported to spring training in Mobile, Alabama for the 1912 season, team captain George Stovall—Jackson's former roommate—did not. In the offseason, owner Charlie Somers had traded Stovall to the St. Louis Browns and hired former Philadelphia Athletics player and manager, Harry Davis, as the new manager of the Cleveland Naps. Davis had earned a reputation as being dependable and hardworking; he had led the American League in home runs four years straight—1904–1907—and Connie Mack had relied greatly upon Davis while he was in Philadelphia.

Davis' strict managerial style differed greatly from that of the hot-tempered yet popular Stovall. Almost immediately upon arriving in Cleveland, Davis banned crap games in the clubhouse, telling the *Cleveland Plain Dealer*, "Some players carry around gambling debts and they cannot do justice to themselves in the games."[2] He also strongly enforced curfews and discouraged social interaction between the often-rowdy Naps and opposing teams.

A younger Jackson might have chafed at this discipline, or been intimidated by the college-educated manager who had replaced his roommate. However, when Jackson arrived at spring training on March 5, 1912, he had just completed a week of extra training with the New Orleans Pelicans, where he had re-

Jackson playing for the Cleveland Indians. *National Baseball Hall of Fame Library, Cooperstown, N.Y.*

laxed and enjoyed vaudeville shows with former mill teammate, Scotty Barr. Jackson was in excellent physical shape and exuded confidence, announcing, "Here I am, boys. Just give me a bat and I'll put a few over the fence," which led the *Plain Dealer* to print, "Joe Jackson needs no press agent. He believes in advertising himself."[3]

His former awkwardness seemingly vanquished, Jackson "adopted the persona of the southern storyteller, and the writers enjoyed his colorful, somewhat exaggerated tales of mill life and playing ball down South. 'Joe himself has a warm, fervid imagination,' said F. C. Lane of *Baseball Magazine*, 'which looks upon facts as hurdles to be surmounted by brief but frequent flights of fancy.' "[4]

Davis' opinion of Jackson probably added to his growing self-esteem. Although Davis publicly complained about many ballplayers, he praised his southern star, calling him the "kind of ballplayer who makes a manager's heart glad."[5]

Although some sportswriters still misquoted and mocked Jackson, many treated him well now; one noted how he acted like a gentleman both on and off the field. This writer also pointed out mild-mannered Jackson was, as well, when dealing with umpires.[6]

Jackson was also gaining a loyal following. In March, the Naps returned to New Orleans to play a few games in the Pelicans' ballpark, and fans turned out in droves to see their favorite player. People wanted to shake his hand and take photos. In April, one fan wrote to Jackson, asking him his "complete" name so he could name his "fat, fine-looking, newly-born twelve-pound baby boy that is somewhat of a ball player" after his favorite batsman.[7] Another fan named Pete always brought a cardboard megaphone to his bleachers seat and "carried on a public monologue" with Jackson. When, for example, Jackson knocked in two late-game runs, putting the Naps in the lead, Pete hollered, "Guess I'll go home now, Joe! You won the game!"[8]

True to his pattern, Jackson played well when he was comfortable with his surroundings and his sense of ease was apparent even before the 1912 season officially began. While still in New Orleans, Jackson hit a long home run over center field, and many observers claimed that was the second longest ball ever hit in that ballpark.

Children often waited for Jackson outside the ballpark, where he helped them with their batting. Not all kids were fortunate enough to watch him play from the comfort of the bleachers, though. A newspaper photo that season showed a group of them lying on the ground near League Park; several are barefoot and one sported a large hole in the sole of his shoe. These children were among the fans who didn't have enough money for admission, so they peeked underneath the right-field gate to follow the action. One child in the photo, who was wearing a floppy hat and torn pants, was quoted as shouting, "Jackson's up, fellers!"[9]

Adults also sought him out; when two railroad workers caught a possum in their depot, they presented it to Jackson before a game. He jokingly lifted its tail, to determine if it was plump enough for possum pie. Several photos were taken of this moment; when Jackson came to bat, he requested that the possum be brought to the plate. He petted the creature, and then hit a single; when the next Naps player came up to bat, he insisted on petting the possum, as well.[10]

Jackson actually had a number of personal entertaining quirks he seemed to enjoy flaunting. When he came up to bat, he often sang the lead line from a popular song, "I'm Sorry I Made You Cry." He didn't know the rest of the words, though, so he'd then simply wave Black Betsy at the pitcher and laugh.[11] Jackson followed other batting rituals, as well; before stepping up to the plate, he drew a line out three inches in length from the front to the back of the batter's box. He then drew another line at a right angle from the point nearest the catcher and then placed his left foot exactly three inches from the plate, keeping his feet together until he was ready to swing.

On April 11, an Opening Day crowd of 19,302 flocked to League Park, breaking previous attendance records. Jackson went 3 for 5, to the fans' delight, and Katie continued her practice of attending all games and keeping a scorecard for her husband, who commented that she gave more errors to fielders than the official scorekeepers. If Katie kept the official score, Jackson said, his batting average would definitely decline; one newspaper headline cheerfully announced, "Joe Jackson's Wife a Strict Judge of Husband's Bingles."[12]

Although Katie continued to leave each game at the seventh inning to cook her husband his evening meal, the couple enjoyed attending theaters and visiting restaurants in Cleveland. Jackson bought a car and the couple drove through the countryside. When they went for walks, fans asked them to stop to partake of iced tea and rhubarb pie, or they'd ask to treat them at the local ice cream parlor.

When the *Plain Dealer* published a photo spread called, "The Wives of the Mighty Naps," Katie's picture was the focus. "Katie's hair was upswept and she was fashionably dressed in a soft silk blouse and a tight-waisted ankle-length skirt. She was smiling."[13]

Besides posing for photos, Katie continued to read and write for Joe, who still fought any attempts to enroll him in formal schooling. The Naps players differed from the Philadelphia Athletics, though; instead of mocking his lack of education, they assigned roommates who would help Jackson whenever he needed to read or write while on the road.

On April 20, the Naps traveled to Michigan to play against Ty Cobb in the Detroit Tiger's brand new ballpark, Navin Field. Jackson scored the first-ever run in the ballpark, and his success continued throughout the season. On June

4, he hit another inside-the-park home run; that month, his batting average reached .401. On June 30, Jackson hit 3 triples, which tied the Naps record for triples in a single game; he also scored 4 runs. On August 11, he stole home twice, the second American League player ever to accomplish this. The second of these occasions, he stole second, third, and home in rapid succession. Only the great Ty Cobb himself was usually capable of such speed and daring on the base paths.

Cobb was not stingy with praise for the upstart rival to his own performance. In fact, he admired the fullness of Jackson's swing. "I could never have hit above .300 with that type of swing. Only Jackson, old Shoeless Joe, had the eye and the timing and the smoothness to do that."[14] Other great players joined in the public admiration for Jackson's batting prowess. Tris Speaker, who tallied a lifetime average of .344, called Jackson's swing "so perfect"[15]; Charles "Chief" Bender, a pitcher who won 180 games before he turned thirty, watched Jackson during half a dozen games, then admitted the following: "I've concluded there's no use trying to fool him."[16] Moreover, his batting style seemed natural. Naps player, Jack Graney, said this about his teammate: "Jackson never seemed to know whether the pitcher was left-handed or right, or whether he hit a fastball, a curve, a spitter or any of the trick deliveries. All he'd say, if you asked him, was that the ball was over. 'Over' for Jackson meant anything he could reach."[17]

His defensive play continued to amaze spectators, as well. The quirky layout of right field at League Park generally meant that a hit towards the right-field wall was at least a double, but Jackson quickly discovered how to play the caroming ball and he often held the batter to a single. "Joe Jackson," wrote one reporter, "is an inventive genius."[18]

Jackson was enjoying unprecedented personal success; unfortunately, the Naps were suffering through a frustrating and inconsistent season in 1912. Veteran Nap Lajoie strained his back, which kept him out of thirty-seven ballgames, and new manager Harry Davis was quickly becoming frustrated with the club. Publicly lambasting his players as "quitters,"[19] he kept switching around the line-up and the team struggled with these unexpected and seemingly random changes.

Tension grew and, on July 16, Davis was forcibly removed from a game when he argued too intensely with the umpire. Rather than mending his relationship with the umpire, Davis filed a protest against him, which only added to the strain. Coupling these feuds with the Naps losing record, the *Plain Dealer* began calling for Davis's resignation; on September 2, the Naps manager did just that, returning to Philadelphia to coach for Connie Mack.

Davis had been the sixth manager in Cleveland over the American League's twelve-year existence; it was now time to select the seventh. Somers named his center fielder, Joe Birmingham, as Davis' replacement and, although the Naps still ended up in fifth place, they won twenty-one of the remaining twenty-eight games of the season. Jackson, whose average had dropped to .377, snagged 50 hits in September—batting .476 for the month—to end the season with a .395 batting average. The only time a Cleveland Naps player ever had a better hitting season was the year before—also set by Jackson.

Unfortunately for Jackson, Ty Cobb refused to relinquish his hold on the batting title. The Tigers star hit .410 for the season, which meant that, once again, Jackson ended up as runner-up in the batting title race. He seemed to take it with good humor, however, commenting, "What a hell of a league this is. I hit .387, .408 and .395 the last three years and I ain't won nothing yet."[20]

During the 1912 season, Jackson hit 26 triples, an American League record that still stands. He led the American League in total bases as well, and finished second in slugging percentage (.579), total hits (226), doubles (44) and runs scored (125). Besides that, he stole 35 bases and notched 30 outfield assists.

Around this time, Jackson also began making business investments, supplementing his income by becoming a soft drink salesman and endorsing products ranging from tobacco to bats and gloves. He also helped market a brand of shoes. "When Shoeless Joe wears 'em," the slogan read, "he wears Selz shoes."[21] He modeled for ads for Boston Garters, which were priced at twenty-five to fifty cents, and were supposed to "hold your sock smooth as your skin"[22]; he appeared in rifle advertisements on the backs of magazines and he endorsed Absorbine Jr. liniment. Jackson also invested in a pool room, bought a larger house for his parents, and purchased a farm. His prosperity seemed ensured and to be rising along with his performance and fame.

Over the winter, he worked on the farm and played in exhibition games. When he reported back to spring training in Pensacola, Florida on March 6, 1913, most people considered him one of the top three or four stars in all of major league baseball. His .394 lifetime batting average was the highest in professional baseball and his defensive skills were extraordinary. When asked to compare Cobb and Jackson, the Naps manager, Joe Birmingham said, "I consider Joe the greater asset to a club of the two."[23]

Jackson started the 1913 season so well that he held the batting lead for a while; on May 10, he hit a bases-loaded triple and, on May 11, he hit his second career grand slam. In June, Jackson's average was .447, the best in the major leagues, and on June 4 against the Yankees, he hit a home run estimated at over 500 feet over the right-field grandstand in the Polo Grounds (the Yankees shared the stadium with New York's Giants). Two days later, the following appeared in the *New York Evening Mail*:

You know where Wagner's landed
We saw where Baker's hit,
But no one ever found the ball
That Joseph Jackson hit.[24]

On June 20, though, Jackson suffered somewhat of a setback. He was hit in the head by a ball and this affected his hearing for several days. Two days later, Jackson got into an uncharacteristic argument with an umpire and was suspended from the league. Jackson protested that even though he had cursed at the umpire, the umpire cursed him first, but it was to no avail. He was suspended for three days and fined twenty-five dollars.

Even more damaging to the Naps season, though, was that Birmingham, the manager, and Lajoie, the veteran player, did not get along. Birmingham resented how Lajoie spoke to him, especially after the player cursed him in public; conversely, Lajoie resented the batting instruction that Birmingham gave. "Birmingham never hit .250 in his life," Lajoie complained bitterly, "so where does he get the license to pose as teacher?"[25]

Then, Jackson injured himself again, this time in a bizarre fashion. While playing the outfield in Washington's Griffith Stadium, he crashed into a bull-shaped sign for the Bull Durham tobacco company and knocked himself unconscious. Although he recovered quickly, his batting average dropped and he ended the season at .373—finishing second, once again, to Ty Cobb.

Although he lost the batting title, Jackson had tagged the most hits that year with 197, hit the most doubles (39) and boasted the highest slugging percentage at .551, this time besting Cobb for the coveted slugging award. In over 500 at-bats, Jackson had struck out only 26 times, and he also had 28 outfield assists. That year, he received the second most votes for the Chalmers Most Valuable Player award, losing to Walter Johnson.[26]

After the regular season ended, the Naps and the Pittsburgh Pirates played a best-of-seven interleague series for additional revenue, which allowed Jackson to bat against the legendary Honus Wagner, a man that many people believe was the best all-around major league baseball player ever. Wagner had won eight National League batting titles since 1900, the most recent being in 1911, and he was frequently the league leader in on-base percentage, slugging percentage, total bases, doubles, triples, and stolen bases.[27]

The Naps won the first two games; during the second game, Jackson drove in the winning run and made an unassisted double play from the outfield. In a seldom-seen move, he caught a line drive in short right field, then ran all the way into the infield, to tag out a runner retreating to first. The Pirates won the next three games, but then the Naps won the final two games to clinch the series. Jackson took home an extra $232.25 for this postseason finale.

Jackson returned home to Greenville that winter, just as he'd done every other winter while playing professional ball. This time, he also brought home "five or six dogs" that were, according to sportswriter Henry Edwards, "more or less pedigreed, particularly less."[28] He also took home eighteen bats. Jackson and Katie spent time in Greenville, but also vacationed in New Orleans, where he played in exhibition games and where the couple was entertained by vaudeville shows, which were not available in Greenville.

Although Joe and Katie enjoyed their time in New Orleans, life in Greenville was uncertain. Jackson's father was ill, a particular concern as some of Jackson's siblings still lived at home and Gertrude, the youngest, was only eight. Without George's income, Joe Jackson would need to assume significantly more financial responsibility for the family's security; at the same time that Jackson and his family were experiencing personal worries, the world of professional baseball was undergoing an upheaval, as well.

In 1913, John T. Powers and a group of entrepreneurs had founded a new minor league baseball system known as the Federal League. This league was to consist of six to eight teams, each managed by former major league players, including Cy Young.[29] During that initial season, the league did not attempt to sign any players who were currently on major league teams, nor did owners claim to want major league status. They simply wanted to offer quality ballgames at a breakeven point, and their 1913 league was a "mixture of highly touted semi-pros from local trolley leagues, marginal minor leaguers and a few over-the-hill major league players."[30]

Attendance figures are hard to find, but the league was successful enough to last the season. At the end of that first season, though, team owners replaced Powers with Chicago millionaire and coal magnate James A. Gilmore; the philosophy of this Spanish-American War veteran was far more aggressive. Gilmore already partly owned the Chicago team in the Federal League and he conducted negotiations with other businessmen, hoping to entice them into transforming the current two-league system, which consisted of the American League and National League, into a three-league system that would include the Federal League.

This idea wasn't original. Renegade leagues had previously been formed during the tenure of the National League, which began in 1876, with officials encouraging players to break their unfavorable and one-sided contracts to join their particular leagues. Starting in 1882, the American Association directly competed with the National League, launching a competition for major league predominance that lasted ten years. To encourage attendance at American Association games, teams charged twenty-five cents per game, as compared to the National

League's admission fee of fifty cents; the renegade league also sold beer and allowed Sunday games, in hopes of attracting a strong fan base.

The American Association was forming at a time when cities were expanding, and some of them—New York, Philadelphia, St. Louis, and Cincinnati, most notably—were without a major league team. Because of these factors, a large enough audience existed to support both leagues, ensuring the success of the American Association for several years. The relationship between the administrations of the National League and the American Association, however, was constantly in flux; during some periods, they organized interleague championship play and seemed relatively at peace with one another. At other times, contractual disputes, which were generally caused when a player left one league to join the other, wreaked havoc.

The situation became more complicated in 1884 when a group of investors formed the Union Association, an aspiring major league system that pledged to provide contracts more favorable to players. This league failed after one year; reasons for the collapse included a lack of financial backing, a dearth of star-quality players, and the fact that the American public did not support a third major league—especially after the American Association, in an attempt to hold on to their players, had expanded from an eight-team system to one with twelve teams.

After the demise of the Union Association, which purported to offer better terms to players, the National League and the American Association tightened their controls on the ballplayers, blacklisting many and fining others, often in a harsh and arbitrary fashion. In response, the Brotherhood of Professional Base Ball Players was formed, which served as both a collective bargaining group for players and the impetus for the Players League, which was founded in 1890. Its founders wanted to protest low salaries, punitive fines, and contract clauses that limited a player's ability to improve his situation. This league also lasted only one year,[31] but during that season, as many as 100 National League players deserted their teams in favor of the Players League, including stars such as Charles Comiskey and Connie Mack; well known and valued players from the American Association also defected.

By the time that the Players League had folded, the American Association was also in trouble; they had expanded when other leagues were forming, which meant that they were expending more financial resources at a time when less support was available for each individual team. Moreover, they had lost many of their fan favorites to the Players League and, although they fought with the National League to regain these contracts, the American Association became absorbed into the more stable National League. Their lasting legacy is that they pioneered the use of professional umpires.

Only a few short years later, in 1900, Ban Johnson formed yet another rival league, the American League, and he also challenged the unique spot that the National League held, once again, in professional baseball. The American League, which incorporated teams from the former minor league, the Western League, as its base, was initially regarded as an outlaw league that was inappropriately luring players away from the National League, but the threat to the established system quickly became apparent.

Johnson began offering top-notch players better contracts, causing hardship for the National League. Not only was he successful at signing stars such as Nap Lajoie, but attendance figures indicated that significantly more fans were attending American League games than National League ones. Johnson began forming teams in cities that already had a National League team, including Boston, Chicago, Philadelphia, St. Louis—and then New York—and by 1903, the American League had successfully established itself as a major league. Therefore, when James Gilmore announced his plan to have the Federal League become the third major league, his plan didn't seem all that preposterous.

To gain support for his proposal, Gilmore needed investors. He must have been quite impressive in his attempts, as National League President John K. Tener said, "not only can [Gilmore] convince a millionaire that the moon is made of green cheese, but he can induce him to invest money in a cheese factory on the moon."[32] Gilmore assured potential backers that they could earn profits by sponsoring the Federal League, and that they could use the teams to advertise their products. One such sponsor, the Victor Sporting Goods Company, praised the league in their advertisements, promising that it would provide quality games, crowds, pitching, batting, and fielding.

Investors, though, weren't enough. Gilmore also needed to entice players, especially fan favorites, to switch to his league; unfortunately, most quality players were under contract to two other leagues. His first move, then, was to play up the all-too-real sources of discontent that players were experiencing in the American and National Leagues, and to exploit their unhappiness with the status quo.

Major league contracts heavily favored the owners. They contained a reserve clause, which basically meant that all contracts automatically extended from the current year until the beginning of the following year, thereby creating a bond between player and owner that was, for all intents and purposes, perpetual. Only team owners could cancel a contract and allow a player to join another team or league. This gave the players little bargaining power and almost no ability to obtain a raise in pay, even when their performance warranted. To protect their collective interests, team owners tacitly agreed not to sign a player who was already under contract with another major league team and they abided by that unwritten agreement. The contracts also contained a ten-day clause, which meant that, although a player could not negotiate or change the contract, the owner could cancel the agreement, for any reason, with only ten days notice.

Under Gilmore's Federal League proposal, however, players could switch teams and also obtain a share of the club's profits. League officials even went on record saying that they were opposed to any form of reserve clause whatsoever. Many players were intrigued by this notion; during the winter of 1913–1914, while Jackson was home with his dying father, three Cleveland pitchers, one of whom won twenty-three games the previous season, signed with the Federal League. George Stovall, the Naps former manager, also broke his contract with the St. Louis Browns to join this upstart league. Stovall posed a particularly dangerous threat; he was so successful at encouraging others to break their contracts that newspapers were calling him "Jesse James of the Federal League."[33]

All told, the Federal League convinced eighty-one major league players, eighteen of whom still had ongoing contracts, to join their rival association. They attempted to sway Ty Cobb and Tris Speaker to join, without success. They nearly convinced pitcher Walter Johnson to leave the Senators; only a counteroffer with a hefty pay raise prevented the "Big Train" from desertion.

National and American League officials threatened to sue the Federal League for illegally luring away their assets. The Federal League threatened to countersue, claiming that the exclusive ownership structure of the current major league system was a monopoly, which violated the 1914 Clayton Anti-Trust Act, a strengthening of the 1890 Sherman Anti-Trust Act.[34]

How much Jackson was aware of these machinations is uncertain. Possibly, because of distractions at home and because of the farm work that he undertook that winter, he was wholly ignorant of them until he was approached directly by Federal League officials, and asked to join their league for an annual salary of $20,000.

Contrary to public perception, Jackson wasn't one of the highest paid major league players. He received only $6,000 from the Naps the previous year, which was $3,000 less than what the aging Lajoie received, and only half of the annual salary of either Cobb or Speaker. So, the sum of $20,000 must have been extraordinarily tempting, especially when his father, George Elmore Jackson, died on February 11 at the age of 57, leaving Joe Jackson the official breadwinner of a large family.

Jackson did not publicly disclose the Federal League's offer until after he signed a three-year contract with the Naps for $6,000 annually. He clearly had no intention of jumping leagues in spite of his low pay. "The Feds got after me when I was in Atlanta," he told the *Plain Dealer*, "but there is no use of their bothering me. I am not going to go to them."[35] Jackson also claimed that he chased off the Federal League representatives by wielding Black Betsy.

It's impossible to know, with certainty, why Jackson refused such a hefty raise. Perhaps he did know that American League officials threatened to ban permanently any player who joined the Federal League and was reluctant to take the risk; or he may have heard rumors about the uncertain financial backing of this new league that was built on corporate promises that might or might not be realistic. Although James Gilmore, a man who made millions of dollars in the coal industry, was sponsoring the new venture, he had no reputation as a baseball man, a distinction that set him apart from Ban Johnson. It also seemed doubtful that Americans could financially support three leagues, and the failure of previous attempts to expand the major leagues signaled that the Federal League's demise was a real possibility. Alternatively, maybe Jackson simply felt comfortable with the Naps and didn't want to change his circumstances; or perhaps he was merely being loyal to the team that had provided him with a solid foundation on which to continue his career.

In any case, Joe Jackson did not break his contract with the Cleveland Naps; instead, he reported to Athens, Georgia, on March 3, 1914 for spring training. As soon as he arrived in his new Ford, he exited the car, picked up a bat and hit several line drives, even before changing into his uniform. He seemed relieved when his swing proved strong, saying, "My eyes are all right. Just watch out for me this year. I just couldn't wait until I had given them a test."[36]

Although Jackson's batting was impressive during the 1914 spring training, Lajoie's wasn't. Several Naps were injured, as well; in addition, three pitchers had left Cleveland for the Federal League, and the Naps looked weak. During spring training, they even lost several games to reserve players known as the "Naplets."

Jackson convinced manager Birmingham to play two exhibition games in Greenville, and he even suggested that Greenville might make a quality permanent site for future spring training. His mother, Martha, attended these contests, and his brother, Earl, played in them. The attendance at the first game, though, was so small that a tongue-in-cheek newspaper reporter stated, "the crowd (was) busy taking a drink by himself."[37] Cleveland writers, who had traveled to Greenville to report on the games, were disappointed with the homespun field, and they mocked the setup. Jackson and the Naps played the second exhibition game, then abandoned the idea of playing in Greenville ever again.

Jackson continued to hit well during spring training, and his batting average rose above .500 in parts of April, while his slugging percentage hovered near .900. During one game, he hit a home run that traveled fifty feet past the right-field fence, the longest home run witnessed in that ballpark.

The Naps season, though, didn't start out well. In the second game, their pitcher broke a bone in his hand; another Naps player jumped to the Federal League and Lajoie was batting poorly, as were many other players. On June 1, there was sparse attendance, with the *Plain Dealer* noting, "That is probably one point in favor of the club. The fewer witnesses to such an affair, the better for the financial end of baseball."[38]

Problems continued as the season progressed. Ray Chapman, their fleet-footed shortstop, broke his leg, which kept him out of the line-up until June 16. Jackson injured his knee during a slide; it became seriously infected and he eventually ended up in the hospital for nearly a week and out of the line-up for almost a month, not returning until July 8. By this point of the season, crowds were numbering under 1,000 during the week and the Naps sank to the bottom of their division.

There were, however, brief moments of top-notch individual play. On July 11, Shoeless Joe Jackson played against George Herman "Babe" Ruth for the first time. Although the Naps lost, Jackson drove in a run against this young pitcher; Ruth later admitted copying Jackson's swing, saying, "I thought he was the greatest hitter I had ever seen, the greatest natural hitter I ever saw. He's the guy who made me a hitter. I copied his swing."[39]

Another personal highlight for Jackson came on August 3 when he hit a double and two singles against future Hall-of-Famer Walter Johnson. "I could throw my fast one past Cobb, Crawford, Lajoie, and all those fellows," Johnson later said, "but Jackson was always a puzzle." When Cobb accused Johnson of pitching more gently against Jackson, Johnson denied that, saying, "If anything, I tried harder against Jackson because he always seemed tougher."[40]

Nevertheless, those moments of success were brief and scattered, and when the 1914 season ended, the Naps must have breathed a collective sigh of relief. Their statistics were dismal. They finished in last place, and attendance was down two-thirds from the previous year. Jackson, once again, lost the American League batting title. He'd led the league as late as August 12 with .360, but ended the season with Boston's Tris Speaker for third with .338, in comparison to Ty Cobb's .368 and Eddie Collins' .344. His slugging percentage was below .500 for the first time in his major league career, and he hit only 22 doubles in 1914. In a sense, Jackson's performance seemed to slump with the team's.

That winter, though, Jackson found a new source of income and entertainment, one that didn't involve Greenville or Katie. He starred in vaudeville acts, showing the crowd "Black Betsy" and demonstrating his powerful swing. These vaudeville appearances were described as a "sob rendition of his rise in the baseball world . . . from a minor place in the cotton mill to a major place in the baseball world." Another writer described his show as a "tabloid musical farce comedy."[41] Although some writers would later claim that Jackson lost money on this venture, he actually made a profit. During his two-week opening in Atlanta, he performed to sold-out audiences each time.

He traveled with a group of beautiful women, known as "Joe Jackson's Baseball Girls," and they toured southern states. Because of his hectic touring schedule, he didn't play exhibition games and he didn't work at the farm. Because he was away from Katie for long stretches of time, he also gained weight from the change in diet.

This circuit tour negatively affected both his physical shape and his marriage, especially when ugly rumors reached Katie. Jackson, it was said, was spending an inordinate amount of time with one actress in particular. The Jacksons' marital situation worsened when, instead of reporting to spring training in 1915, Jackson stayed with the vaudeville troupe. At this point, Katie hired an attorney and filed suit for divorce, citing Cuyahoga County, Ohio, as their legal residence, because such an action would have been illegal in South Carolina.

Katie contacted the sheriff of Greenville, South Carolina, and he traveled to where Jackson was staying to serve him papers. Upon learning of the suit, the new vaudeville star became angry. A quick fistfight ensued and a newspaper reporter said that the sheriff was "badly battered."[42]

After sparring with the sheriff, that evening effectively ended Jackson's vaudeville tour and possibly gave him second thoughts about exploiting his personal celebrity. Instead of returning to his hotel room, Jackson got on a train to Greenville, where he posted bond for the charges filed against him. He then returned home to Katie; the following morning, he headed to spring training camp. On April 12, the *Cleveland Plain Dealer* announced that Jackson had suffered a nervous collapse over the matter; shortly thereafter, though, the *Sporting News* shared that Jackson's common sense and "forgiving little wife"[43] had contributed to the couple's new understanding with one another. Katie withdrew her request for divorce and their life returned to its more familiar pattern.

NOTES

1. Gropman, *Say It Ain't So, Joe!*, 102.
2. Fleitz, *Shoeless*, 61.
3. Ibid., 62.
4. Ibid.
5. Gropman, *Say It Ain't So, Joe!*, 126.
6. Ibid., 121.
7. Fleitz, *Shoeless*, 63.
8. Gropman, *Say It Ain't So, Joe!*, 122.
9. Ibid., 119.
10. Ibid., 119–120.

11. Frommer, *Shoeless Joe and Ragtime Baseball*, 44.

12. Gropman, *Say It Ain't So, Joe!*, 115.

13. Ibid., 117.

14. Fleitz, *Shoeless*, 81.

15. Ibid., 72.

16. Gropman, *Say It Ain't So, Joe!*, 123.

17. Frommer, *Shoeless Joe and Ragtime Baseball*, 42.

18. Gropman, *Say It Ain't So, Joe!*, 127.

19. Fleitz, *Shoeless*, 66.

20. Frommer, *Shoeless Joe and Ragtime Baseball*, 41.

21. Fleitz, *Shoeless*, 73.

22. Frommer, *Shoeless Joe and Ragtime Baseball*, 44.

23. Fleitz, *Shoeless*, 71.

24. Ibid., 76.

25. Ibid., 77.

26. Ibid., 78.

27. See http://www.baseball.reference.com/w/wagneho01.shtml.

28. Fleitz, *Shoeless*, 79.

29. See http://www.baseballlibrary.com/baseballlibrary/ballplayers/F/Federal_League.stm.

30. Marc Okkonen, *Federal League: Baseball's Third Major League* (New York: Society for American Baseball Research, 1989), 4.

31. For information about the Federal League and other leagues of the era, see Okkonen's Federal League; also see David Pietrusza, *Major Leagues: The Formation, Sometimes Absorption, and Mostly Inevitable Demise of eighteen Professional Baseball Organizations, 1871 to Present* (Jefferson, NC: McFarland and Company, 1991). As the subtitle implies, the beginnings and endings of leagues weren't always clear or distinct.

32. Pietrusza, *Major Leagues*, 220.

33. Fleitz, *Shoeless*, 82.

34. David Pietrusza, *Judge and Jury: The Life and Times of Judge Kenesaw Mountain Landis* (South Bend, IN: Diamond Communications, Inc., 1998), 154.

35. Fleitz, *Shoeless*, 86.

36. Ibid., 86.

37. Ibid., 87.

38. Ibid., 89.

39. Frommer, *Shoeless Joe and Ragtime Baseball*, 50.

40. Fleitz, *Shoeless*, 92.

41. Gropman, *Say It Ain't So, Joe!*, 129.

42. Ibid., 130.

43. Fleitz, *Shoeless*, 98–99.

Jackson, who became known as baseball's "Beau Brummell" because of his natty and stylish clothing, shows off his trophies. *Cleveland Public Library.*

CHANGES IN THE AIR, 1915–1917

"If the White Sox ever held a victory banquet," Ring Lardner once told Heywood Broun, "they'd ask the caterer for twenty separate checks."

It was true. The Sox rarely did anything together, except win.
  —Told from the point-of-view of the fictional character, Sport
  Sullivan[1]

Joe Jackson's personal life seemed to be unraveling during the 1915 off-season. His father's illness and death the previous year had upset him, and now he struggled to regain equilibrium in his marriage. He could obtain little solace from work, either. During 1914–1915, professional baseball had been falling into disarray, and bickering between Federal League officials and established major league clubs had moved from the ballparks into the courtroom. Principally, contract disputes were at the center of the problem, at least at first, but in January 1915, the Federal League followed through on its threat and filed an antitrust lawsuit against the major league system. The Federal League owners had reason for optimism; they had won lesser contractual disputes and felt that, because of recent federal legislation, they had a good opportunity to tackle the monopolistic nature of the American and National Leagues.

In the early part of the twentieth century, President Theodore Roosevelt, known as the "Trust Buster," began focusing his energy on breaking up monopolies that he felt used deceptive business practices. Accordingly, the government filed over forty lawsuits against gigantic monopolies, including the Northern Securities Company, the American Tobacco Company, the Du Pont Corporation, and the New Haven Railroad. The largest monopoly of all, John D. Rockefeller's Standard Oil, was also in Roosevelt's sights. This company controlled 85 percent of the nation's refined oil and brought in enormous profits each year. Even more monopolistic, Standard Oil employed a railway rebate system that allowed the oil company to double and triple the railway freight costs of their other rail carriers, virtually ensuring the competitors' failure—and the continuing dominance of Standard Oil.[2]

In February 1903, under Roosevelt's presidency, the Elkins Anti-Rebate Act disallowed these large and powerful shipper rebates; by 1906, it was clear that Standard Oil was ignoring the law, and indictments were handed down in several states where rebating occurred. Proceedings in *United States v. Standard Oil Company of Indiana* began on March 4, 1907 in the courtroom of Judge Kenesaw Mountain Landis, a man known for making tough and dramatic decisions.[3]

Rockefeller, who was required to appear in court, went into hiding while his attorneys attempted to negotiate a deal with Landis whereby the case could be tried by proxy; the judge, though, insisted upon Rockefeller's personal appearance. The multimillionaire eventually acquiesced, testifying on July 6; on August 3, Landis delivered a 7,500-word opinion that upheld the constitutionality of the Elkins Act. He also fined Rockefeller and Standard Oil an astounding $29,240,000, the largest fine to date imposed by a court in the United States.[4]

Although that penalty was eventually overturned, there was much celebration around the country when the financial consequence was first announced. "One honest judge," wrote Landis's biographer, David Pietrusza, "had at last been found. Someone had *finally* brought the trusts to their knees."[5]

The *Chicago Record-Herald* put the fine in perspective, alluding to the controversial shipping rebates in its comparison. "Twenty-nine million silver dollars would weigh 980 tons and require 58 freight cars for its transport."[6]

Journalist Fred Lieb, referring to the fact that the judge was named after Kennesaw Mountain, Georgia, where his surgeon father was wounded in a Civil War battle, said that, "Landis was as hard on offenders in civil courts . . . as a chip of granite from Kennesaw Mountain, and when he reached a decision he was as firm as the mountain itself in making it stand."[7]

Although he was physically unimpressive, standing about five feet, seven inches, and weighing around 130 pounds, Kenesaw[8] Mountain Landis exuded power, nevertheless. His white hair sprouted in a bold and unkempt fashion, and his face was craggy and raw. People summarized his personality as flinty, colorful, quirky and flamboyant; because of his hardline approach toward Rockefeller and the Standard Oil monopoly, Federal League officials initially applauded his overseeing their case against the American and National League.

As time went by, though, Landis' procrastination—and his unwillingness to rule against the current major league structure—became apparent. Landis didn't rule for the major league system, he just didn't rule against it, and Federal League officials came to realize that this no-nonsense judge harbored a special affection for the game of baseball. "Both sides," he said, "must understand that any blows at the thing called baseball would be regarded by this court as a blow to a national institution."[9]

The longer that Landis delayed making a decision, the more deeply in debt the Federal League fell. Although players appreciated the more generous salaries paid by the Federal League, those benefits also caused the burgeoning organization significant financial difficulties. By December 1915, it was obvious that the Federal League must dissolve; shortly afterwards, the *Sporting News* displayed a two-column photo of Landis with a caption that read, simply, "He's the game's good friend."[10]

In the midst of this combination of stasis and inaction, Jackson had returned to 1915 spring training, where newspaper reporters mocked his recent foray into vaudeville. The *Cleveland Plain Dealer*, noting how Jackson had spent an hour before the regular-season opener chatting with Ty Cobb, had this caustic comment: "Perhaps Ty was getting pointers on running a burlesque show."[11]

Jackson's batting performance, though, didn't seem to suffer from the mockery. He hit a two-run double on Opening Day, and his batting average quickly climbed to .350. However, Cleveland—now renamed the Indians—hadn't improved upon the previous year's desultory performance. Contributing to their malaise, perhaps, was the fact that the team had lost a fan favorite; Indians owner, Charles Somers, had sold Nap Lajoie to Jackson's old team, the Philadelphia Athletics.

Perhaps desperate for any change that might improve the dynamics of his struggling team, Somers insisted that manager Joe Birmingham move Jackson to first base, a position that the slugger sometimes played in practice. This demand increased the growing tension between the two men. Birmingham resented the owner's interference, and Somers must have been disappointed in his new manager's win-loss record. By mid-May, Birmingham, Cleveland's seventh manager, was fired, causing some to label that city as the graveyard for baseball managers.

Somers appointed former catcher Lee Fohl to an interim manager position; after a fruitless search for a permanent manager, he gave Fohl the job. Jackson, in the meantime, was nursing a sore arm; people who were looking to rationalize away the Indians struggles blamed Jackson's ailment on the change in his fielding position.

Jackson's physical problems continued to multiply. On June 16, Boston Red Sox pitcher Ernie Shore beaned him, and the slugger was unconscious for several minutes. Although he returned to work the following day, a car accident on July 7 almost took him out of the game for good. No bones were broken, but Jackson suffered from numerous cuts and bruises, and knee and elbow injuries kept him out of the line-up, other than minor exhibition play, until July 30.

Meanwhile, the troubles for Jackson's club continued. Attendance was down, thanks to a year and a half of dismal play; on July 1, the *Plain Dealer* lambasted their home team as the "joke of the big leagues."[12] Somers, who had already sold the popular Lajoie, began shopping around for a Jackson trade. Rumors surfaced that Jackson was going to play for the Washington Senators, and the Federal League, which hadn't yet dissolved, bid again for his services. The potential for a contract-breaking switch to the Federal League eventually disturbed Somers enough that he insisted Jackson sign a three-year contract with the Indians for $6,000 per year.[13]

Although Katie Jackson had been displeased with the behavior of her formerly errant husband, she never stopped assisting with his business affairs, and she was reported to be highly upset over her husband's negotiations with the Federal League. She attended the contract signing with Somers, where the Cleveland Indians owner praised her business sense; from that point on, she completely controlled the family finances.

Ironically, the firm contract that Katie insisted upon made it very difficult for Jackson to switch to the Federal League; which, in turn, made him a much more attractive prospect for other teams in the National and American Leagues. The Washington Senators were interested in Jackson, but so was Charles Comiskey, owner of the Chicago White Sox. "Go to Cleveland," Comiskey reportedly said to his secretary, "watch the bidding for Jackson, [and] raise the highest one made by any club until they all drop out."[14]

The secretary followed his instructions, and Somers and Comiskey finally settled on a price of $31,500 for Jackson, along with three players sent to Cleveland: outfielders Robert "Braggo" Roth and Larry Chappell, and pitcher Ed Klepfer. All told, the value of Jackson in the trade was $65,500, the largest in professional baseball history up to that point.

As news of Jackson's impending departure became public, Ohio newspapers began summarizing his batting accomplishments for Cleveland's team. In 673 games, he had garnered 937 hits, with 400-plus of them for extra bases; when he left, his cumulative average was .374. When one fan was asked about the Indians chances without Jackson, he replied, "Team? What team? They sold *him* to Chicago!"[15]

Cleveland's loss, though, was Chicago's potential gain. In his quest for a baseball dynasty, Comiskey had already built a new stadium, dubbed White Sox Park (soon renamed Comiskey Park), completed in 1910. Built on property that once served as the city dump, Comiskey envisioned a grandiose Roman design. Costs were prohibitive, though, and so he compromised on the architectural plans. Nevertheless, the stadium was nicknamed the "Baseball Palace of the World," and the setting was picturesque. "The steeples of several churches," wrote author Harvey Frommer, "the facades of brand-new buildings, and the languid leafiness of old trees formed a pleasing backdrop."[16]

Just a few short years after completing Comiskey Park, the White Sox owner began building a team with winning potential; he already owned pitcher Ed Walsh and second baseman Eddie Collins, and Joe Jackson would be the next step in his quest for a pennant. Comiskey hadn't won a league championship since 1906, but he saw an opportunity in 1915 because his perennial competition, Connie Mack's Philadelphia Athletics, was the only team with a poorer playing record than the Indians.

Thirty-two thousand fans streamed into the red-bricked ballpark on July 1, 1910, filling the two-tiered grandstand that included one row of wooden bleachers and brilliant bunting. To please fans, Comiskey had installed showers by the bleachers behind center field, so that spectators could find relief from the summer heat. He also provided large picnic areas that were available to groups free of charge, and he incorporated Bavarian and Mexican restaurants—complete with beer halls—in his ballpark.

It was reported that Comiskey had consulted with pitcher Ed Walsh on the design of the field; Walsh, understandably enough, wanted a layout that favored pitchers, and so that park did. Fences in left and right field were located 362 feet from home plate, while center field was 420 feet away. This ballpark clearly wasn't as favorable to hitters as League Park in Cleveland.[17]

Although these less-than-ideal conditions might have intimidated a younger Jackson, Shoeless Joe was a far different individual from the nervous country boy who had fled his train ride to Philadelphia, Pennsylvania, years before. Jackson was also different from the rising star who had arrived in Cleveland to be seriously tested in the major leagues; now, he was an established presence in professional baseball and more likely to look out for his own interests.

"While he does not admit it," a *Cleveland Plain Dealer* reporter wrote, "he was becoming . . . a purely individual player who sacrificed team work for Joe

Jackson."[18] While this reporter's view of Jackson's lack of teamwork seems exaggerated and jaundiced, Jackson was more confident in his abilities and beginning to see himself as a star.

It was inaccurately reported that Jackson's salary in Chicago would be $10,000; the reality was $6,000. When compared to other baseball stars of his caliber, the pay was low; on the other hand, the annual salary for an average worker in America during that era was only $750,[19] which made Jackson comparatively well off.

At the time Jackson arrived in Chicago on August 20, 1915, the city boasted a population of over two million (many of them immigrant) and was the second largest metropolis in the country.[20] A somewhat cynical view of Chicago is as follows: an "ugly, muscular mass of people, places, and plans. Its brick pavements where horse-drawn wagons and cars vied for space symbolized an old century dying and a new one beginning its crest. In Chicago, all came together: racial tensions, union tensions, the shimmy and the shake, sex and crime and women on the prowl, men and boys looking for trouble, and trouble looking for them."[21]

Although that description painted a negative picture of Chicago, its fans welcomed Jackson, and Comiskey dubbed him the "greatest straightaway hitter in all of baseball."[22] Newspapers called Katie the "White Sox Mascot," probably because she traveled with her husband, something unusual in that era.[23]

The atmosphere in Chicago was fairly pleasant, which usually foretold a good season for Jackson, but he batted only .272 during the forty-five games of his partial season with the White Sox. Even when scorekeepers factored in the .327 that he'd batted for the Cleveland Naps that year, Jackson's batting average totaled .308, the worst of his professional career.[24]

Several factors mitigated. He was still recovering from his July car accident; he had endured a stressful period in his marriage, and had completed yet another move. Jackson must have also felt the effects of being surrounded by a new set of teammates, some of whom were college educated, a situation similar to what he had experienced in Philadelphia. Therefore, although Jackson experienced a professional low, circumstances seemed temporary. Meanwhile, personal troubles lingered; although he and Katie had reconciled, his reputation in Greenville was quite shaky.

Jackson did not return to his hometown that winter, hesitant because of bad feelings that still festered with the sheriff that he had assaulted. People gossiped about his near divorce, something still considered scandalous in Greenville, South Carolina—at that time, only one in every 1,000 persons was divorced[25]—and besides that, his pool hall and farm were losing money, probably because of mismanagement that occurred while Jackson and Katie were away.

Therefore, the Jacksons returned to Cleveland during the off-season, a city where they felt comfortable. Before spring training began in 1916, they moved again—this time to Savannah, Georgia, where Jackson's newly wed sister, Lula, had just moved. Jackson had enjoyed playing semipro ball in that town; after selling his farm and pool hall, he and Katie bought a $10,000 waterfront home, and Jackson also invested in a pool hall in his new hometown.[26] Everything, however, wasn't ideal.

During this off-season, sportswriters weren't consistently kind to Jackson. One story in *Baseball Magazine* called, "The Greatest Player That Might Have Been," claimed that Jackson had a "judgment not always adequate . . . wayward temperament and an erratic ambition scarce fitted to develop his wondrous abilities to their fullest measure." Although Jackson must have felt somewhat insulted, articles such as this one also caused him to realize that he must, once again, become more serious about his training and ballplaying.[27]

Spring training started up again in March 1916 at Mineral Wells, Texas. There, Jackson quickly discovered that the owner of Chicago's team, Charles Comiskey, prodded his players into a hectic schedule of exhibition games, presumably to put more money into the owner's pocket. When the regular season began on April 12, 31,000 fans attended Opening Day in Chicago, only to watch the Detroit Tigers win 4–0. Jackson had performed well in spring training, but in this home opener, he hit only one single, giving rise to the talk that the slugger's best years were already behind him.

Comiskey considered trading Jackson to build up his infield; the owner was intent on building a pennant-winning team. Towards that end, Comiskey acquired two new pitchers, Claude "Lefty" Williams, a young curveball pitcher who quickly befriended Jackson, and Dave Danforth, a "shine ball" pitcher who taught Chicago veteran Eddie Cicotte how to use oil and dust to cause a fastball to unexpectedly dip near the plate. Cicotte hoped that this new trick would revitalize his sagging career and allow him to be part of a pennant-winning team.[28]

During the first two months of the 1916 season, the White Sox played only average ball. In the middle of June, though, manager Clarence "Pants" Rowland moved Jackson, who had been batting in the fifth position, back to the cleanup spot, fourth in the order. From June 15 to 18, the White Sox won three out of four games against the Boston Red Sox, the defending American League champions. Jackson racked up 10 hits out of 14 trips to the plate, which raised his batting average to .372. From May 31 until July 4, he connected for 55 hits out of 104 times at bat. His average, if one isolated that time period, was an amazing .524.[29]

By the end of August, the White Sox were in third place. Although their overall performances were sporadic, Cicotte had used the shine ball to his advantage that summer and had a 15–7 record. "Lefty" Williams and "Red" Faber were also winning games, and outfielder Oscar "Happy" Felsch began hitting well, ending up with a .300 season. That combination was not enough to beat the Red Sox, who boasted pitchers Babe Ruth and Ernie Shore on their roster, but the White Sox did end the season in a satisfying second place.[30]

Jackson finished the year with a .341 average, third in the batting title race. His 21 triples were tops in the league, as were his total bases (293). His slugging percentage was second in the league at .495; he also boasted the third highest number of doubles (40) and the fifth highest number of runs batted in (78), a new statistic that was gaining popularity. When the White Sox challenged the Chicago Cubs in their traditional post season City Series, Jackson hit 3 doubles in the third game and a home run in the fourth. His average during that series was .571.[31]

In a reversal of *Baseball Magazine*'s denigrating article from the previous year, the *Sporting News* published a long editorial on Jackson, praising his positive attitude and team loyalty. The reporter extolled his batting skills and described him in this manner: "Unlettered and unlearned in the ways of the world when he broke into the limelight a few years back, he is today a person in whose company one finds pleasure and profit, a gentleman of manners, at ease in any gathering, his homely wisdom a delight to those who meet him, and his sheer honesty and straightforwardness a relief in these sordid times."[32]

By this time, rumors about a Jackson trade had faded. Comiskey continued his team building after the season, acquiring first baseman Arnold "Chick" Gandil and shortstop Charles "Swede" Risberg; the second purchase allowed Comiskey and Rowland to move George "Buck" Weaver from the shortstop position to third base, a position where he excelled.

Although the infield was greatly strengthened by these moves, the team was not cohesive behind scenes. Gandil, who had grown up in the mining camps of California and Arizona, and who had run away from home as a teenager, strongly disliked the educated team captain, Eddie Collins. Gandil, who once earned a living in the rough sport of boxing, drank heavily and gravitated to the company of Risberg, a hot-tempered man who had once knocked out an umpire with one punch.

Moreover, Comiskey favored his college-educated and more refined players, and he apparently didn't attempt to mediate or smooth over the differences in style among players who came from disparate backgrounds. He did, however, want to inspire his players to work together, so he promised them a bonus—specifics not revealed to the players—if they won the pennant in 1917; when Jackson and his teammates returned to spring training camp in March, the Chicago White Sox were predicted to do just that. Jackson, though, was once again plagued by physical problems. He started the season with an ankle injury—there was concern that he had damaged tendons—and his back was bothering him; Rowland moved him from center field to left field. By mid-May, his average was only .265 and, on July 1, had climbed only to .283.

Fortunately, Felsch was batting over .300, slightly higher than in 1916, and the White Sox and the Red Sox began battling once more for the American League pennant. In June, the White Sox won sixteen out of seventeen games and held a slight lead in the pennant race.[33]

On July 5, Jackson, still "off his feed"[34] with back and ankle problems, took a few days off to rest and recover. During that time, the Red Sox and White Sox continued to exchange first- and second-place bragging rights. Jackson returned to play on July 15, somewhat rejuvenated, and he tagged two hits that day; two days later, he hit a home run over the fence in Washington, and the White Sox won four games in just two days to regain the lead.

On August 14, a shine ball thrown by Dave Danforth—the player who taught Eddie Cicotte how to throw this controversial pitch—hit Tris Speaker in the head, knocking him unconscious. After that, American League president, Ban Johnson, forbade that pitch; Comiskey, felt that this was a deliberate attack on his team and vehemently protested the ban. Several times that season, there were protracted debates with umpires over whether or not a Chicago pitcher threw a shine ball. (Felsch thought the debate was meaningless, telling reporters that shine balls only existed in one's imagination.)[35]

By September, the White Sox held a four-game lead; by September 8, they held a seven-game lead, and they officially clinched the pennant on September 21 by beating the Red Sox. The White Sox had won one hundred games that season and ended up with an eight-game lead over their Boston rivals. They led the league in stolen bases, as well as in triples and runs scored.[36] Their winning percentage at Comiskey Park was an amazing .740, which surely must have pleased hometown fans.

Although Jackson's year wasn't stellar, he tagged 17 hits during 30 at-bats in September, raising his average to .294. By the end of the season, he climbed over the .300 mark, ending the season with .301. He also had the second most triples (17).

Between the end of the season and the beginning of the World Series, Jackson participated in a fundraising all-star game, to benefit the family of Tim Murnane, a sportswriter who had died suddenly. During that game, Jackson competed in a long-distance throwing contest, winning with a distance of 396 feet and 8 inches. For his efforts, he received a large silver bowl with an inscription calling Jackson the "World's Greatest Slugger."[37] He beat out Babe

Ruth and Tris Speaker, among other top-level players, but fans from Greenville lamented this throw, remembering when their hometown hero regularly threw over 400 feet. Their explanation was that ten years of major league play had taken some of the snap out of Jackson's arm.

Nevertheless, the Chicago White Sox won the American League pennant and the 1917 World Series loomed ahead. So did many other challenges, including the pressure on players to enlist as soldiers in World War I and the growing factionalism among players on the White Sox team, including the increasingly more obvious split between the "city slickers versus farm boys like Joe Jackson." As Frommer describes, "There were schisms springing from ethnic background." As important—and maybe even more importantly—there were also "problems stemming from disproportionate salaries." Although this was occurring in more places that just this particular team, "Nowhere was this more evident than on the Chicago White Sox."[38]

NOTES

1. Brendan Boyd, *Blue Ruin: A Novel of the 1919 World Series* (New York: W.W. Norton and Company, 1991), 36.

2. David Pietrusza, *Judge and Jury: The Life and Times of Judge Kenesaw Mountain Landis* (South Bend, IN: Diamond Communications, 1998), 47–48.

3. Ibid., 49.

4. Ibid., 63.

5. Ibid., 65 (emphasis Pietrusza's).

6. Ibid., 64.

7. Fred Lieb, *Baseball As I Have Known It* (New York: Coward, McCann and Geoghegan, 1977), 115.

8. Although some believe that "Kenesaw" was a misspelling of "Kennesaw," both were used in the nineteenth century when referring to the mountain.

9. Frommer, *Shoeless Joe and Ragtime Baseball*, 54.

10. Ibid., 55.

11. Fleitz, *Shoeless*, 99.

12. Ibid., 102.

13. The *Sporting News*, February 11, 1915, reported that Jackson claimed to have turned down a three-year, $60,000 contract with the Federal League. The reporter quoted Jackson as saying that there are things in this world more important than money, including "keeping faith with your friends, for instance. All of which goes to show that you don't have to know how to read and write to be a man of principle and conscience." See http://www.baseball1.com/carney/index.php?storyid=177.

14. Fleitz, *Shoeless*, 104.

15. Gropman, *Say It Ain't So, Joe!*, 137 (emphasis Gropman's).

16. Frommer, *Shoeless Joe and Ragtime Baseball*, 60.

17. See http://www.ballparksofbaseball.com/past/ComiskeyPark.htm.

18. Fleitz, *Shoeless*, 105.

19. See Kingswood College Library at http://kclibrary.nhmccd.edu/decade10.html.

20. See http://cdcga.org/HTMLs/decades/1910s.htm.

21. Frommer, *Shoeless Joe and Ragtime Baseball*, 63.

22. Ibid., 57.

23. Gropman, *Say It Ain't So, Joe!*, 140.

24. Jackson did have a lower batting average in 1908 and 1909, but he only batted five games in each of those seasons. See http://www.baseball-reference.com/j/jacksjo01.shtml.

25. See Kingswood College Library at http://kclibrary.nhmccd.edu/decade10.html.

26. Fleitz, *Shoeless*, 115.

27. Ibid., 115–116.

28. Ibid., 119.

29. Frommer, *Shoeless Joe and Ragtime Baseball*, 66.

30. Fleitz, *Shoeless*, 121–122.

31. Ibid., 122; see also http://www.baseball-reference.com/j/jacksjo01.shtml.

32. Gropman, *Say It Ain't So, Joe!*, 142.

33. Fleitz, *Shoeless*, 129–130.

34. Ibid., 130.

35. Ibid., 132.

36. Frommer, *Shoeless Joe and Ragtime Baseball*, 76; see also http://www.baseball-reference.com/games/standings.cgi?date=1917-09-00.

37. A photo of this trophy can be seen in Joe Thompson, *Growing Up With Shoeless Joe: The Greatest Natural Player in Baseball History* (Laurel Fork, VA: JTI Publishing, 1998), 28.

38. Frommer, *Shoeless Joe and Ragtime Baseball*, 76.

WORLD SERIES AND A WAR, 1917–1918

He [Charles Comiskey] threw nickels around for players like they were manhole covers.

—Harvey Frommer[1]

Although Charles Comiskey willingly paid whatever it took to get the team that he wanted, he was frugal—many called it stingy—with his players once they were under contract. The salaries that he paid weren't significantly lower than average, but they were lower than many other clubs; coupled with the fact that the Chicago White Sox had boasted the highest attendance figures every year since 1910, his players felt they had every reason to resent his closeness with a dollar.

As an example of this thriftiness, nearly every player in the major leagues received a daily food allowance of four dollars; Comiskey gave his players only three. He also charged his players twenty-five cents per day to launder their uniforms; although other owners also charged for laundry services, this was an added insult for Comiskey's White Sox, since his players already received smaller wages and food allowances. (The White Sox players refused to pay this laundry fee, and their unwashed uniforms earned them the nickname of "Black Sox.")

There was also the issue of the players' one-sided contracts. During the negotiation process, Comiskey's secretary, Harry Grabiner, would present a contract with a narrow range of options, then tell the players that they could either take it or leave it. Although this uncompromising contract signing wasn't unique to Comiskey, it did highlight his unwillingness to give extra money to his players.

Besides the limited range of choices for players, Comiskey's contracts seemed unfair when comparing the disparate terms granted his ballplayers. For example, while Eddie Collins, admittedly a highly talented ballplayer, earned $14,500 per year; Jackson, another remarkably skilled player, was earning only $6,000.

Comiskey's managers struggled with the owner's intense, hands-on approach; partly because of this clash, the White Sox had gone through six managers by 1915. The seventh manager, Clarence "Pants" Rowland, may have worked well with Comiskey precisely because his lack of any major league experience whatsoever allowed him to more easily acquiesce to Comiskey's judgment.

It would, however, be unfair to portray only one side of Comiskey. Sportswriters, whom he wined and dined, spoke highly of him. Even if more cynical minds might suggest that this move was well calculated to garner good press, fans also appreciated his generosity and most contemporaries would have labeled him as a well-respected and knowledgeable baseball magnate.

Charles Albert Comiskey actually began his baseball career decades before the 1917 season, initially playing first base for the St. Louis Browns of the American Association in 1882. While playing in St. Louis, he was credited with a revolutionary new defensive style. In that era, first basemen traditionally kept one foot on the base, even if there were no runners on board. Although it's unlikely that Comiskey was literally the first to employ the strategy of playing off the base whenever no runners were on them, he did popularize the tactic. This strategy allowed him to cover a larger expanse of the right portion of the infield. This style also encouraged the pitchers to take a more active role in defensive plays at first base, particularly on bunts and infield choppers.

In 1883, Comiskey also began managing the Browns; as player-manager, he led the Browns to pennants for four years straight (1885–1888). This winning streak didn't come from a passive approach, of course, and author David Fleitz points out that Comiskey also "introduced fan violence and umpire intimidation as essential facets of team strategy."[2] After his streak of winning seasons, Comiskey left the Browns organization for one year to participate in the outlaw league known as the Players League. He then returned to the Browns, but the American Association disbanded in 1891, leaving Comiskey without a team.[3]

Never one to remain idle, he quickly joined the Cincinnati Reds in the National League; in 1895, he purchased a team in Sioux City from the Western League, and moved this team to St. Paul, Minnesota. In 1900, he moved the team again, this time to Chicago. He renamed them the White Stockings and this team became part of the original American League line-up.[4]

The White Stockings (shortened to the "White Sox" for the benefit of sportswriters and those who compiled box scores) won American League pennants in

1900 and 1901, and then they won the "Horseless Carriage" World Series in 1906 against the Chicago Cubs. Sportswriters were calling Comiskey "The Noblest Roman of Baseball," which was then shortened to "The Old Roman."

Comiskey's public persona, just like the moniker of the ballpark he created, went through a transition; during the first three decades of Comiskey's major league baseball career, he transformed himself from the "thuggish player and rule-breaking manager of the 1880s" to one who "loved the limelight of civic respectability."[5]

In 1917, as team magnate and civic citizen, Comiskey put together a talented team with World Series potential. He didn't recruit rookies; rather, he pieced together an experienced team, which included catcher Ray Schalk. Often described as "fiery," Schalk caught four no-hitters in his professional career and he revolutionized the position of catcher. He aggressively backed up plays at first and third base; he also handled wild pitches resourcefully, which prevented many runners from advancing on the base paths. It was this swift and uncompromising style of play, along with the fact that he caught a record-breaking four major league no-hitters, that ensured Schalk's place in the Baseball Hall of Fame.[6]

The infield of the 1917 Chicago White Sox was also exemplary. At first base, Comiskey had placed Arnold "Chick" Gandil, a fierce man who had played professional ball since 1910. Gandil was a decent hitter, batting over .300 in 1912 and 1913.[7] More importantly, his fielding skills were superb. Gandil, a former boxer, also flaunted an intimidating style; at six-two and two hundred pounds, he was muscular and solid.

At second base was Eddie "Cocky" Collins, one of the premiere second baseman—and base stealers—of his time. Collins, also a future Hall-of-Famer, boasted the most stolen bases during four seasons and is the seventh all-time base stealer. "He was an adroit bunter, a slashing, left-handed-batting hit-and-run man, and a brilliant baserunner. In the dugout or on the coaching lines, he was a canny, sign-stealing, intuitive strategist."[8] He served as the White Sox team captain; as a college educated ballplayer, he also led one of the two unofficial—yet all too real—factions of the 1917 team in Chicago. The leader of the other splinter group, the rougher and more unpredictable one, was Gandil.

Shortstop Charles "Swede" Risberg was fairly new to the team; while his batting was only average, his strong arm added enormous depth to the White Sox infield.[9] Unfortunately, he suffered an injury and could not play in the 1917 World Series. Therefore, George "Buck" Weaver was moved back to the shortstop position. (Utility man, Fred McMullin, played third base in the World Series.)

Fleet-footed Buck Weaver was a tremendous fielder at the base, and even the great Ty Cobb was reluctant to use his trademark bunt against him.[10] Moreover, the infield combination of Schalk, Gandil, Collins and Weaver could be extremely effective, which was especially important to a team's defense in the dead ball era, when fewer balls were hit out of the infield.

The Chicago outfield was also strong, with Oscar "Happy" Felsch, Joe Jackson, and John "Shano" Collins serving as its components. Not only was Felsch effective in the outfield, with a strong arm and the ability to cover large spans of ground, he'd batted .300 in 1916 and .308 in 1917. His 15 double plays from the outfield stand as a record, even today.[11] Collins was powerful and capable, and Jackson, of course, had certainly proven his worth in Cleveland.

The pitching staff of the White Sox was formidable, as well, with Eddie Cicotte boasting the lowest earned run average of the season (1.53) in the American League. Claude "Lefty" Williams and Urban "Red" Faber, both young and upcoming pitchers, also excelled at their craft.

The 1917 Chicago White Sox, then, were clearly one of the finest teams of its era,[12] and they would challenge another of the premiere teams, the New York Giants, in the 1917 World Series. Although both teams contained talented line-ups, huge contrasts existed between the two managers. John McGraw, manager of the New York Giants, had significant major league experience. He served as third baseman and shortstop for the Baltimore Orioles of the National League for most of his sixteen-year playing career. McGraw, nicknamed the "Little Napoleon," was scrawny and scrappy and abrasive. According to baseball legend, it was McGraw's antics that increased the number of umpires required in a game.[13]

Fans were eagerly anticipating the match-up between the White Sox and Giants; to add to the excitement of the Series, these two teams had a history of strife. Just four years before, they had traveled much of the world together and nearly had a major brawl in Egypt. During the near riot, Weaver warned McGraw that, if their two teams ever met in the World Series, the White Sox would "show you what a real fighting ball club is—you and your yellowbellies."[14]

The first game was October 6, 1917, in Comiskey Park with 32,000 people in attendance. The White Sox sported brand new stockings in red, white and blue in honor of the war effort overseas; some considered the spangled outfits as overdone, while others perceived them as patriotic. "Slim" Sallee, who had a record of 18–7 that season with a league-high four saves, was pitching for the Giants.[15] Cicotte was pitching for the White Sox; as writer James T. Farrell later recalled, when he [Cicotte] "was right, he was almost unbeatable."[16] New York fans cheered when Cicotte gave up a single, but that, plus a steal at second base, was their only cause for celebration.

In the bottom of the first inning, the Sox nearly scored off of Sallee; unfortunately for Joe Jackson, his potential RBI was eliminated when the Giants second baseman, Charles "Buck" Herzog, snagged an incredible catch over his shoulder. The White Sox scored in the third inning when McMullin batted in Collins; they scored again in the fourth inning with an over-the-fence home run by Felsch. At this point, White Sox were winning 2–0.

The Sox lead was cut in half in the fifth inning, though, and a dispute over who should catch a pop-up between Collins and Gandil in the sixth nearly resulted in a collision. Collins backed off at the last moment, and Gandil caught the ball. This near disaster lead one *New York Times* reporter—whether in utter seriousness or tongue in cheek is hard to determine—to write, "There were times that it seemed that the White Sox team play lacked harmony."[17]

In retrospect, that comment is hard to dispute. In the spirit of the moment, though, the White Sox were clinging to a tight lead and they desperately wanted to preserve that edge. In the seventh inning, Jackson performed momentum-stealing outfield magic, catching a ball with a "spectacular diving, tumbling catch, stealing a sure triple."[18] At that point, according to Farrell, "The umpires rushed out to left field as Jackson lay sprawled with the ball safe in his hands and thumbed an out signal amidst many cheers."[19] The final score for the game was White Sox 2, Giants 1, with Cicotte pitching a seven-hitter.[20]

The second game of the World Series was played the following day, and was the first Sunday game in World Series history. Red Faber, a young spit ball throwing right-hander, served as pitcher for the White Sox, while Ferdie Schupp, who'd won twenty-one games, pitched for New York. The first inning was quiet, but the Giants scored two runs in the second when a ball thrown by Jackson tumbled past the catcher, Ray Schalk. That same inning, Jackson retaliated with a single and secured third base when Felsch hit his own one-bagger. Gandil knocked in Jackson, and Weaver notched another RBI when his hit allowed Felsch to score the tying run.

In the fourth, the White Sox earned five more runs, including two that Jackson batted in with a sharp single. This raised their lead to 7–2.

Faber, who was pitching a fabulous game, came up to bat in the fifth inning, when he made an embarassing offensive error. While on second base, he attempted to steal third; unfortunately, bases were loaded and, when Faber arrived at third, he saw Weaver standing on that base. When Weaver snarled and asked Faber where he thought he was going, Faber sheepishly—and quite accurately—told him, "Back out to pitch."[21] No further runs were scored in the game, and the White Sox were winning the Series, two games to none.

The White Sox and Giants traveled to New York for Games 3 and 4. During both, Jackson went hitless; the Giants won both games, tying the Series at 2–2. In Game 3, with over 33,600 people in attendance, Cicotte lost to John "Rube" Benton 2–0. Faber lost Game 4 to Schupp 5–0, with Benny Kauff hitting two home runs for the Giants.

Acrimony between the two teams increased tensions and added color to the Series. The Giants had mercilessly taunted the White Sox, perhaps remembering how easily they were riled in Egypt, and probably hoping that bench jockeying could distract Chicago's team. During the first four games of the Series, the White Sox players ignored the insults; not as a noble gesture, but as a deliberate strategy. During the fifth game, however, they changed their tactics, and this game became one of the roughest World Series games ever witnessed. Players slid into bases, sharpened spikes "up," and they bellowed out insults constantly; one Giants player even attempted to kick the ball out of Schalk's catcher's mitt.

The game proved to be an exciting contest in other ways, as well. Ewell "Reb" Russell pitched for Chicago, and he gave up two runs in the first. Before the inning was finished, Rowland replaced Russell with Cicotte, who retired the side; Sallee pitched for the Giants. The Sox cut the Giants lead in half in the third with Jackson contributing a single to the effort. New York scored two more runs in the fourth, bringing their lead to 4–1.

In the fifth, Felsch collided with the first baseman; the New York infield, seeing it as a deliberate assault, charged him. McGraw rushed out to the infield and broke up the skirmish. In the sixth, the White Sox once again sliced the Giants lead in half, and the score stood at 4–2. In the seventh, the Giants scored; by this time, Lefty Williams had replaced Cicotte on the mound.

Jackson hit another single in the seventh; both he and Felsch scored off of a double by Gandil who advanced to third base when Weaver grounded out. Schalk walked; he stole second base, and an overthrow to that base by the pitcher allowed Gandil to score. This tied the game.

In the eighth inning, Jackson tagged his third hit of the day; during that rally, the White Sox scored three runs, to advance to an 8–5 lead. Although the rough play continued, prompting Chicago's manager to challenge the umpire to a fight, no more runs were scored. Faber finished the pitching chores of the day and the White Sox won the fifth game, 8–5. The seven-game Series stood at 3–2, with Chicago holding the advantage.

The following day, Faber started for Chicago, and Benton for the Giants. The first three innings were quiet for both pitchers; in the fourth, however, the defense of the Giants fell apart in a spectacular fashion. When Eddie Collins slapped a soft grounder, one that looked like a certain out, the throw to first base was wild. Collins ran to second base. Jackson hit a fly ball that should have been caught, but the right fielder dropped the ball. Collins advanced to third, while Jackson remained on first. Felsch then hit the ball right to the pitcher, which should have ensured another out, but it wasn't to be.

Collins started running towards home plate, and he became caught between third base and home plate. The Giants third baseman and catcher became engaged in a run-down; while this footwork was taking place, Felsch and Jackson safely landed on first and second base, respectively. As the Giants third baseman, Heinie Zimmerman, chased Collins toward home plate, Felsch and Jackson moved to second and third base, respectively; Collins evaded Zimmerman's tag and scored.

Gandil was next at the plate and his single allowed both Jackson and Felsch to score; the White Sox led 3–0. Although the Giants scored two runs in the fifth inning, that wasn't enough to even the score; the White Sox scored another run in the ninth, clinching the World Series championship in the sixth game.

Years later, Weaver recalled that the Giants manager shook his hand, saying, "You're the best, and I want to take my hat off to you."[22] Rowland, though, had less fond memories of the parting words that McGraw spit out at him.

In postgame analysis, sportswriters frequently noted that it was McGraw's fear of Jackson's bat that caused New York's manager to overuse his left-handed pitchers, thus opening the gate for a White Sox championship. Overall, Jackson batted .304 in the Series, driving in two runs. Moreover, his extraordinary catch effectively ended Game 1, leading Chicago to the Series-opening win.

Jackson and his teammates returned to Chicago by train and enjoyed a celebratory parade on their arrival. They also received their long-anticipated bonus from Comiskey—but not in the expected manner. Instead of the anticipated cash bonus, players received a case of stale champagne that, according to sportswriter Ring Lardner, tasted like "stale piss."[23]

As world champions, though, each player earned an additional $3,669.32 for the World Series win. Jackson spent his winnings on a brand new Oldsmobile Pacemaker, which became one of his favorite cars.

For the off-season, he and Katie returned to their waterfront home in Savannah amid rumors that New York Giants player, Buck Herzog, had deliberately bungled plays in the World Series. McGraw didn't actively pursue an investigation; instead, he simply traded Herzog to the Boston Red Sox, and disturbing rumors were no longer the Little Napoleon's problem.

Even more momentous was the effect that America's entry into the World War would have on professional baseball after the World Series ended. On May 18, 1917, Congress had passed the Selective Service Act that required all men between the ages of twenty-one and thirty-one to register for the draft; numbers were drawn to determine who would head to basic training, then overseas. This greatly affected major league baseball, because the majority of players fell within the prescribed age range for conscription.

There were other effects on the national pastime, as well. In the spring of 1918, the White Sox postponed spring training until March 18 because of wartime travel restrictions, and when the season began, players practiced military drills in addition to batting practice. Players dressed in full military uniforms, including boots and unloaded guns, during pregame ceremonies. Baseball team owners hoped that these exercises would convince the government that ballplayers should be exempt from the draft because they could boost morale of Americans during a dark time.

On May 18, 1918, though, the secretary of war issued the now-famous "Work or Fight" proclamation; baseball, along with other forms of entertainment, was declared nonessential, which meant that all players of conscription age were required either to join the army or to find employment in a defense-related industry by July 1. This order meant that all but four White Sox players needed to either "work or fight." Professional baseball was allowed to continue, but the regular season needed to end by September 2.[24] "Because of its high visibility and symbolic value," writes author Donald Gropman, "baseball was singled out as one of the expendable luxuries."[25]

Jackson originally applied for an exemption from the draft, citing his marital status. Although an exemption had been granted in Greenville in 1917, it was lifted in 1918. Jackson had played seventeen games for the White Sox that aborted season, hitting .354, before being ordered to report to the army.

Jackson then received an offer from the Harlan and Hollingsworth Shipbuilding Company in Delaware, a company that was putting together its own baseball team for the Bethlehem Steel League. Because shipbuilding was essential to the war effort, and because many of the shipbuilders were fighting overseas, Jackson did not need to report to basic training. Instead, he moved to Delaware. There, Jackson led his team to the championship series; in the final game of that series, he hit two home runs and the game needed to stop so that coins tossed by fans in celebration could be removed from the field.

Jackson was not the only well-known ballplayer to work at a shipbuilding facility rather than fight overseas, but he was among the first do so; therefore, he served as a symbol of the "shipyard slackers." American League President Ban Johnson harshly criticized the players who chose to work in shipbuilding and other defense-related industries, as did sportswriters. Newspapers branded Jackson and others as draft evaders, and Comiskey joined the public bashing. "There is no room on my club," he announced, "for players who wish to evade the army draft by entering the employ of ship builders!"[26] Rowland, upon raising a flag decorated with thirteen stars—one each for the White Sox players and employees involved in the war effort—made sure that people knew Jackson did not earn a star.

Jackson's rationale for staying stateside included the fact that he needed to support his wife and widowed mother. He was also supporting a younger brother and sister; besides, three of his brothers were already in uniform, so he felt that his family was well represented in the wartime effort.

Even so, Jackson contributed to the war effort in his own way. He played in exhibition games that benefited numerous charities, especially the American Red Cross. Indeed, his efforts helped the Red Cross to garner $6,000 from one game alone; still, whenever a player chose to work at a shipbuilding facility rather than go overseas, he was taunted as "pulling a Joe Jackson."[27] The *Chicago Tribune* wrote that Jackson was a man of "unusual physical development, and presumably would make an excellent fighting man, but it appears that Mr. Jackson would prefer not to fight."[28] Another article scathingly accused, "The fighting blood of the Jacksons is not as red as it used to be in the days of Old Stonewall and Old Hickory, for General Joe of the White Sox has fled to the refuge of a shipyard."[29]

While Jackson was working at the shipbuilding plant and playing baseball for the Bethlehem Steel League, the Boston Red Sox won the American League pennant. Interestingly, Babe Ruth merely joined a reserve unit and was permitted to continue playing major league ball with none of the approbation or criticism that was lobbed at Jackson. This gives rise to the question of why Jackson was the target of so much criticism when he was performing a charitable war-related function, while many other players—such as Ruth—continued to play major league ball for their own promotion and profit. Jackson's reputation as a coward from the Philadelphia days may possibly have been a factor; Comiskey's vocal condemnation surely couldn't have helped, either. It may, however, merely have been a difference in civic attitudes between Boston or New York and Chicago. Anti-war sentiment and conscientious objection was more common in the East Coast cities than in the Midwest, where the agitation for the United States involvement had been active from early in the conflict. As a "home town hero" of Chicago, Jackson's demurring from the draft may well have been perceived as a betrayal of local values.

In any case, as the shortened 1918 season drew to a close, there was speculation about the future of major league baseball in wartime. Ban Johnson cancelled the 1919 season; his edict didn't cause much of a panic, though, because he'd also cancelled the 1918 season after the "work or fight" order was issued, and that hadn't become reality.

Operating under the assumption that major league play would not resume in 1919, the shipyard leagues offered to spearhead the baseball season. That made sense because many of the major league players were already working in their facilities and playing on their teams. When the Armistice was declared on November 11, 1918, though, this initiative ended, and the 1919 season was set to resume in the traditional major league format. Because of the decreased attendance during the previous season, only a 140-game season was scheduled.

Jackson, like many other ballplayers, left the shipbuilding plant to return home. His situation, though, was unlike that of most fellow ballplayers. Because the magnate who owned his contract had previously declared that he would not welcome back those players who did not join the army, Jackson was uncertain about what his return to Chicago—and the 1919 season—would bring for him.

NOTES

1. Frommer, *Shoeless Joe and Ragtime Baseball*, 64. In contrast, the owner of the Cleveland Indians, Charlie Somers, would walk down the aisles of the players' train and give them $20 gold pieces as a token of his appreciation.

2. Fleitz, *Shoeless*, 106.

3. See http://www.baseball-reference.com/managers/comisch01.shtml.

4. See http://www.baseballlibrary.com/baseballlibrary/ballplayers/C/Comiskey_Charlie.stm.

5. Fleitz, *Shoeless*, 107.

6. See http://www.baseballhalloffame.org/hofers_and_honorees/hofer_bios/schalk_ray.htm and http://www.baseballlibrary.com/baseballlibrary/ballplayers/S/Schalk_Ray.stm.

7. See http://www.baseball-reference.com/g/gandich01.shtml.

8. See http://www.baseballlibrary.com/baseballlibrary/ballplayers/C/Collins_Eddie.stm and http://www.cmgww.com/baseball/collins/biography.htm.

9. See http://www.baseballlibrary.com/baseballlibrary/ballplayers/R/Risberg_Swede.stm.

10. See http://www.baseballlibrary.com/baseballlibrary/ballplayers/W/Weaver_Buck.stm. See also Frommer, *Shoeless Joe and Ragtime Baseball*, 70.

11. See http://www.baseballlibrary.com/baseballlibrary/ballplayers/F/Felsch_Happy.stm.

12. For more specifics about this team, see Frommer, *Shoeless Joe and Ragtime Baseball*, 69–71.

13. See http://www.baseballlibrary.com/baseballlibrary/ballplayers/M/McGraw_John.stm.

14. Fleitz, *Shoeless*, 136.

15. See http://www.baseballlibrary.com/baseballlibrary/ballplayers/S/Sallee_Slim.stm.

16. James T. Farrell, *My Baseball Diary; A Famed American Actor Recalls the Wonderful World of Baseball, Yesterday and Today* (New York: A.S. Barnes and Company, 1957), 62.

17. Fleitz, *Shoeless*, 138.

18. Ibid.

19. Farrell, *My Baseball Diary*, 65.

20. For box scores, see http://blackbetsy.com/1917ws.htm.

21. Fleitz, *Shoeless*, 139.

22. Ibid., 143.

23. Frommer, *Shoeless Joe and Ragtime Baseball*, 77.
24. For an excellent overview of this subject, see Fleitz, *Shoeless*, 147–155.
25. Gropman, *Say It Ain't So, Joe!*, 146.
26. Ibid., 149.
27. Fleitz, *Shoeless*, 152.
28. Gropman, *Say It Ain't So, Joe!*, 148.
29. Ibid., 149.

TANGLED ALLIANCES

It's the best bunch of fighters I ever saw. It's a wonderful combo, the greatest team I ever had.

—Charles Comiskey[1]

On September 10, 1919, Arnold "Chick" Gandil—a sour, ill-tempered man at best—waited impatiently in his small but well appointed hotel room, agitated with little area to pace. His associate, Joseph "Sport" Sullivan, was supposed to meet him at the hotel, but he hadn't yet arrived. This gave Gandil even more time to brood. Although the White Sox played well this season, and although it seemed likely that his team would play for the World Series championship again, Gandil felt angry and vindictive. Such traits were part of his general nature, but this day he was feeling especially irritated because the owner of the Chicago White Sox, Charles Comiskey, wasn't financially rewarding his game-winning players, even though Comiskey himself was raking in high revenues from the gate receipts that a winning season brought him.

Gandil, who was known as a "professional malcontent,"[2] wanted more, and he wanted it in hard money; he was earning only $3,500 per year and, at 32 years of age, he knew his baseball career would soon wind down. He had no hope of earning more money under Comiskey because the owner had already brusquely denied his players a raise, so Gandil was plotting other ways to get the cash he believed he deserved. Besides wishing to receive money for himself, Gandil also longed for Comiskey to suffer financially for his miserliness, something that would especially happen if the White Sox lost the World Series. Fortunately, Gandil knew just the people who could assist in meting out that type of retribution.

As a teenager, Gandil had competed in brutal bare-fisted boxing matches in outlaw mining towns located along the wild border between Arizona and Mexico; there, he associated with rough, aggressive men and also fell into the company of professional gamblers, men whose characters and reputations were less than sterling. During this experience he developed a name for himself as one who had a toughness of mind and body. When Gandil switched to professional baseball, he didn't change his attitude, and he soon earned a reputation as the only first baseman who still spurned a glove. He also continued his associations with gamblers.

From 1912 to 1915, Gandil played first base for the Washington Senators; during that time, he also began pool-hall drinking with "Sport" Sullivan, an Irish racetrack gambler and bookmaker. Their friendship continued to progress with Sullivan supplying the booze and Gandil providing his new associate with "tips," such as an unexpected change in starting pitchers or the status of a teammate's injury. Armed with such insider knowledge, Sullivan began to develop a reputation among his fellow gamblers as a baseball expert, and the two men continued to develop a friendship.

Gandil admired Sullivan's ability to benefit financially from others and his slick ways of chatting up the monied type; he also envied and somewhat resented Sullivan, as he "moved so easily in the night life demimonde" with "a pocket full of cash."[3] Nevertheless, Sullivan had the connections that Gandil needed to pull off his scheme, and he wasn't going to allow envy to stand in the way of big personal profits.

On September 10, when Sullivan, a "tall, beefy, red-faced man in a white suit and bright red bow tie stepped out of a taxi and walked into Boston's Hotel Buckminster," the gambler probably wondered at Gandil's choice of hotels, for it was far more reputable than usual.[4] The explanation, though, was simple. The White Sox were scheduled to play against the Red Sox, in Boston; lodging had presented a problem for the White Sox management because the past behavior of certain players hadn't been exemplary, and some hotels were reluctant to house the White Sox team. One of the last times that the Chicago team had traveled to Boston, things had really gotten out of hand. Rowdy and volatile, the White Sox players drank far too much and trashed their rooms; they smashed chairs, tables, and beds, and threw the broken pieces out the window and into the courtyard. That particular hotel, understandably enough, asked the players to leave—adding that they shouldn't ever return.

Rather than search for another cheap hotel that seemed to invite such abuse, the White Sox management attempted another strategy for the September games: renting rooms in a more respectable establishment, Hotel Buckminster. Although the hotel didn't boast such luxuries as a restaurant or room service, the hotel—built in 1897 on Boston's Kenmore Square—was fairly new, as well as clean and well kept. Club management hoped its tidy and more respectable atmosphere would subdue the more rambunctious White Sox players.

Discreet signage might have made the hotel difficult to locate, which could have accounted for Sullivan's tardiness that night. He was also something of a dandy, so possibly he stopped in front of one of the lobby's many mirrors to comb his hair or straighten his bow tie before heading to Gandil's room. When Sullivan finally picked up the house phone to ring for Gandil, the ballplayer's voice was strangled with tension, and he barked at his friend, telling him to come up immediately.

Once Sullivan arrived, conversation between the two men was intense—and hushed. In spite of the hotel's relative opulence, the rooms were closely connected, and any loud or heated conversation might filter through the thin walls. Although no one knows, exactly, what transpired between Gandil and Sullivan that September day, and while no one knows who owed favors and who needed to repay them, this conversation almost certainly launched the scheme that changed professional baseball forever: the notion to "fix" the 1919 World Series.

Merely concocting this plan, though, wasn't enough. For this scheme to work, Gandil needed the cooperation of Eddie Cicotte and Lefty Williams, the two star pitchers who would have the most starts during the World Series. Gandil had already begun murmuring suggestions to Cicotte; so far, they hadn't borne fruit. Gandil was confident, though, that he could persuade the pitcher—who disliked Comiskey intensely—to participate in the plot.

Two years before, Cicotte had won twenty-eight games for the White Sox, helping to lead them—and Comiskey—to a World Series win. In 1919, an often-repeated story says that Comiskey promised his winning pitcher a $10,000 bonus if he won thirty games that year. According to this anecdote, the owner benched his winning pitcher after he'd won twenty-nine games, to avoid paying the bonus. Although there is no proof that this incident actually occurred, and compelling rebuttals have been made suggesting that it did not happen, it is without question that Cicotte felt that Comiskey underpaid him, and that must have left the pitcher more vulnerable to gambler overtures.[5]

Therefore, during Gandil's conversation with Sullivan in the hotel, the first baseman must have mentioned Cicotte's bitterness, sharing his belief that he could be persuaded to deliberately lose games in exchange for cash. Gandil may have also shared specifics about Cicotte's $4,000 mortgage on a newly purchased farm and the fact that Cicotte, already age 35 and nearing the end of his baseball career, had no other way to support his wife and children. In addition, if Cicotte—who was scheduled to pitch the first game of the World Series—agreed to the fix, then the more reluctant Williams could certainly be made to see reason, as well.

How easy or difficult it was to persuade Sullivan will never be known. Perhaps, as author Eliot Asinof has suggested, Sullivan believed that the "biggest gambling bonanza in the history of baseball was being dropped magnificently into his lap like manna from heaven." Perhaps he did see this meeting as a "payoff for all his efforts, the return for all those beers, the pool games, the fifty-cent cigars" he had bought for Gandil.[6] In any case, he saw grand possibilities for glorious profit, and he agreed to consider the plan, vague and unshaped as it was. Before leaving Hotel Buckminster, Sullivan tentatively agreed to provide Gandil with $80,000 in cash, a portion of which could be used to persuade Cicotte to abandon his moral stance against game-fixing; meanwhile, Gandil promised to entice other key players, including Joe Jackson, to throw the games. The only real impediment to the scheme was that Sullivan didn't have $80,000; he didn't even have $10,000. But he was a gambler, and this was too good a chance to pass up because of such a "petty" detail.[7]

When Jackson returned from the shipbuilding yard after the war ended, less than a year before this meeting between Gandil and Sullivan took place, he couldn't have imagined how much his life would change in the upcoming season. In November 1918, the outfielder was focusing on Comiskey's brash words that players who had chosen to work in defense-related industries in the United States, rather than fight in the war overseas, would not be welcomed back on the Chicago team. The threat was empty, though, and it was more or less forgotten, now that the war was over and life in the United States was getting back to normal. Comiskey censored no players for their "work or fight" choices; he concentrated instead on the goal of winning the 1919 World Series. Jackson, of course, could help Comiskey achieve this, so the White Sox owner sent him a contract for $6,000, which Jackson signed and returned in February. Although that contract did not contain a raise, it was not the decrease that many White Sox and other players saw after the war.

Comiskey's indifference to Jackson's shipbuilding adventure must have been comforting to the slugger, as well as the sustenance of his salary without a cut, but he still worried about fan reception. Newspapers had branded the slugger with antipatriotic insults, with *Chicago Tribune* reporter Hugh Fullerton implying that Jackson was the most likely target for boos, even suggesting that fan hostility might cause Jackson to leave professional baseball.

Jackson's apprehension grew because, as a postwar cost-cutting measure, team owners did not begin spring training until mid-March. Jackson ultimately discovered, though, that he had no real reason to fear fan hostility. During the first game of the regular season, hundreds of people known as "Jackson Rooters" brought a band that played rousing songs in Shoeless Joe's honor. These rooters marched around the stadium waving banners; their enthusiasm halted White Sox play when Jackson came to bat for the first time. They rushed the batter's box to present their hero with a $200 gold pocket watch, a gift he treasured for the rest of his life. After presenting him with his watch, the fans also began to chant, "Give 'em Black Betsy! Give 'em Black Betsy!" In the fifth inning, they draped a bed sheet over right field, with the words "Jackson Rooters" printed in large letters. Their support must have greatly reassured Jackson.

Comiskey, always one to read a crowd and seek public approval, announced to the press that he was glad he didn't listen to those who called Jackson a slacker. Savvy Katie cut out articles quoting Comiskey and pasted them in an album— right next to Comiskey's published statements to the contrary.

Jackson chalked up ten hits, including three doubles and a home run, against the St. Louis Browns during the opening series of the 1919 season. He normally used dark bats such as "Black Betsy," but for this outing, he selected a brand new, all white bat—nicknamed "Blond Betsy"—for the four-game series. He quickly settled back into his baseball routine, posting a .420 average by May 15. Even though he did not maintain that pace, he did keep his average well above .300 throughout the entire season.

Jackson generally played well in a familiar environment and, overall, the team looked the same as when he had left for his shipbuilding job. One major change, though, had taken place. After the club's poor performances in 1918, Comiskey replaced manager, Clarence Rowland, with William Gleason. Nicknamed "Kid" for his short stature and enthusiasm for baseball, Gleason peaked as a pitcher in 1890 when he won thirty-eight games for Philadelphia. Switching to the position of second base when the distance between the pitcher's mound and home plate increased to sixty feet, six inches, he contributed to the Baltimore Orioles pennant win in 1895. In addition, as team captain for the New York Giants from 1896 to 1900, he is sometimes credited with being the first to use the intentional base on balls as a deliberate strategy to avoid pitching to a powerful hitter.[8]

Gleason's first season as the manager of the Chicago White Sox started out well; by the end of May, his team was in first place. They occasionally struggled to hold their lead and sporadically lost it to the New York Yankees or the Cleveland Indians. An Indians player pitched the only no-hitter in the American League that season, while center fielder Tris Speaker led the team well. Jackson's former team spun out admirable winning streaks, but the Indians simply couldn't keep up with Chicago's powerhouse team of 1919.

On September 24, playing against the St. Louis Browns, Jackson smashed in the winning run during the ninth inning, to clinch the American League pennant. That season, Jackson finished with a .351 average, earning the third most hits (181) and RBIs (a career-high 96) in the league, as well as the fourth most total bases (261); Jackson's slugging percentage, at .506, was fifth in the league.[9] One sportswriter said, "Joe Jackson is one of the most frequent busters of ball-games known to the game."[10] Other White Sox players also performed well. Eddie Collins batted .319 and led the league with thirty-three stolen bases,[11] while utility player, Fred McMullin, batted .294.[12] In addition to Cicotte's twenty-nine wins, Lefty Williams won a respectable twenty-three. White Sox pitching seemed unbeatable.

Tension between the players and Comiskey, though, continued to escalate. Like Gandil, most of the players felt that the owner was being deliberately stingy and was, in their view, unable to keep his word to them about financial rewards. Several of the White Sox players had tried a reasonable approach and asked Gleason to intercede with the team's owner about pay raises, but Comiskey refused to consider the request, and resentment toward his parsimonious practices only increased.

Team factions were becoming even more disparate, as well, with the players' level of education being a prime factor in choosing sides; college-educated Eddie Collins, for example, associated with the more learned players—pitcher Red Faber and catcher Ray Schalk—and avoided the less educated and more rowdy Gandil, Risberg, Weaver and McMullin. Gandil, in turn, disliked the more privileged Collins; Weaver, when expressing his own disenchantment with Collins, said that he was "a great guy to look out for himself. If there was a tough gent comin' down to second, he'd yell at the shortstop to take the play."[13]

Williams, along with Happy Felsch, who had only a sixth-grade education, and Jackson, who had no formal education at all, stayed out of the worst of the sniping, but gravitated to the rougher, more earthy group of Gandil, Risberg, Weaver and McMullin; not because they necessarily resented or disliked Collins, but because they had so little in common with him. Years later, Collins recalled the extreme degree of the cliques, noting that, "Players would even double cross each other on the field and yet, despite those things, we still managed the win the pennant."[14]

Besides winning the American League pennant for the second time in three years, the Chicago White Sox were expected by fans and pundits alike to sweep the series against the National League champions, the Cincinnati Reds. Led by manager Pat Moran, the Reds won their division title by nine games, but they were considered the underdogs of the Series. As one headline of the *Sporting*

News pointed out next to a photo of the Reds team, "Joy If Reds Win—But a Shock If They Do."[15]

This headline wasn't intended as a disparaging remark about the manager of the Reds. Moran, who was known as "Old Whiskey Face," was knowledgeable about baseball and those who played the game. Because of that skill, Moran had pieced together a quality team. At first base, Moran had Jake Daubert, who had won the National League batting title in 1913 and 1914; the first-sacker racked up an average of .350 and .329 in those seasons, respectively, and was also known as a solid and steady fielder. In 1913, Daubert won the Most Valuable Player award for the National League and, during the 1919 season, he came into the World Series with a respectable, if unspectacular, .276 average to show for trips to the plate.

Playing second base for Cincinnati was Morrie Rath. Although Rath never became a star player, he was reliable; that season, he had the most assists, putouts, and double plays of any second baseman in the National League. On August 26, Rath boasted thirteen assists in a fifteen-inning game, the second highest number of assists in any National League game, a record that still stands. In 1919, he batted .264 with 29 RBIs.

The Reds shortstop, Larry Kopf, hit .270 that season, while catcher Ivey Wingo batted .273. Third baseman, Heinie Groh, was one of the Reds stars. Easily recognizable because of his uniquely shaped "bottle bat," Groh played strategically, using a mixture of bunts and walks to get on base. During the 1919 season, Groh hit .310.

Although this infield was better than average, and although some Reds fans would dispute this claim, the Cincinnati team did not field anywhere near as powerful an infield as the White Sox combination of Schalk, Gandil, Collins, Risberg, and Weaver.[16]

The Cincinnati outfield was comprised of left fielder Pat Duncan, center fielder Edd Roush, and right fielder Alfred "Greasy" Neale. Duncan played for the Pittsburgh Pirates in 1915, batting .200; he didn't play in the major leagues again until 1919, when he batted .244. Neale hit .242 during the 1919 season. The big star of the Cincinnati team was center fielder Roush, who posted a .321 average during the season. Roush, who eventually was inducted into Baseball's Hall of Fame, won the Golden Glove Award in 1915, and played for the All-Star teams in 1916 and 1917. He also won the National League batting title in 1917 (.341) and in 1919 (.321).

The pitching staff of the Cincinnati Reds included left-handers Slim Sallee—who had faced the White Sox as a Giant in 1917—and Walter "Dutch" Ruether; they also had right-handed Horace "Hod" Eller, Jimmy Ring, Ray Fisher, and

Adolfo "Dolf" Luque. Although this was a fine pitching staff, the Chicago White Sox were still strongly favored to win the World Series during this newly-expanded nine-game format. Although anything can happen in baseball—and often does—most historians agree that, had Gandil not chosen to entice players to deliberately lose games, the Chicago team would, indeed, have won the 1919 World Series.

Certainly, Gandil seemed to believe that a Chicago win was more than a fifty-fifty proposition. After his meeting with Sullivan, he went to work to convince key players to participate in the game-throwing plot, something that took on momentum when he convinced Cicotte to participate. The pitcher's resentment towards Comiskey likely was a major factor in his decision, although what else nettled the pitcher is not known.

Gandil now approached other players. First there was Swede Risberg, who had no qualms about participating; such was his resentment of the owner's abuse of the players, particularly after Comiskey's refusal to be moved by Gleason's plea for raises. Utility player Fred McMullin overheard the conversation between Gandil and Risberg and asked to be included. That wasn't part of the original plan because McMullin wasn't likely to play a significant role in the World Series; obviously, the more people who became involved, the less money would be made for each participant, and naturally, every person added to the scheme increased the risk of discovery. But as McMullin might rat out the plan if he was excluded, Gandil had little choice but to include him.

When Cicotte asked Buck Weaver to join the conspiracy, Weaver replied that the notion was crazy and such a fix couldn't be done. Meanwhile, Gandil discussed the plan with Williams and Felsch; the outfielder—who was making only $3,750 despite his .300 batting average and record-setting outfield assists—agreed, but Williams still resisted. Gandil then told Williams that the fix was going to occur with or without his participation, so the young pitcher, a twenty-three game winner who was earning only $2,600 annually, changed his mind and agreed to help in exchange for a payoff. Weaver still wasn't swayed.

In spite of Gandil and Sullivan's attempt to keep matters quiet, rumors of a game-fixing conspiracy began circulating, giving rise to further complications. "Sleepy" Bill Burns, a former major league pitcher and friend of Cicotte, heard whispers that a scheme was afoot. Burns was a shifty character who played on five teams in his five-season major league career. Notorious for his association with underworld thugs and riff-raff, he had a reputation as a crap-shooting and card-playing gambler with "good stuff but no ambition."[17] He had tended to read newspapers or doze on the bench as a player; after baseball, he began speculating in the oil business, something that he would exploit later in life in a variety of nefarious get-rich-quick schemes that would actually net him a decent amount of money. Predictably, the rumors about fixing a game appealed to him and he had some oil income available to wager; so he approached Cicotte and asked point blank if the game-fixing rumors were true. Cicotte attempted to laugh off Burns' questions, but his denials apparently weren't convincing. Burns continued to press Cicotte for details, and finally, the pitcher shared them with his ex-teammate.

Burns begged Cicotte not to make any firm commitments with Sullivan, figuring that he, a former major league baseball player who saw himself as a successful gambler, would be a far better choice as ringleader of the plot. He immediately began looking for a partner in this venture and hooked up with Billy Maharg, a former boxer; the two gamblers then met with Cicotte and Gandil and offered to pay the White Sox players $100,000 to throw the games.[18] This was $20,000 more than what Sullivan had offered, and Gandil, thrilled with an unanticipated bidding war, agreed to the arrangement. Perhaps Gandil planned to double-cross all of the gamblers and accept two sets of payoff funds; perhaps he also planned to double-cross the other players involved and keep all of the excess funds himself. Regardless, the plot was now moving forward, and the question was no longer a matter of "if," but of who and how.

In spite of all the talk, though, no money had yet changed hands. It is highly unlikely that any of the gamblers—Burns and Maharg, or even Sullivan, for that matter—had any real notion of where they would get these funds; whatever funds Burns had access to would not have been anywhere in the neighborhood of $100,000, and Sullivan was, by all accounts, virtually tapped out. Still, Gandil's deal simply sounded too intriguing to pass up, for this was no typical game; nor was it a typical Series. Indeed, several factors caused the 1919 World Series to potentially be the perfect Series to throw. The Chicago White Sox were clearly expected to win; this meant that, if rumors of a fix could be kept quiet, bookmakers would set the betting odds in a fashion that would make betting on Cincinnati a greater risk at longer odds; for the privileged insiders, then, who knew that the Cincinnati Reds would win the Series, the financial rewards would be unimaginably grand.

Besides, to successfully fix a World Series, one team must dominate the games to such a degree that its players genuinely could determine which games they would win—and which they would lose. Such a team is rare, but the 1919 Chicago White Sox was that team.

Another factor could not be discounted: player discontent. Comiskey's miserliness, demonstrated in the low salaries he paid, caused a continually building resentment among his players. Their morale and attitude was in such a state that any sense of natural competitiveness or team loyalty was subordinated to their resentment of the owner's stinginess. Few players had forgotten their collective 1917 World Series "bonus": a case of stale champagne.

There were other unique factors. Because of injuries, the White Sox were using a three-man starting rotation. This meant that fewer pitchers needed to be in on the fix for it to work. Because managers seldom used relief pitchers in this era, at least not unless a game was well in hand or, conversely, the possibility of a win was out of sight, the cooperation of two thirds of the pitching staff nearly assured the success of a fix.

Other elements were also in play, and these may have convinced White Sox players that throwing games wasn't so bad, after all. Connections between gambling and baseball had existed for decades, and the current White Sox roster had seen several other players "get away with" deliberately losing games in exchange for cash, most notably Hal Chase. Moreover, the attitude towards the combination of baseball and gambling had been mixed. Some saw it as evil, as witnessed in the 1869 *New York Times* article, "Baseball in Danger."[19] The writer warned that baseball must distance itself from gamblers. Others, though, saw gambling as an acceptable sideline of the sport. According to author Daniel E. Ginsburg,

> Baseball initially became popular among "gentlemen"—members of the upper class playing for leisure and fun. As part of this activity, a wager was usually made—perhaps dinner, perhaps a small sum of money—all in a "sporting" fashion.
>
> As the game grew in popularity, "sportsmen"—that is, gamblers—began to take an interest in the game. Baseball provided a good opportunity to make a friendly wager. Many people found watching games more enjoyable with a small wager, and this was often handled very privately.[20]

During the earliest days of professional baseball, betting was loosely arranged, which made collection of funds difficult. If someone refused to acknowledge that he had made a losing bet, what acceptable recourse did the other bettor have? The money could, of course, be given to an appointed individual ahead of time for safekeeping, so that he could appropriately distribute funds after the game; but on more than one occasion, the person with the money disappeared. So, as stakes rose and wagers became more intense, a formal system developed. Betting among individuals began evolving into a betting pool, whereby a forerunner of a modern-day bookmaker would quote fluctuating odds, collect all the dollars before the game was played, and then pay out accordingly, keeping a percentage for himself. This system caught the attention of bettors, and the number of participants began to increase—as did the amount of money that they bet.

Wagering among gentlemen, or even among the less substantial class of the general public, is quite different from game-fixing; as the betting system evolved, though, the pool of money became more centralized, the bookmakers more tightly knit (as they exchanged the "book" or odds on any given game for purposes of consistency and to prevent undercutting), which made game fixing more feasible. Moreover, less honorable players quickly discovered that their "salaries represented a fraction of what they could make by dealing with the gamblers" so these players "travelled from city to city like princes, sporting diamonds, drinking champagne at dinner every night, and ostentatiously paying the tab by peeling off folding money from wads of the stuff that mysteriously reproduced themselves"; in many, although by no means all, cases, such baubles were the fruits of illicit play and gambling connections.[21]

Although the particulars of many illegitimate arrangements were never made public, baseball game-fixing scandals did erupt—fairly frequently—during the mid-to-late nineteenth century. On September 28, 1865, for example, three players from the New York Mutuals allegedly accepted money to lose a game against the Brooklyn Eckfords. The players (and the amount of money accepted) were shortstop Thomas Devyr ($30), third baseman Ed Duffy ($30), and catcher William Wansley ($100). The accused players insisted that they were "victims of a wicked conspiracy,"[22] but were nevertheless kicked off the team and banned from baseball. Their punishment, though, was fairly short in duration. Devyr was reinstated in 1867, Duffy in 1868, and Wansley in 1870.

Twelve years later, another scandal shook the sport, causing some to suggest that baseball's integrity was forever tainted. The *St. Louis Globe-Democrat* even predicted the end of the game.[23]

This particular debacle involved a charter team of the National League, the Louisville Grays. On May 30, Jim Devlin of the Grays pitched against the New York Mutuals, the same team involved in the 1865 controversy. During that game, right fielder George Bechtel mishandled three balls, and the Louisville team posted a loss. Management suspected a fixed game and began investigating. Evidence quickly suggested that Bechtel had also sent Devlin a telegram saying that, if they lost the game scheduled on June 10, "We can make $500." Although an anonymous source from Philadelphia backed up Bechtel's denial of foul play, management told Bechtel to resign. When he didn't, they banned him from professional baseball.

During the off-season, the management of the Louisville Grays hustled to improve their team's chances to win during their second season, acquiring catcher Bill Craver and left fielder George Hall. (Craver, it should be noted, had been expelled from the Chicago White Sox in 1870 because he had accepted money to lose games.) The Grays were predicted to win the pennant and, on August 16, they were in first place, five and one-half games ahead of the Boston Red Caps. A series of losses then transpired, and Louisville dropped to second place.

On August 31 and September 1, 1877, the vice president of the ball club received telegrams warning him to watch his men and informing him that his team planned to lose upcoming games. When the team did lose those games, the vice president confronted Devlin and insisted that he put his confession in writing. Accusations flew between management and players, with an investigation ensuing, targeting the actions of Devlin, Hall, Craver, and third baseman, Al Nichols. Craver refused to cooperate with the investigation and, as a result, management banned him. (Ironically, he switched careers to law enforcement, becoming a police officer.)

The other three players allowed the team's management to review their telegram communications, and officials determined that these players were indeed conspiring with gamblers, using basic codes to decide which games would be fixed losses. Devlin, Hall, and Nichols then confessed and, on October 30, 1877, the Louisville Grays fired them from their team; on December 4, the National League banned them from professional baseball. Devlin relocated to Philadelphia where he also served his community as a police officer. Hall found work as an engraver, while Nichols played semipro ball and became involved in other suspect situations.

The result of this scandal wasn't the end of baseball, as some had feared. Instead, the Louisville Grays dissolved, and the four participants were, just like the New York Mutuals players, banned from the game—but this time, not reinstated. Those in charge took a hard line, telling players that, if they participated in game fixing, they would be permanently banned from professional baseball.[24]

Rumors of game-fixing had polluted previous interleague championship play, as well. In 1886, for example, the Chicago Colts were accused of deliberately losing games. In that era, players were paid a portion of game receipts, and the Colts allegedly lost games to lengthen the interleague championship series and thereby increase the amount of revenue. Ironically, they were playing against the St. Louis Browns, who were led by player-manager Charles Comiskey.

Some baseball officials attempted to control gambling at ballparks, in part because of the game-fixing possibilities that gambling presented. Concerned about the corruptness of professional baseball, the president of the newly formed American League, Ban Johnson, officially forbade betting in American League parks in 1903.

In reality, though, despite Johnson's rules, baseball gambling intensified during the first two decades of the twentieth century. Sportsmen wagered increasingly larger amounts of money, especially in eastern cities; moreover, during World War I, most racetracks on the East Coast closed, leaving many heavy gamblers without a place to congregate. Many of them chose baseball parks as their new location. This wasn't necessarily seen as a negative; there was a "general perception among [baseball] owners," writes Ginsburg, "that a certain amount of gambling was good for business, since it created more interest in the games. As a result, despite an occasional raid on nickel-and-dime gamblers at ball parks, the high-stakes gambling element was able to move their operations from the race track to the ball park relatively unmolested."[25]

Ginsburg continues in that vein, commenting that the "stage for the Black Sox scandal was set by the way baseball handled . . . other instances of corruption. Baseball owners ignored the growing corruption because they felt that negative publicity would damage their industry. This laissez-faire attitude, of course, merely encouraged more corruption."[26]

Therefore, as the 1919 World Series approached, anyone aware of the gambling undercurrents of professional baseball also knew that officials enforced rules and meted out discipline erratically. Consequently, taking a gambling-related risk might not have seemed all that risky in the inconsistent and uncertain climate of 1919, especially when the potential payoff was so very high.

That, in fact, is what Gandil and the others were counting on. If they got caught—and they certainly did not plan to be caught—their punishments might be mild in comparison to the profits. If they succeeded without detection, they not only would have the profits, but also the glory of having played in the 1919 World Series and, for those who had active career years ahead of them, of increasing their contract value as individual players.

NOTES

1. Frommer, *Shoeless Joe and Ragtime Baseball*, 86.
2. See http://www.blackbetsy.com/soxplayr.htm.
3. Fleitz, *Shoeless*, 169.
4. Asinof, *Eight Men Out*, 6.
5. Asinof includes this incident in *Eight Men Out*, and it is also included in the movie by the same name. David Fleitz offers a detailed rebuttal in *Shoeless*, 111–112.
6. Asinof, *Eight Men Out*, 9.
7. See Asinof, *Eight Men Out*, 6–9 for more specifics.
8. See http://www.baseballlibrary.com/baseballlibrary/ballplayers/G/Gleason_Kid.stm.
9. See http://www.baseball-reference.com/j/jacksjo01.shtml.
10. Gropman, *Say It Ain't So, Joe!*, 158.
11. See http://www.baseball-reference.com/c/collied01.shtml.

12. See http://www.baseball-reference.com/m/mcmulfr01.shtml.

13. Fleitz, *Shoeless*, 167.

14. Ibid.

15. Frommer, *Shoeless Joe and Ragtime Baseball*, 91.

16. William A. Cook, author of *The 1919 World Series: What Really Happened?* (Jefferson, NC: McFarland and Company, 2001) offers a detailed and passionate rebuttal to this assertion. According to Cook, "The Reds would probably have won no matter how the game was played. They were, in fact, an excellent team capable of beating the seemingly superhuman White Sox." Another version of this argument appears in Victor Luhrs' book, *The Great Baseball Mystery: The 1919 World Series* (New York: A.S. Barnes and Company, 1966).

17. See http://www.baseballlibrary.com/baseballlibrary/ballplayers/B/Burns_Bill.stm.

18. Asinof, *Eight Men Out*, 22–24.

19. Daniel E. Ginsberg, *The Fix Is In: A History of Baseball Gambling and Game Fixing Scandals* (Jefferson, NC: McFarland and Company, 1995), 11.

20. Ibid., 2.

21. Lee Allen quoted in Ginsberg, *The Fix Is In*, 17.

22. See http://www.1919blacksox.com/banished.htm.

23. Pietrusza, *Major Leagues*, 38.

24. For information about this scandal, see Pietrusza, *Major Leagues*, and Ginsberg, *The Fix Is In*.

25. Ginsberg, *The Fix Is In*, 85.

26. Ibid., 100.

WEBS OF TREACHERY

Any man who insinuates that the 1919 World's Series was not honorably played
by every participant therein not only does not know what he is talking about,
but is a menace to the game quite as much as the gamblers would be if they
had the ghost of a chance to get in their nefarious work.
— Francis C. Richter[1]

Advise All Not to Bet on This Series. Ugly Rumors Afloat.
— Hugh Fullerton[2]

The 1919 World Series was less than two weeks away, and Arnold Gandil found himself in an exhilarating and enviable position. Not only had he successfully masterminded a game-fixing scheme that would shower him with magnificent sums of money—$80,000 from his associate, Joseph "Sport" Sullivan, and $100,000 from the duo of former White Sox player Sleepy Bill Burns and former boxer Billy Maharg—he had also brilliantly secured the cooperation of Eddie Cicotte and Lefty Williams, the pitchers who would start Games 1 and 2, respectively, as well as other games during the Series.

Specifics of how the games would be lost hadn't yet been finalized; but on September 21, Gandil, Cicotte, and Williams, along with Happy Felsch, Buck Weaver, Swede Risberg, and Fred McMullin, met in the Ansonia Hotel in Manhattan.[3] There, they decided that precise strategies could wait until Kid Gleason finalized the roster. Gandil wasn't worried. The trickiest discussions had already taken place, so he allowed himself to become as close to elated as he ever did. After all, he must have reasoned, what could go wrong now?

Jackson in his White Sox uniform during the 1920 season. *National Baseball Hall of Fame Library, Cooperstown, N.Y.*

It's unlikely that Gandil was aware of the problems that Burns and Maharg were encountering as they searched for financial backing; after contacting numerous big name gamblers, they were without a cent. To attempt to rectify the situation, Burns and Maharg undertook a big venture, traveling to New York to meet the most notorious and well-heeled gambler in America: Arnold Rothstein.[4]

Although there were many nicknames associated with Rothstein, including "Mr. Big," "The Fixer," "Big Bankroll," "The Man Uptown," and "The Brain," perhaps his attorney described him best.[5] "Arnold Rothstein," William J. Fallon said, "is a man who waits in doorways . . . a mouse, waiting in the doorway for his cheese."[6]

It was said that when Rothstein was only twelve,[7] he was already gambling. On Friday evenings, his pious father, known as "Abe the Just," would empty his pockets of money and jewelry before attending Friday evening prayers. Arnold would pawn his father's watch, using the cash to gamble for the next twenty-four hours. He would always get the watch out of hock before his father returned home on Saturday evening, and no one was the wiser. Rothstein dropped out of high school at age 16 and began hanging around pool halls. There, he met a corrupt politician with ties to Tammany Hall, the popular synecdoche for the Democratic political machine in Manhattan. Through these connections, Rothstein eventually became the contact between New York politicians and the underworld crime syndicate.

Rothstein continued to nurture a wide network with the underworld; he also formed relationships with police and politicians, paying them kickbacks and bribes so that they would not interfere with illegal dealings going on in the gambling houses that he established throughout New York. Rothstein was low-key and conservative, but he was also well-connected and could be deadly when crossed. Historian Robert Rockaway noted, "Rothstein is recognized as the pioneer big businessman of organized crime in the United States;" historian Leo Katcher added a further spin, calling Rothstein the "J. P. Morgan of the underworld; its banker and master of strategy."[8] For all these reasons, Rothstein was a logical—if somewhat overly ambitious—choice for Burns and Maharg's plan.

Rothstein was also notoriously cautious and protective of his public image. Instead of meeting with the two gamblers directly, Rothstein sent his bodyguard, former featherweight boxing champion Abe Attell, to find out what the small timers wanted. Attell was sufficiently impressed with their plan to carry the idea back to his boss; for reasons of his own, though, Rothstein declined to participate. Later, the two gamblers tried again and met with Rothstein personally, but his answer remained the same: "Big Bankroll" did not want to get involved; in his view, the scheme would not work.

Financing of the game-fixing conspiracy, never well thought out to begin with, kept getting murkier, this time because of Attell, a man who knew how to look out for himself. Born in 1884 to Jewish parents in an Irish neighborhood, he learned to brawl at a young age; he fought up to ten times daily, protecting himself from Irish bullies roaming the streets. When he was thirteen, his father abandoned him, his mother, and his many siblings, and Attell began selling newspapers to earn money. In 1897, while standing at his newspaper corner, he observed a boxing match and decided to join in the action. Fighting, he decided, could pay in coin more valuable than mere survival.

After promising his mother that he'd fight only once, she granted him permission to participate in a boxing match. Attell returned home with fifteen dollars in prize money—and no injuries—after knocking out his opponent in the second round. After that, his mother encouraged him to continue boxing, and even started betting on her son to win. In 1901, the current featherweight champion did not meet the weight requirements of the boxing classification. Attell, who had just beaten a former champion in a match, sensed an opportunity for advancement and pronounced himself the new national featherweight champion. By 1904, after Attell had won a significant amount of fights, his claim was generally accepted. By 1906, it was undisputed, and he held the title until 1912.[9]

Attell didn't always fight fairly. During one fight, he bent back his opponent's arm; referees also had to wipe unknown material off Attell's body, a substance that was allegedly applied to make his opponent groggy. (Attell insisted that the substance was not chloroform, as it was alleged, but instead was merely cocoa butter.)[10] As he kept fighting and winning, Attell started betting on himself—not an uncommon practice among prize fighters[11]—and he also assisted gamblers in their bets, letting them know ahead of time in which round he intended to finish the fight with a knock-out. In one such fight, his opponent, having learned which round Attell had predicted, fled the ring before it began, preferring to scamper away than be knocked out by this fierce fighter.[12] Opponents often feared Attell, while gamblers appreciated his ability in "arranging a realistic-looking dive for the right amount of money."[13] Whenever Attell lost a fight, people assumed that he hadn't really lost; instead, he was merely "doing business."[14]

Known as the "Little Champ" because he was only five feet, four inches tall, Attell won ninety-two matches in his illustrious boxing career, fifty-one of them knockouts,[15] and many of them against larger men in other weight divisions. He "gloried in being small and whacking around bigger men"[16] and this attitude made him an ideal bodyguard for a man such as Rothstein. Attell was also a "dazzling, dapper young champion, darting in and out of prestigious saloons where the powerful politicians and sporting crowd gathered, an ambitious young operator looking to get into the action."[17]

So, never one to back down from a fight or miss an opportunity, Attell refused to let go of the chance to get on a fix of the World Series. He figured that, by using Rothstein's name, he could get a piece of the action. Accordingly, he arranged a clandestine meeting with Burns and told him that Rothstein had changed his mind and would furnish the necessary $100,000. He also insisted that, for security purposes, Burns keep Rothstein's name out of the scheme.

Burns and Maharg were now satisfied that they had enough money to fund their scheme and they stopped looking for sources of financing. Sullivan, though, was still on the make, so he contacted Rothstein to discuss the potential backing of his own plan. Rothstein knew of Sullivan, perhaps because of his growing reputation as a baseball expert earned through information that Gandil secretly fed him; regardless of the reasons why, the gambling kingpin agreed to grant an audience to Sullivan.

Moreover, while the gamblers were frantically trying to obtain financing, Gandil was working on gaining Jackson's cooperation; a few errors in the outfield and a cooled-down bat would provide the insurance the plan needed. Therefore, Gandil approached Jackson earlier in September with an offer of $10,000, which "Shoeless Joe" refused; when the offer escalated to $20,000, though, Jackson agreed to participate.[18]

Why Jackson agreed to join in a game-fixing conspiracy will never be known. Perhaps he figured that the fix would be in; regardless of whether he agreed to cooperate or not, the outcome would be the same. Possibly, because of his life-long habit of accepting extra cash from sideline sources—dating back to his mill-town baseball days, when fans supplemented his pay with their own hard-earned coins—Jackson convinced himself, at least temporarily, that accepting the money wouldn't hurt anyone, and so long as it was offered, he might as well take it.

It goes without saying that Jackson, like Cicotte and Gandil, also resented Comiskey's penny-pinching ways. Jackson was about to compete against players who were far less skilled than he, but who were making more money. Jake Daubert, for example, the first baseman for the Cincinnati Reds was earning $9,000, compared to Jackson's $6,000. Heinie Groh was making $8,000, while Edd Roush was bringing home $10,000. (By comparison, Ty Cobb and Tris Speaker, players of Jackson's commiserate ability, were earning $20,000 and $16,000, respectively.)[19] There was no question that the Reds players were talented, but they were nowhere near the caliber of Jackson. Knowing that they were outstripping him at the bank when they couldn't touch him on the field doubtlessly rankled him.

It's possible, though, that the answer is even simpler. Jackson was supporting himself and Katie, along with his widowed mother, handicapped brother, and youngest sister; maybe he just couldn't say "no" to the money. Alternatively, as Eddie Collins said about Jackson, years later, he was "easily led."[20] But Jackson was no rube. He had been around professional baseball long enough to know the risks such a plan would offer, and whether he was pinched for ready cash or not, he was a long way from being destitute.

Sullivan's proposal intrigued Rothstein enough for him to send his associate,

Nat Evans, to Chicago. Before leaving, Evans expressed his fear that too many people already knew of the fix, which might prevent its success. Rothstein suggested that the opposite might be true. "If nine guys go to bed with a girl," he reasoned, "then she'll have a tough time proving the tenth is the father."[21]

Evans used the alias of "Brown" to conceal his identity, and on September 29, he and Sullivan discussed the potential fix with Gandil. Other unnamed players also attended the illicit meeting. Gandil again demanded $80,000 in cash before the Series—which was now only two days away—began. Brown didn't commit to the plan, merely telling the players that he'd see what he could do.

Evans then talked to Rothstein, who wired him $40,000 in cash to begin the process, and then sent another forty grand to keep it moving. Rothstein was no fool, though. He insisted that the second $40,000 go into a safe, to be distributed after the Series was successfully fixed.[22]

The seed money was given to Sullivan, who added another twist to the already-convoluted proceedings. Instead of handing over the money to the involved players or to Gandil for distribution, Sullivan furnished only $10,000 to Gandil; he then used the bulk of the money ($29,000) to place his own bets on the Series in an obvious attempt to make money on the side from the capital Rothstein had provided. Unfortunately, this jeopardized the entire scheme.

Gandil was furious at the shortfall. He instantly saw it as a double cross that could spoil everything. He'd already promised $10,000 to Cicotte to throw the first game. If that didn't happen, then the entire deal was off. If he handed over the entire $10,000 to Cicotte, how was he to guarantee the cooperation of the other players, who also expected payoffs in advance? It's possible that Gandil hoped that Burns and Maharg would come up with the promised $100,000, but that was no more likely at that juncture than it had ever been, because things were unraveling there as well.

The players certainly could have backed off at this point, but the gamblers were rough men who could turn dangerous if they were double-crossed, and things had already gone too far, inasmuch as their commitment to throw the games was concerned. Also, the potential for financial gain was still large enough—or their anger at Comiskey heated enough—that they didn't abandon the plan when upfront money didn't appear as anticipated. Therefore, the players decided to go ahead with the fix. The gamblers didn't insist on any particular pattern of wins and losses, as long as the White Sox lost in the end. Cicotte, though, needed to hit the leadoff batter during the first inning of the first game to signal that the fix was on. Because Cicotte rarely hit batters, this unusual incident would serve well as a signal.

On September 30, the White Sox team departed for Cincinnati. Seven players in the fix then gathered at the Sinton Hotel, where they decided to throw the first three games, then try to win the fourth. Jackson, it should be noted, was not at the meeting. Attell and Burns also met with the players, assuring them that they would be paid an aggregate fee of $20,000 after each of the five losses of the best-of-nine series. In actuality, of course, Attell had no cash from Rothstein to give to the players; besides, he was using the money that he was raising from various sources—estimated at $40,000—to place his own bets.[23]

Two other pivotal events also occurred—one important to the entire fix, the other vital to those who want to analyze whether or not Jackson intended to deliberately lose games or had merely agreed to accept cash and then played as best he could. First, on September 29, Cicotte found $10,000 under his hotel pillow and he secreted the money into the lining of his jacket. These were the initial funds that Sullivan had supplied to Gandil; the first baseman forwarded that money to Cicotte. In addition, when the team arrived in Cincinnati, Jackson approached Gleason and told him that he didn't want to play. Gleason angrily refused the request, officially making Jackson part of the ill-fated line-up of the 1919 Black Sox.[24] It's reasonable to assume that Jackson wanted to avoid being an actual part of the fix; perhaps Jackson considered derailing the entire scheme, but didn't follow through.

Even though Jackson didn't tell what he knew, game-fixing rumors spread. Sports writer Hugh Fullerton contacted the newspapers that carried his column and advised reporters and editors not to bet on any games. Williams began counseling friends not to bet on the Sox, while Risberg sent a telegram to his friend, Joe Gedeon from the St. Louis Browns, suggesting that he bet on the Reds. Attell shared confidential information with his closest friends, as well. The secret, by now, was open knowledge, at least in the underworld. Ironically, Sullivan, who had held back $29,000 from the seed money to place his own bets, found that the flurry of rumors had already driven down the odds. On September 29, he was unable to get anything better than an even bet, a serious drop in odds from the 8-to-5 spread available the morning before. Clearly, the news was out; the fix was in.

As gamblers were frantically placing bets and attempting to parlay their money into something greater, and schemers were trying to double-cross their coconspirators, the general public was thrilling to the opening-day atmosphere of the 1919 World Series. It was the first Series since the war ended, and people were in a carefree mood, relieved to be free of daily anxiety and grisly news. The Series offered an exciting and delightful diversion, capped off by a rivalry between two Midwestern teams with long traditions.

Enthusiastic Chicago fans were confident of victory, anticipating "Shoeless Joe's slugging, the amazing shine ball of Eddie Cicotte, the magnificent all-around play of Eddie Collins, the fiery personality of little Ray Schalk, the flashiness and color of the incredible Buck Weaver."[25] Meanwhile, Cincinnati fans, eagerly accepting the role of scrappy underdogs, flooded Redland Field, refusing to believe that their hometown heroes would fail to give the dominant Chicago White Sox a run for their money.

Even though Redland Field officially seated only 20,000,[26] folding chairs were set up in breezeways and aisles, and standing room tickets were soon sold out. On October 1, Jackson trotted to the outfield in front of screaming 30,511 fans who were eager to see topnotch play. The game, though, started out quietly as Reds pitcher "Dutch" Ruether held the White Sox scoreless for the first inning. Edd Roush made a stunning one-handed catch that delighted fans, but the top of the inning was otherwise uneventful.

The first Reds batter was second baseman, Morrie Rath. Cicotte threw a fat strike, but Rath left the bat on his shoulder. Cicotte's second pitch beaned Rath, just as planned, and the fix was officially on. After gambling kingpin Rothstein heard about this errant pitch, he immediately bet $100,000 of his own money on the Reds. (Rothstein cautiously refused to bet on any one game; instead, he placed his money on the overall outcome of the Series.) Jake Daubert was up next. He hit a single and Rath raced to third base. Heinie Groh lofted a long fly to left field; Jackson caught the ball for the first out, but Rath scored on the sacrifice. At the end of the first inning, the Reds were winning, 1–0.

In the second, Jackson dribbled the ball into the infield, but a wild throw advanced him safely to second base. Felsch hit a sacrifice fly, moving Jackson to third; then, on a hit by Gandil, Jackson scored the only Chicago run of the inning. The game remained tied in the second, and neither team hit or scored in the third, where Jackson hauled in two fly balls for quick outs.

In the fourth, Jackson was thrown out at first base; the bottom half of the inning was a treat for Cincinnati fans. The batters could do no wrong, it seemed. They scored five runs on just six hits, including a triple that Ruether hit between Jackson and Felsch. In the top of the sixth, Jackson was tagged out at first, but two players advanced on the fielders' choice. Cincinnati scored two more runs in the bottom of the seventh, and another in the eighth, raising the score to 9–1, where it remained. The Reds led the Series by a game, and the fix had apparently not been necessary. Or had it?

Chicago's catcher, Ray Schalk, thought something was definitely wrong. With the instincts that only a veteran backstop can have, he was convinced that Cicotte was intentionally throwing his worst stuff and was at the very least inconsistent. It infuriated him. He wanted to confront Cicotte after the game, but the pitcher had slipped away.

Gleason, who had replaced Cicotte with Roy Wilkinson near the end of the disastrous fourth and then called Grover Lowdermilk to the mound in the eighth, was possibly more frustrated than Schalk. He had heard the rumors of a fix, which were reinforced by telegrams from around the country cautioning about dishonest play. Later that evening, Gleason spotted Cicotte and accosted him. Never a subtle man, Gleason stood screaming at the pitcher on the sidewalk outside the hotel, an outburst witnessed by dozens of startled onlookers. Gleason soon realized the futility of his gesture, though, and retired to his room in frustration where, apparently, he began cogitating over the increasing rumors coming to his attention and allowing his suspicions to grow.

Gandil and the other players involved in the fix must have been equally as frustrated, but for entirely different reasons. Attell and Burns now owed them $20,000. Attell actually had thousands of dollars in his hotel room but he planned to use it to place bets on Game 2. Even so, the former boxer suddenly turned big-time gambler knew that he needed to ensure the players' continued cooperation. Accordingly, he and Burns and Maharg met with the disgruntled players the next morning, promising them that they would receive their money the following day. Burns doubted that Attell would come across, but Williams apparently didn't; that was far more important to the plan, because Williams was starting the second game.[27]

There were 29,960 fans in attendance for Game 2, with Slim Sallee dueling Williams on the mound. Gleason, who had spent a sleepless night, was now suspicious of many players, including Williams. He told Schalk, "Watch him."

The first inning was quiet. In the second, Jackson looped a double over Roush's head; he advanced to third on Felsch's sacrifice but remained stranded there. Williams held the Reds hitless in the second, and the third inning produced only one lone single, from Williams himself.

In the fourth, Buck Weaver and Jackson singled. They advanced on a sacrifice, but neither man could score. Cincinnati, though, put numbers on the board during their half of the inning. Williams walked Rath, and Daubert's sacrifice allowed him to take second. Heinie Groh was also given a free pass, and Roush scored Rath on a single that moved Groh to third. Roush attempted to steal second, but he was tagged out. After Pat Duncan walked, Larry Kopf tripled, scoring two more runs. The Reds led 3–0.

Chicago did not score in the fifth, but a quick defensive play by Jackson held a Cincinnati line drive to a single. In the sixth, Weaver doubled, but Jackson struck out. Cincinnati added another run that inning, bringing the score to 4–0. Chicago came back with two runs in the seventh, cutting the Cincinnati lead in half; then Jackson smashed a blue darter in the eighth and scampered to second base on a muffled play. No additional runs, though, were scored. In the second game of the World Series, Jackson went 3 for 4, but the White Sox lost again, 4–2, and were now down in the Series 0–2.

After the game ended, Schalk, who was beside himself with frustration, vented to Gleason, saying that Williams had "crossed him"[28] three times by not throwing the curve ball that had been anticipated. Gleason, furious, spotted Gandil in the locker room calmly smoking a cigar, and the fiery manager, already stricken with stress, exploded. He grabbed his first baseman by his throat. A melee began and the frustrated catcher joined in, punching Williams several times.

After the donnybrook quieted down, Gleason composed himself enough to speak to reporters, diplomatically speaking of "Williams' wildness" and "mistakes in our defense."[29] While Gleason may have assuaged some suspicious questions, he didn't fool sportswriter Ring Lardner, who composed a drunken ditty about corrupt Chicago; that night, he sang that tune loudly in a Cincinnati tavern, replacing the words, "I'm forever blowing bubbles" to "I'm forever blowing ballgames."[30]

At 11:00 P.M., Comiskey and Gleason met. Rumors of a fix were growing in number, and both were now seriously alarmed. The manager admitted he was suspicious that some players were involved in something nefarious, but he had no real proof. Comiskey, never shy about acting impulsively, didn't need much more than that. At 2:30 A.M., a sleepless Comiskey aroused National League President John Heydler, then Ban Johnson, the president of the American League, and announced his suspicions. Johnson, a former friend of Comiskey's and now one of his most bitter enemies, told the White Sox owner that his assertions were nothing but the "yelp of a whipped cur."[31] That was the end of the matter—for then.

Other darker skirmishes were taking place that evening, as well. Burns confronted Attell and demanded the $40,000 now owed the players, but the former boxer demurred; Burns received only $10,000, which he forwarded to Gandil, who assured the gambler that, even though Chicago's rookie pitcher, "busher" Dickie Kerr, wasn't part of the fix, the White Sox would lose Game 3 as well. So assured, Burns and Maharg bet all of their available funds on Game 3.

Jackson reportedly confronted Gandil that night, as well, asking him about the $20,000 that was promised. When the first baseman responded that he didn't have the cash, Jackson was at a loss. He dared not complain to Katie, his practical, no-nonsense wife, who knew nothing about the scheme. He'd already asked Gleason for permission to sit out the Series, and was denied. Therefore, Shoeless Joe could only bide his time.

After two consecutive White Sox losses, the situation was unsettling, at best, for the players involved in the game-fixing scheme. They'd been guaranteed a combined $180,000 from two sets of gamblers; but only $20,000 had exchanged hands, and half of that money remained with Gandil, who had yet to distribute it. (Actually, Gandil never did share any of that $10,000 with the players; he kept it for himself.) Game 3 was supposed to be another loss; as was becoming the pattern, though, the players with knowledge of the fix weren't certain how, specifically, they were to play a role. All they knew is that, somehow or the other, they needed to lose.

For the third outing, the teams moved to Chicago, where Ray Fisher was starting for Cincinnati.[32] For Chicago, Kerr, unaware of the fix, toed the rubber in front of 29,126 excited fans. According to author Harvey Frommer, Comiskey Park seats were jammed with people "ready with streamers of blue and white, noisemakers to accentuate the moment, and sweaters and coats to stave off the cutting edge of the chill that blew in off the lake."[33] Cincinnati fans had come up to the Windy City, as well.

Neither team put any hits on the board during the first inning; during the second, the Cincinnati Reds got one hit, but the runner was stranded. Jackson started off the second inning for Chicago, connecting for such a powerful single that the crowd roared. He reached second base on a weak bunt by Felsch, slipping as he rounded second, but made it to third safely; in the play's confusion, Felsch took second. Gandil then tapped a ball between Daubert and Rath, scoring Jackson and Felsch. Chicago was now ahead, 2–0, the first lead they'd had in the entire 1919 World Series. Gandil's racking up two RBIs early in the game doubtlessly unnerved his gambling associates, but he probably expected Cincinnati players to hit well against the inexperienced Kerr. He might have also been sensitive to the steadily increasing rumors and wanted to divert suspicion from himself. Or, it's possibly that he wanted to demonstrate to the gamblers that his abilities were in no way impaired by the scheme, and that he could perform as well as he wished.

The third inning was unproductive for both clubs, with Jackson offering an attempted sacrifice that failed. In the fourth, Chicago scored another run, thanks to Schalk's sacrifice bunt. In the sixth, Jackson made a good catch and also rapped a single; he was thrown out, though, in an attempted steal. He went 2 for 3 that game, scoring one of the three runs, and the Chicago White Sox won 3–0. The game took less than ninety minutes to complete and the Series now stood at Cincinnati Reds 2, Chicago White Sox 1.[34]

Gandil's RBIs didn't make a difference, truly, in the game's outcome, for the Sox had a winning run to spare; but his guarantee to Burns and Maharg—that the White Sox would definitely lose Game 3—was not fulfilled. Burns lost his entire $12,000 fortune by betting on the Reds. Maharg also lost all of his money, and needed to pawn his diamond stickpin for train fare home. The two small-timers were through with the scheme, so their contact, Attell, was now free to wager the money in his possession entirely for his own benefit.

When it came time for Gandil to pressure a gambler for more money, he now had to choose Sport Sullivan, but Sullivan was under pressure of his own. Arnold Rothstein had placed almost $300,000 in personal bets on an overall Cincinnati World Series win, and Sullivan dreaded the consequences if the scheme went awry. He therefore needed to reassure the White Sox players who were skittish about late payoffs, to ensure that the Reds would, indeed, win the Series. Gandil's actions in Game 3 had suddenly put the entire plan in a different light, one that would shine brightly on Game 4.

NOTES

1. Fleitz, *Shoeless*, 195.
2. Ibid., 175.
3. According to Fleitz, by "all reliable accounts," Jackson was not at this meeting (*Shoeless*, 172). In *Say It Ain't So, Joe!*, Donald Gropman implies that Jackson wasn't present by saying that on October 1, Burns gave Jackson the first corroboration that the "fix was actually in" (169). However, in *Eight Men Out*, Eliot Asinof notes Jackson's presence at this meeting directly (19) and indirectly (33). Although this is one of the main cruxes of the matter regarding Jackson's degree of guilt, there is no real way to determine the truth. Fleitz puts the meeting date as September 18.
4. Asinof, *Eight Men Out*, 24.
5. See http://www.crimelibrary.com/gangsters_outlaws/mob_bosses/rothstein/index_1.html.
6. Asinof, *Eight Men Out*, unnumbered page that starts Chapter 1.
7. By the time he was fourteen, Asinof, in *Eight Men Out*, says that he was "gambling seriously" (25).
8. See the Jewish Virtual Library of the American Jewish History Society at http://www.us-israel.org/jsource/biography/Rothstein.html.
9. For information about young Attell, see http://www.cyberboxingzone.com/boxing/attell.htm.
10. See the International Boxing Hall of Fame Web site at http://www.ibhof.com/kilbane.htm.
11. See the International Boxing Hall of Fame Web site at http://www.ibhof.com/attell.htm.
12. See http://www.jewsinsports.org/profile.asp?sport=boxing&ID=5.
13. Fleitz, *Shoeless*, 172.
14. Asinof, *Eight Men Out*, 27.
15. See http://www.ibhof.com/attell.htm.
16. See http://www.cyberboxingzone.com/boxing/attell.htm.
17. Eliot Asinof, *Bleeding Between the Lines* (New York: Holt, Rinehart, and Winston, 1979), 104.
18. In *Shoeless*, Fleitz supports this view (172) but Gropman in *Say It Ain't So, Joe!*

says that Gandil offered Jackson $10,000 and then $20,000, but Jackson refused (165). In *Eight Men Out*, Asinof implies Jackson's compliance, placing him at the meeting where the payoff was being discussed (19) and also mentioning Jackson's insistence on $20,000 (34). In Jackson's 1920 Grand Jury testimony, he talks of being promised $20,000. Gropman counters that Jackson's testimony was coerced, previously rehearsed with Charles Comiskey's attorney, and inaccurate.

19. Fleitz, *Shoeless*, 160–161.

20. Ibid., 170.

21. Asinof, *Eight Men Out*, 30.

22. Ibid., 33–34.

23. Decades later, when Attell described "cheaters cheating cheaters," Asinof said that the sounds of Attells' "amorality kept ringing in my ears, his deviousness the guiding ethic of my writing." See *Bleeding Between the Lines*, 108–109.

24. Asinof (*Eight Men Out*) has Jackson telling Gleason, before the Series began, that he doesn't want to play (59) and so does Fleitz in *Shoeless* (176). Gropman (*Say It Ain't So, Joe!*) has him telling Charles Comiskey himself (169); in a 1949 interview with *Sport* magazine, that was Jackson's version of what happened. In 1920, Jackson testified that he intended to inform Comiskey of the scheme, but Gandil allegedly warned that it wouldn't go well for Jackson if he did.

25. Asinof, *Eight Men Out*, 31.

26. See http://www.baseball-statistics.com/Ballparks/Cin/Crosley.htm.

27. Fleitz, *Shoeless*, 179–180.

28. Ibid., 182.

29. Ibid.

30. Ibid.

31. Some sources say "crying of a whipped cur" while others list "yelp of a beaten cur."

32. He was relieved in the eighth inning by "Dolf" Luque, one of the first players from Cuba to join the major league system, and the first Latin American to pitch in a World Series.

33. Frommer, *Shoeless Joe and Ragtime Baseball*, 107.

34. For more specifics about Games 1–3, see www.blackbetsy.com and Fleitz's *Shoeless*, 178–185.

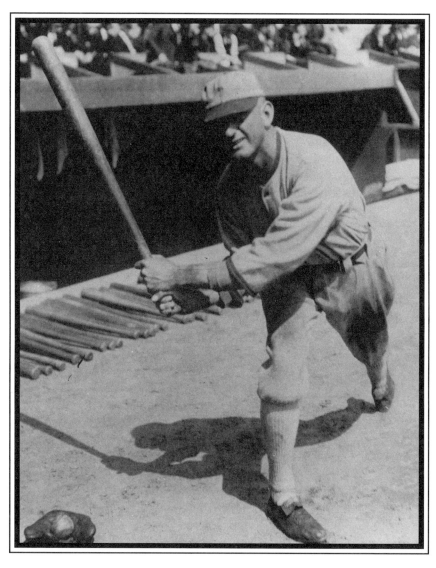

Jackson swinging the bat before the 1917 World Series. *Cleveland Public Library.*

GETTING A "LITTLE JAZZ"

No one will ever know the whole story, I suppose. There will always be gaps, to be filled in, as I have tried to, over the years. There is no truth, only versions.
—Point of view of the fictional character, Sport Sullivan[1]

Arnold Rothstein, according to one contemporary, had a "mild and pleasing" voice, with graceful mannerisms. He also had "white, skillful hands, and amazingly vital, sparkling, dark brown eyes . . . laughing, brilliant, restless eyes glowing in the pale but expressive face." Rothstein didn't drink or smoke, and overall, was a "quiet, medium-sized man, inconspicuously dressed, in this restaurant or that, in this courtroom or that, or strolling on a sidewalk with a friend, frequently reaching down to snap the garter on his sock, his ready laughter revealing those white, even, artificial teeth, hardly whiter than his pallid skin, which was like a woman's."[2]

This wasn't the sketch of an intimidating man, but Sport Sullivan wasn't deceived by Rothstein's respectable appearance; he instinctively understood that Rothstein's congenial manifestation was a facade. If crossed, this pallid, placid gambler, who took enormous pride in his ability to estimate accurately the character of other men, would respond demonstratively. If offended or betrayed, Rothstein would not—maybe could not—forgive. Therefore, to appease the "Big Bankroll" after the unexpected White Sox win in the third game, Sullivan called Chick Gandil to ensure that the fix was still on and that all would run smoothly.

From Gandil's perspective, of course, the crux of the matter was money; if the promised cash didn't appear, then the entire deal was off, and the Sox would play to win the World Series. Sullivan—dreading Rothstein's wrath, and knowing the gambler had bet $270,000 of his personal funds on the Reds to win the Series—assured Gandil that all would be taken care of promptly, and that he would receive $20,000 after Game 4 and another $20,000 after Game 5. With that confirmation, Sullivan and Gandil reached an accord. By the time the fourth game began, though, Sullivan was already devising a method to cheat the players out of the second of the two agreed-upon payoffs.

Although Gandil was relieved, manager Kid Gleason and catcher Ray Schalk were more than uneasy. Earlier in the season, future Hall-of-Famer Red Faber was injured, which meant that the White Sox were relying upon a three-man pitching rotation for the World Series. Because of that, Eddie Cicotte, the pitcher who lost Game 1 of the Series, was starting Game 4 as well; this was a source of significant apprehension for both Gleason and Schalk.

On Saturday, October 4, nearly 35,000 people, 3,000 more than capacity, descended on Comiskey Park to watch Cicotte challenge Jimmy Ring of the Cincinnati Reds. Those anticipating a pitcher's duel were well rewarded through the first four innings when neither team could score. In that time frame, Jackson caught a ball hit by Edd Roush, and he also rapped out a solid double, reaching third base on Happy Felsch's sacrifice. Jackson tapped a single in the third inning, as well, but he was stranded both times. In the fourth, Jackson snagged Morrie Rath's sharp line drive, preventing a hit.

For many, controversial play in the fifth inning confirmed that dishonesty was afoot. As Ring affirmed years later, "That's when we knew for sure there was some horseshit going on."[3] Reds left fielder Pat Duncan hit a grounder to Cicotte, who scooped the ball and threw wildly to first; the ball bounced out of reach and Duncan ran safely to second. Larry Kopf then singled and Duncan ran to third; the ball was still in play when Jackson accurately threw toward the plate to hold Duncan, but he rounded the third sack and was galloping home, anyway. The out at the plate seemed certain, but Cicotte then inexplicably tried to cut off Jackson's throw, even though it was not in his reach. Cicotte touched the ball, deflecting it from its path toward the plate, and thereby prevented Schalk from making the catch and tagging Duncan, who was nowhere near home. The ball rolled away and Duncan scored easily; Cicotte stared morosely towards center field, avoiding Schalk's intense gaze.

This play must have significantly increased the suspicions of sportswriter Hugh Fullerton and former pitching star and future Hall-of-Famer Christy Mathewson, who was reporting for the *New York Evening World*. Before the World Series even started, Fullerton and Mathewson had spotted well-known and flashy gamblers congregating at the Sinton Hotel in Cincinnati, along with other suspicious characters who were lurking about the hotel and ballpark. Fullerton and Mathewson were also alert to the game-fixing rumors before the onset of the Series; for future analyses, they carefully recorded each play, circling in red those that didn't seem quite right. When Cicotte deflected Jackson's throw, both men reached for their pens.

It's also possible that this savvy duo shook their heads about the next play; the mistake, this time, was Jackson's. Greasy Neale lined a high fly over Jackson's head, who ran in circles before sticking out his mitt in an attempt to catch the ball. Kopf scored, which prompted a *Cleveland Plain Dealer* reporter to chide Jackson in print.[4] The rest of the game didn't go well for him, either. Jackson made contact with the ball in the sixth inning, but he flied out to Kopf; in the eighth, Jackson struck out. The Reds notched another win 2–0, and they were leading the Series 3–1.

After the game, an incensed Gleason held a mandatory meeting. He probably chastised Jackson, but was livid with Cicotte, and he blasted the players with the conviction of his suspicions. He accused them of deliberately losing the games; the majority of the team remained silent after hearing those charges, although Gandil spoke up, vehemently denying any and all accusations. Meanwhile, Fred McMullin threatened to punch anyone who questioned his integrity.

Once the postgame ordeal was over, Gandil met with Sullivan and collected $20,000; he separated the bills into four envelopes, each containing $5,000. One envelope was for Felsch and another was for Swede Risberg. Gandil gave the other two to Lefty Williams, asking him to forward one envelope to Jackson.

Although Williams did deliver the money, there are differing accounts about the specifics. Some say that, after Williams handed over the cash, Jackson felt cheated and argued that he needed the entire $20,000. Perhaps Jackson then rushed to Gandil, demanding more money; in this version, Gandil reportedly snapped back that Attell had "given us a jazzing"[5] by keeping most of the money for himself. Another version states that Williams and Jackson were silent throughout the transaction; in another, Jackson tried to reject the money. In any case, when Katie discovered why her husband had the cash, she broke down and cried, thinking it "an awful thing to do."[6]

Katie had thus far been unaware of her husband's behind-the-scene machinations, but Jackson now needed to confess some particulars. He, along with the other players with knowledge of the game-fixing, still hoped that the scheme would continue to remain a secret from the general public. However, allegations—up until now merely whispered rumors—began appearing in print. "There is more ugly talk and more suspicions among the fans than there ever has been in any World's Series," wrote Fullerton. "The rumors of crookedness, of fixed games and plots, are thick. It is not necessary to dignify them by telling what they are, but the sad part is that such suspicions of baseball is so wide-spread."[7] Tension among the factions of players, and between management and the players involved in the fix, must have been nearly unbearable, and it's reasonable to assume that the end of the World Series, regardless of its final outcome, would come as a relief to everyone. Two more games should do it, if Gandil and his cohorts had their way.

Rain, however, delayed Game 5, stretching out anxiety. While waiting to hear if the game would be cancelled, Gleason was interviewed by writers and, during the interview, he threatened to pitch Game 5 himself. Although the manager never intended to follow through on that notion, he did consider sending Dickie Kerr to the mound instead of Williams, thereby using a pitcher he believed to be honest. Perhaps Gleason thought that this alteration might disrupt the flow of the fix. Game 5, though, was ultimately cancelled for weather, granting Gleason time to reconsider his decision.

The game was rescheduled for the next day, and Gleason reluctantly sent Williams back to the mound, while Hod Eller pitched for the Reds in front of a crowd of 34,379. Fans witnessed little action during the first four innings; in fact, Williams didn't give up one hit, and Eller struck out six batters in a row in the second and third innings, setting a World Series record for consecutive strike-outs. Jackson saw little play, flying out the first inning and being thrown out in the fourth. That inning, he caught one ball for a Cincinnati out.

In the sixth inning, though, Eller placed a hit between Jackson and Felsch, and Felsch's throw was high; Jackson "seemed to be daydreaming."[8] Eller ended up on third, and Rath singled him in. Jake Daubert sacrificed to move Rath to second, and Heinie Groh walked on four pitches. Roush then knocked in both Rath and Groh, sliding into third with a triple. Many spectators believed that Schalk had successfully tagged out Groh at the plate; Schalk, infuriated at the call and frustrated by the entire World Series debacle, lunged at the umpire and was ejected from the game. But the situation was desperate. The Reds were winning 3–0, and the Sox were now without their agile catcher. After the Schalk ejection, Duncan lofted a fly ball to Jackson, whose throw was good enough to reach home plate; but the substitute catcher, Byrd Lynn, didn't make the tag in time. The Reds now led, 4–0.

Jackson was thrown out at first base in the seventh inning, and he caught Rath's fly ball in the eighth. Cincinnati scored again in the ninth, and Jackson grounded out to end the game. The final score was 4–0 in the Reds second shutout of Chicago. The White Sox were now just one game away from losing the 1919 World Series.

Gleason, understandably distressed, snapped at writers that his team couldn't beat a rag tag team from high school. "His Sox had not scored a single run in 23 innings," writes David Fleitz, "and had suffered back-to-back shutouts from Jimmy Ring and Hod Eller, two pitchers not to be mistaken for Cy Young and Walter Johnson."9 Gleason even suggested that he might allow Kerr, the only White Sox pitcher to win a game in the Series so far, to pitch all remaining games. Gleason didn't even bother to search out Williams, knowing that to be futile.

The manager, though, wasn't the only White Sox to be upset. Gandil was expecting another payoff of $20,000 from Sullivan, but the money didn't arrive. Sullivan, ever elusive, had now utterly disappeared. Frustration was mounting among the players who had expected cash for their bungled play; as they traveled back to Cincinnati for Game 6, they decided that they'd been cheated and vowed to win the Series after all. If they did, they would rebuff the gamblers for their dishonesty; besides, each man on the winning World Series team would garner a $5,000 bonus. That wasn't the kind of money they'd hoped for, but it was better than nothing.

Neither Cicotte nor Williams, though, would pitch Game 6. Instead, the starting pitcher for the White Sox was Kerr. For Cincinnati, it was the return of Dutch Ruether, who may have been somewhat overconfident, not realizing that he would be the first Reds pitcher to face the White Sox after the game-fixing players decided to win the 1919 World Series. Early game play, though, belied their change of intent. The Sox were scoreless until the fifth; Jackson flied out in the first and then again in the fourth. In the interim, the Reds scored two runs on Duncan's double in the third, and then they scored two more. The score was now 4–0, and the Reds fans smelled victory.

In the fifth inning, Ruether permitted two walks, and then a single by Kerr and a sacrifice by Eddie Collins served as the impetus for the first Sox run. When Jackson came to the plate in the sixth, Buck Weaver was at second base; Jackson's single scored him. Felsch then doubled, scoring Jackson easily, and Schalk tagged a single, scoring Felsch. The game was now tied 4–4.

The game remained tied until extra innings, when Weaver doubled in the tenth. Jackson successfully bunted, which advanced Weaver to third, and Gandil singled, bringing in what ended up to be the winning run. The White Sox won the sixth game 5–4, bringing the Series tally to 4–2.

Cicotte was scheduled to pitch for Game 7 but Gleason was understandably reluctant; the pitcher, though, begged the manager for a chance to pitch and win a game for his team. Perhaps Cicotte was considering that a win at this crucial moment would be helpful when his contract was renegotiated for 1920, or maybe he wanted to ensure that the double-crossing gamblers wouldn't benefit from their tainted scheme. Or perhaps he wanted to remove the stain that the rumors and Gleason's anger had already put on him. In any case, Gleason relented and Cicotte headed to the mound.

Only 13,923 fans attended this game, a startling small crowd.[10] White Sox outfielder Shano Collins singled to start the game and a sacrifice by Eddie Collins advanced him to second; Jackson's single brought Collins home. In the third, Jackson batted in Collins again. In the fifth, Felsch came to the plate with the bases loaded and he hit a two-run single, bringing the score to 4–0. The Reds scored one run, but lost the game 4–1, and the White Sox, now closing the gap, were down only one game in the Series. Perhaps, Chicago fans must have hoped, the team was now on track.

At this point, though, the "Big Bankroll," Arnold Rothstein, intervened. He had invested significant capital wagering on a Reds win that now didn't look very likely. Unlike Gandil, he knew how to reach Sullivan. He informed the gambler that the Sox must lose the next game, and substandard play must begin in the very first inning. Sullivan, desperate and doubtlessly terrified of what Rothstein might do to him, contacted "Harry F.," a cigar-smoking thug from Chicago. Sullivan requested that Harry F. deliver a message to White Sox pitcher, Lefty Williams: lose game eight, or else fear for your personal safety—and that of Mrs. Williams, as well.

Gleason also increased the pressure on his players, announcing that he'd "use an iron [gun]"[11] on any player who intentionally lost Game 8. Although that might have sounded intimidating under more ordinary circumstances, Williams surely must have realized the more deadly threat: that of Harry F., messenger of kingpin Arnold Rothstein.

Williams, understandably enough, didn't make Rothstein wait to see results. In the first fifteen pitches of the eighth game, Williams gave up four hits and allowed three runs to score. Gleason didn't hesitate. He stormed to the mound and angrily removed Williams from the game, replacing him with Bill James, who gave up yet another run. After just one inning, the Reds were winning 4–0, and by the end of the second 5–0.

In the third inning, Jackson swung hard and hit the ball over the right field fence, notching the first—and only—home run by anyone on either team in the 1919 World Series. The Reds scored in the fifth, as well, erasing Jackson's run, and the Cincinnati team scored another three runs in the sixth. The score was now 9–1; although Jackson drove in two more runs, and Chicago scored another two in the eighth, the Reds also scored in the eighth and the Sox lost the deciding game 10–5. The Cincinnati Reds, the clear underdogs at the outset of the competition, had just won the 1919 World Series.

Joe Jackson's World Series statistics—1 home run, 6 RBIs, 5 runs scored, a .375 batting average and a .563 slugging percentage—were impressive for a variety of reasons. His batting average was the highest of all players on either team, and seventy-one points above what he'd batted in the 1917 Series. In fact, Jackson's 12 hits tied the previous World Series record; had one of his hits not been changed to an error, he would have set a new record. He also handled thirty chances in the outfield without errors. In comparison, Eddie Collins, the well-respected team captain and future Hall-of-Famer, batted .226 and had 2 errors. Roush and Groh, the stars of the Cincinnati Reds, batted .214 and .172, respectively.[12]

Jackson's supporters point to these statistics and accomplishments to show as evidence that, even if he did accept money from the gamblers, he did not deliberately participate in any game-losing activities. An alternative theory has been put forth, however, the underlying thesis being that Jackson, being the quality of player that he was, could select the plays to blow on purpose. Such contentions have become the subject of frequent and heated debate.

David L. Fleitz offers a compelling and thoughtful presentation of this viewpoint. He suggests that Jackson did, indeed, choose when to play well and when to play poorly. Highlights of Fleitz's reasoning include the fact that the Reds hit 3 triples into left field, balls that Jackson was usually able to field easily; the notion that Jackson may have played out of position during portions of the World Series, including when Neale hit the crucial double over his head in Game 4, scoring one run; and the fact that, even though Jackson tied Buck Herzog of the New York Giants World Series record of twelve hits, that statistic is misleading. The 1919 World Series lasted eight games, because this particular Series was a best of nine, rather than a best of seven, giving Jackson more opportunities for hits than was typical. Fleitz also notes that Jackson's best play occurred in the latter games of the Series, when the Reds overall win was practically a foregone conclusion.[13]

Prior to the publication of Fleitz's book *Shoeless: The Life and Times of Joe Jackson* in 1992, statistician Jay Bennett attempted to resolve this debate scientifically by calculating Jackson's "Player Game Percentage" and comparing those results to the computations of others who played in the Series. This calculation would factor in hitting, fielding, and reaction to game situations to determine the overall quality of World Series play; Bennett's conclusions would please those who believe that Jackson did not deliberately help lose games or actively participate in staged play. Bennett reported that, out of all the White Sox players, only Jackson had an "overall positive contribution." Jackson's batting statistics were high in most clutch moments, including leadoff and late inning pressure situations, and were higher during the Series than during the regular season. Besides, he also had a greater "batting contribution" than anyone else in the 1919 World Series.[14]

Less scientific, perhaps, but even more compelling than Bennett's conclusions, is an anecdotal but important detail: in the fifth inning of Game 4, Jackson attempted to throw out a runner at home, and was quite accurate in his throw, but Cicotte—who was actively involved in game-fixing—deliberately deflected the ball from its path. It's possible to infer that Cicotte knew that Jackson was *not* attempting to lose the Series, although it's also conversely possible that Jackson's throw was inadvertently more accurate than the outfielder intended, and Cicotte was providing a macabre "assist."[15]

Such particulars and detailed arguments, though, were not on the minds of the White Sox at that time; they had more immediate concerns, ranging from disappointment, anger, and embarrassment over the loss, to frustration and fury over less-than-promised payoffs. The payoff situation was eased somewhat when, the morning after the World Series ended, Sullivan resurfaced with cash in hand. He had emptied the safe of the $40,000 that Rothstein had put away as insurance money and gave it to Gandil. The first baseman of the White Sox disbursed $15,000 to Swede Risberg, asking him to give $5,000 of that to Fred McMullin. Gandil kept the other $25,000 for himself, along with the $10,000 given to him by Sleepy Bill Burns after the second game. Shortly after that, a drunken and somewhat disoriented Gandil made plans to return to California, with ten years' worth of salary stashed in his back pocket.

After the Series ended, Jackson headed to Comiskey's office and asked to speak to the team's owner. His motivation is unknown; although, perhaps, as some have suggested, he wanted to return the money, or reveal details about the fix. Jackson waited for hours, but Comiskey did not appear, and one can only speculate how Jackson felt at this staggering moment. He had displayed conflicting emotions about the scheme throughout the World Series, agreeing to accept cash from the gamblers—even bargaining for a higher dollar figure than what was originally offered—and yet, he also asked the team manager to be benched for the entire Series. This indicates a distaste for the whole scenario, or at least demonstrates Jackson's ambivalent attitude about the whole sordid scheme. Such apparent contradictions opened the debate about Jackson's actual involvement in what would become known as the "Black Sox Scandal"; whether Shoeless Joe was a willing and active participant or a reluctant fellow traveler in the scheme simply cannot be known for sure.

What is known is that Jackson did accept the cash. Although his defenders have attempted to demonstrate otherwise and/or ignore the evidence, the slugger's 1920 testimony clearly confirms this as the fact. But the matter remains more complex than that. Jackson may have attempted to see Comiskey to turn over the money and make a clean breast of the entire affair, but was snubbed in the attempt. (As some have suggested, Comiskey's secretary, Harry Grabiner, may have even told Jackson to keep the money.) Or Jackson might have had other motives in mind for seeing the owner.

Although the quality of Jackson's 1919 World Series play has been debated and interpreted in a variety of fashions, his batting and fielding statistics speak volumes. Analysts such as Fleitz argue, often in a gripping and convincing style, that Jackson's game-fixing efforts were handled in a subtle and calculated manner, to the degree that he threw the game while appearing to play to win. After pondering Jackson's personality and intellect, though, and taking into account the fact that, even after all the seasons he'd played professional baseball, he remained, at heart, a somewhat naïve country boy, eager to make his place among more sophisticated and better-educated teammates, it seems far more likely that, if Jackson had actively and willingly played to lose, his contributions would have been as apparent—or rather, as transparent—as Cicotte's and Williams' deliberate blunders and clumsy mishaps. Perhaps, as some contemporary critics have suggested, the truth lies here: Jackson's lack of education and sophistication prevented him from doing anything but respond to his baseball instincts—to hit the ball hard and well, and to field fiercely, no matter what he was instructed to do.

As the loss of the World Series sunk into Jackson's consciousness, it's likely that he felt hollow and distraught. Here he was, a man whose life had been transformed by the sport of baseball and there he was, on the losing team—even worse, on the team that had crumbled and dissembled on purpose. All of this had garnered him only $5,000, less than a year's salary. Moreover, Jackson relied heavily upon his wife for emotional and pragmatic support, and his actions and secrecy probably drove a wedge between them.

In any case, after the Series ended and he was snubbed by Comiskey, Jackson, along with Williams, headed for Savannah. As he spent his winter in Georgia, Jackson worked in his poolroom and newly-established dry cleaning business, and Katie reportedly deposited Jackson's ill-gotten $5,000 into their bank account, most of which was used to pay for his sister Gertrude's hospital bills. (Years later, Jackson said that he "donated" his $5,000 to a hospital.)

Meanwhile, Fullerton wrote another column about his suspicions, stating that the world may have witnessed its last interleague baseball competition. "There are seven men on the [White Sox] team," he added, "who will not be there when the gong sounds next Spring."[16] Surely Jackson and others involved in the game-fixing scheme must have shuddered, at least a bit, when hearing Fullerton's ominous predictions and pronouncements; the ultimate "eighth man," whoever he supposed himself to be, was at least temporarily relieved.

NOTES

1. Boyd, *Blue Ruin*, 7.

2. Donald Henderson Clarke quoted at http://www.crimelibrary.com/gangsters_out laws/mob_bosses/rothstein/index_1.html.

3. Fleitz, *Shoeless*, 186.

4. Ibid.

5. Ibid., 187.

6. This may be the most contested point about Jackson's actions during 1919. Fleitz believes that Jackson received the money directly from Williams after the fourth game, and then he confronted Gandil over the shortage (*Shoeless*, 187). In Jackson's 1920 Grand Jury testimony, he states that Williams "threw" the money down following what he recalled to be the fourth game; Jackson added that he asked Gandil about the shortage, and stated his belief that Gandil himself held back the money, rather than the gamblers. Eliot Asinof has Williams silently handing the money to Jackson, who silently accepted the cash. "Nobody talked about it" (*Eight Men Out*, 104–105). Donald Gropman shows Williams handing Jackson the money, but Jackson refusing; Williams, rather than Jackson, complains about the amount, saying it should have been $10,000, not $5,000; when Jackson once again refused the money, the two got into a shouting match and Williams threw the money down. Jackson, the following day, tried to return it to Charles Comiskey (*Say It Ain't So, Joe!*, 171–172). In a court hearing in 1924, Jackson claimed that Williams offered him the money after the entire World Series had ended. The quote by Katie was from Jackson's Grand Jury testimony.

7. Ken Burns and Geoffrey C. Ward, *Baseball: An Illustrated History* (New York: A. A. Knopf, 1994), quoted by Fleitz, *Shoeless*, 186.

8. 1920 *Reach Guide*, quoted by Fleitz, *Shoeless*, 188.

9. Fleitz, *Shoeless*, 188–189.

10. Conflicting explanations exist for this remarkably small crowd. Asinof suggests that traffic problems and a lack of choice seats from the day before, coupled with Cincinnati fans' "sinking, undeniable, uncontrollable premonition of another defeat" kept them away. There were even rumors that the Reds had been bribed to lose games to lengthen the Series; therefore, this game was already in the loss column for them (*Eight Men Out*, 110). Harvey Frommer says that the disappointment of the previous day's loss kept fans away in droves (*Shoeless Joe and Ragtime Baseball*, 112). Gene Carney (http://www.base ball1.com/carney) has provided alternative explanations, including sportswriter Fred Lieb's statement that the Reds marketing department sold tickets in strips of three; most fans, not expecting a lengthy Series against the powerful White Sox, used them on games 1, 2, and 6 (Fred Lieb, *The Story of the World Series* [New York: G.P. Putnam's Sons, 1949]). Yet another explanation is that Garry Herrmann, the owner of the Reds, drank heavily the night before this game, and overslept with the tickets still in his possession. Carney uncovered this explanation in an article, written by Tom Swope in 1935, in the Cooperstown archives. Although in and of itself the answer is not vital, this example does illustrate the confusing complexity of the times.

11. Asinof, *Eight Men Out*, 115.

12. Frommer, *Shoeless Joe and Ragtime Baseball*, 113–114.

13. Fleitz, *Shoeless*, 277–278.

14. Jay Bennett, "Did Shoeless Joe Jackson Throw the 1919 World Series?" *The American Statistician* 47, no. 4, 1993, 241.

15. In 1956, Chick Gandil told a *Sports Illustrated* writer that he had told Cicotte to cut off Jackson's throw; this assertion adds credence to the notion that Gandil knew that Jackson was playing to win. Christopher H. Evans and William R. Herzog II, eds., *The Faith of Fifty Million: Baseball, Religion, and American Culture* (Louisville, KY: Westminster John Knox Press, 2002), 102.

16. Fleitz, *Shoeless*, 192.

SAY IT AIN'T SO, JOE!

I've lived a thousand years in the last twelve months.
—Eddie Cicotte[1]

Hugh Fullerton was a respected journalist, renowned for his entertaining and sensational writing style, which was chock full of baseball slang and insider knowledge. Prior to Fullerton's appearance on newspaper pages, sportswriters tended to list plays in a dusty, encyclopedic fashion; some writers regularly interviewed athletes and attempted to provide readers with their perspectives on games and surrounding events, but Fullerton was one of the first to successfully exploit this journalistic tool and make it an ordinary part of fan expectations.[2]

Fullerton had also gained fame for his uncanny ability to predict baseball game outcomes; this skill, garnered through the careful study of statistics, earned him a reputation as a "dopester"[3] and first drew widespread notice during the 1906 World Series when he correctly predicted that the Chicago Cubs, who had won an astonishing 116 games during the regular season, would lose to the underdog White Sox. When asked how he accomplished such a feat, he replied, somewhat tongue-in-cheek, "I took a large lead pencil, nine sheets of white glazed copy paper, and figured it out."[4]

He continued to predict World Series' play and took great pride in correctly forecasting outcomes. In 1919, Fullerton had announced that the White Sox would win the Series—and easily, at that.[5] When the conclusion was dramatically different, he decided to decipher what went wrong and then publish his findings.

This wasn't the first time that Fullerton and Joe Jackson found themselves in conflict; the journalist had previously chastised the slugger for his lack of education and was especially hard on Jackson when he chose to work at a shipbuilding plant, rather than fight in the war. When asked, point blank, his feelings about Jackson, Fullerton was somewhat evasive, stating his admiration of the Southerner's batting ability, but making no comment on Jackson as a person.[6]

Jackson couldn't have had a worse nemesis in the media. Thousands enjoyed reading Fullerton's columns; even more damaging, the writer often sensationalized and glamorized details. His detractors claimed that he intentionally exaggerated for effect, but his fans generally accepted whatever he wrote as gospel.[7]

Fullerton, though, wasn't Jackson's only problem in the off-season. Team owner Charles Comiskey was also a concern, as he publicly decried the notion that the 1919 World Series had deliberately been lost. "There is always some scandal of some kind following a big sporting event like the World Series," Comiskey pronounced. "These yarns are manufactured out of whole cloth and grow out of bitterness due to losing wagers. I believe my boys fought the battles of the recent World Series on the level, as they have always done, and I would be the first to want information to the contrary."[8]

On October 15, Comiskey followed through on his declaration, offering $20,000 for information about game-fixing activities in the Series.[9] On the surface, this move would suggest that he was unaware of the scheme, but that wasn't the case. He had already hired detectives to investigate the rumors and was quite knowledgeable about what had transpired[10]; his true motivation in offering the reward appears to have been to sniff out how many others were also "in the know," in order to avert a scandal that could potentially destroy his money-making team. Meanwhile, Comiskey's shrewd, Harvard-educated attorney, Alfred Austrian, was working hard in the background to lay the groundwork that would allow Comiskey to distance himself from the plot if it, indeed, became public.

Shortly after offering the reward, Comiskey had a taker: Swede Risberg's friend, Joe Gedeon of the St. Louis Browns. Risberg had wired Gedeon before the Series began, advising him to bet on the Reds; when the reward money was offered, Gedeon was more than willing to sell out his friend. Comiskey and Austrian agreed to listen to Gedeon's story; after gathering information, though, they refused to pay him.

Comiskey and Austrian also spoke to a man named Harry Redmon, a St. Louis gambler and theater owner. Although it's uncertain how Redmon knew what he claimed he did, one thing is certain: he provided Comiskey and Austrian with the names of eight White Sox players involved in the plot, as well as the names of several gamblers associated with Attell.

After gathering information from Redmon and Gedeon, Comiskey did nothing; he didn't even contact the tarnished players to let them know what the informants had to say. In a typical move that underscored his miserly reputation, Comiskey withheld World Series bonus checks—$3,154.27 per man—from Chick Gandil, Swede Risberg, Buck Weaver, Fred McMullin, Eddie Cicotte, Lefty Williams, Happy Felsch, and Joe Jackson.

Neither Jackson nor any of the others knew, with certainty, why their checks didn't come, but Jackson soon became impatient for his money. On October 27, Katie Jackson wrote to Comiskey on behalf of her husband. An excerpt reads as follows: "As I haven't heard anything from the club in Regards to my Saries check and would like to know why you are Holding it as I kneed the money Would like to have something as earley as possiable. And if possiable send it to me this week."[11]

On November 11, Comiskey responded, stating there had been a "great deal of adverse talk in which your name has been mentioned, along with several others, referring to and reflecting on your integrity in the recent World Series."[12] He then offered to pay Jackson's expenses for a trip to Chicago, so they could discuss rumors about the Series.

In Jackson's next letter, the slugger expressed surprise over the rumors, stating, "my playing proved that I did all I could to win."[13] He also agreed to come to Chicago, if that would help clear his name. Although Comiskey never sent travel expenses, he inexplicably relented, mailing checks to the eight players whose money had been withheld.

Perhaps the owner thought that paying the players would provide closure to the corrupt Series and its potential ramifications. The situation was not that simple, though. Comiskey was not the only one who had discovered damning information, and others were far less reluctant to reveal it. Ban Johnson, who despised Comiskey, had also hired detectives; meanwhile, Fullerton continued his research. Once the journalist had compiled enough information, he attempted to publish an article, but his Chicago editors were hesitant. After all, baseball was the national pastime, a pillar of American life, and if rumors of a World Series scandal became widespread, then the reputation of the sport might suffer a crippling blow. Frustrated, Fullerton took his column, which contained specific dates and names, to the editors of the *New York Evening World*. They were also cautious; but after convincing Fullerton to tone down his charges, they printed his text.

The article, published on December 15, didn't name any White Sox players.

Instead, Fullerton merely shared how he'd seen Abe Attell and Arnold Roth-stein, among others, at the ballparks; he also revealed that a gambler had told him before the eighth game had even begun that the Chicago team would play poorly in the first inning. Fullerton also noted how rumors of a fix were wide-spread in gambling circles even before the Series began and he faulted owners for not paying closer attention to those warnings.[14]

Although that column must have alarmed some of those involved in the fix, the overall reaction was fairly muted. The loudest response was from owners and fellow writers who chastised Fullerton for publishing his information. *Baseball Magazine* criticized Fullerton as writer of "sensational stories"[15] who was fool-ish in believing that the game of baseball could be fixed.

Comiskey then repeated his offer of reward money for anyone who had knowledge of a fix; his previous figure of $20,000, though, had inexplicably been cut in half, to $10,000.[16] Perhaps he figured that repeating his offer would en-hance his reputation as a man unaware of wrongdoing.

Meanwhile, Comiskey and Jackson (via Katie) continued to exchange letters, now about Jackson's salary for the upcoming season. Although Jackson had pre-viously been passive about contract negotiations, this time he wanted to know why other players received more money than he did; he also complained about a "pare of Shoes and new Glove" that had been stolen from the clubhouse. Jack-son took a hardline approach, stating that, if he didn't receive a "three year iron-clad contract for ten thousand a year I cant signe as living expenses are going up all the time. . . . I am going to open a nother Billiard parlor in Birmingham and can make more by Beeing with the Business all the time than I can at my present Salrie there."[17] (The term "ironclad" meant, to Jackson, that there would be no clause allowing Comiskey to cancel his contract, without cause, after a ten-day period.)

On January 29, 1920, Comiskey countered Jackson's demands with an offer of $7,000—an out-of-character move for the take-it-or-leave-it owner—warn-ing Jackson that he couldn't allow anyone without a signed contract to partici-pate in spring training. Jackson showed atypical backbone, returning the contract and stating that "You may think a thousand dollars is a liberal en-creas. . . . I consider myself as good a Ballplayer as you have on the club. . . . I can make more money in the Billiard Buisness. . . . So if I Don't get ten thou-sand and a three year ironclad contract I will not signe."[18]

Comiskey counteroffered once again, offering a two-year contract for $7,000 annually; interestingly, he didn't mention the ten-day clause in this letter. Jack-son, though, still insisted upon a three-year contract. Comiskey must have felt somewhat backed into a corner; although he had undoubtedly heard, either from the player himself or through other sources, that Jackson had accepted $5,000 from gamblers, it would not benefit the owner to reveal those details. Instead, Comiskey wanted to sign Jackson and the other players suspected of game-fixing, and keep the particulars quiet. A scandal might shake up his winning ballclub, which would cost Comiskey money in the end. (It seemed unlikely that Comiskey could obtain a good trade for Jackson, either; baseball owners had, by now, heard nasty game-fixing rumors and wanted no tainted players.)

After one more round of letters, Comiskey, knowing that he needed Jackson's bat in his 1920 line-up if he wanted another chance at a pennant, decided to partially accede to contract demands. He sent his secretary, Harry Grabiner, to Jackson's town, instructing him to obtain the player's signature on a three-year contract that would pay $8,000 each year. Grabiner arrived at the depot and called Jackson's house; the player, who was leaving to visit his sister at the hospital, picked up Grabiner at the train station and reviewed the contract with him. Jackson, who could recognize numbers, saw that he'd edged Comiskey up by $2,000 per year; satisfied, he signed the contract the same day. Later, however, he claimed two things that Grabiner disputed: that he had asked to have Katie read the contract, but Grabiner refused; and that the team secretary assured him that the ten-day clause had been removed. (It was buried on page three of a complicated four-page document.) Jackson's claims were probably true; he certainly relied upon Katie for business matters, and he had been adamant about the removal of the clause. It seems unlikely that he would have signed without Grabiner's reassurance that all was as the player wanted it.

Meanwhile, Comiskey traveled to the West Coast to obtain signed contracts from Risberg, Weaver, and Gandil. Despite the owner's best efforts to re-sign his first baseman—even offering him a $2,000 raise—Gandil refused to return to Chicago. Instead, he remained in California, where he played semipro baseball for $75 per game and lathered his wife in diamonds—after depositing thirty $1,000 bills into the local bank.[19] He also talked of opening up his own restaurant.

By this time, spring training for the White Sox had finally started, two or three weeks after other professional teams were already underway. The rationale given for the later start was that this experienced team didn't need significant preseason warm-ups; the real reason for the delay, though, was that Risberg, Cicotte, and Felsch hadn't signed contracts and were fiercely negotiating raises. Weaver hadn't signed yet, either, and he was actually insisting upon a trade to the New York Yankees, citing Babe Ruth as a man who had negotiated a similar contract-breaking deal.

Comiskey must have been furious that these players who had, just a few scant months earlier, benefited from gamblers' dollars were now insisting upon raises. Moreover, it's ironic that a dishonest act would ultimately force Comiskey's hand in a way that top-notch World Series play in 1917 had failed.

The owner, though, had little choice but to give in. Cicotte's pay was raised to $10,000, while Felsch's went from $3,750 to $7,000. McMullin received an unanticipated raise, as well, and William's salary more than doubled, from $2,600 to $6,000. Weaver settled with the owner for a sum of $7,000 and no ten-day reserve clause, something that Jackson requested, but failed to receive. (Decades later, when Grabiner's diary was found, it was discovered that the secretary had called Jackson the "world's worst negotiator.")[20]

The atmosphere at spring training camp in 1920 must have been exquisitely tense. Comiskey, who loved his money, must have despised the players who had basically blackmailed him for raises; the fact that these raises were well deserved and long overdue wouldn't have altered the stingy owner's perspective. The animosity between team factions, even without the presence of Gandil, who had served as leader of the rougher group, surely must have intensified; Ray Schalk's rage during the Series had been fierce, and he and manager Kid Gleason had even resorted to physical violence against Williams and Gandil when emotions ran particularly high.

Astonishingly enough, though, this fractured team won its first six games of the season and, by May 1, was in second place, just one and one-half games behind the Boston Red Sox. Jackson's statistics were also incredible; the slugger, certainly no longer a young rookie, batted an extraordinary .469 during the month of April.

During the month of June, Ruth gifted Jackson with one of his bats, with the proviso that the Southerner couldn't use it against his team. By July, Jackson was in third place for the batting title, behind George Sisler and Tris Speaker; he was finally consistently ahead of Ty Cobb in the hitting department. His defensive moves weren't slowing down, either. On July 6, in the eleventh inning, Jackson prevented an almost certain triple with a "diving, tumbling"[21] catch. On July 16, he hit an inside-the-park grand slam; in August, his batting average once again reached .400. When Jackson tagged a home run in each of the two games of a double-header in August, the White Sox were, once again, in first place.

If it wasn't for one disturbing factor—the gamblers who had tasted monetary success during the fixed World Series—it's possible that the White Sox could have won another pennant. That wasn't going to happen, though, because some gamblers who had profited from the scheme threatened to expose the involved players if they didn't continue to lose strategic games that would assist them monetarily. Because of the gamblers' intimidating connections with organized crime, and because of continuing greed, some of the players—most notable Risberg and Felsch—cooperated and accepted payoffs,[22] while disenchanted journalists began publishing the most obvious player missteps. Significantly, Jackson wasn't one of their targets.

As the month of August began winding down, several White Sox players bungled even more easy plays, causing the rumors of game-throwing to increase. On September 1, Dickie Kerr, a pitcher who wasn't involved in the game-fixing the previous season, angrily confronted Risberg and Weaver, accusing them of deliberately losing the game. Risberg lost his temper and punched Kerr, and the Chicago bench erupted into a brawl.[23]

Besides the gambler-related pressures that coerced some players into losing games, financially savvy players realized that winning the pennant wouldn't bring the largest cash reward; they could, in fact, earn more money if the New York Yankees, with their huge fan base, won the American League title, especially if their rivals, the New York Giants, won the National League title. The success of two New York teams would increase the gate receipt revenues that were shared, incrementally, with the second, third, and fourth place teams in each league; in addition, if the White Sox did not win the pennant, they would be available to play a city series against the Chicago Cubs, a match-up that was generally lucrative for the players involved.[24]

It was clear, in any case, that the situation with the White Sox ballclub was disintegrating beyond repair. To add to the escalating tension, the president of the Chicago Cubs, William Veeck, received several telegrams on August 31, warning him that the upcoming Cubs-Phillies game was fixed, and that his team would deliberately lose the game.[25] Veeck changed his starting pitcher and offered his replacement a $500 incentive to win; his team lost 3–0, nevertheless.

Veeck, like Comiskey and Johnson before him, hired a detective agency to investigate the rumors. Any hopes of hushing up the situation, though, were crushed on September 4 when the *Chicago Herald and Examiner* published a story of the alleged scam. Jim Crusinberry, a reporter for the rival *Chicago Tribune*, took advantage of the moment and enticed a reader to write a letter to the *Tribune's* editor, demanding a full investigation into the rumors that the 1919 World Series had, indeed, been fixed by gamblers and then deliberately lost by a group of White Sox players who benefited financially from the scheme.

This letter, published on September 5, created an enormous outcry from readers who demanded that something be done about this injustice; within two days, the Illinois State Attorney, Maclay Hoyne, had assembled a grand jury. On September 15, however, Hoyne lost his bid for reelection, which meant that, once again, the crisis—soon to be labeled the Black Sox Scandal—might die down. Perhaps it would have, had it not been for Ban Johnson, whose grudge against Charles Comiskey seemed to grow more intense with each passing season. Johnson's own private detectives had completed their work; now he took their discoveries, which were roughly the same as what Comiskey's gumshoes had learned, to Circuit Court Judge Charles McDonald and insisted that the investigation continue. While some questioned Johnson's motivation, suggesting that he really wanted to oust Comiskey from professional baseball—and perhaps buy the winning White Sox team at a greatly reduced price—momentum was now running at full throttle, and an investigation was officially in progress.

The court agreed with Johnson—not surprising, because Judge McDonald was Johnson's friend—and subpoenaed Comiskey, who testified under oath that his own private investigation had turned up nothing of substance. (Decades later, when Harry Grabiner's diary surfaced, the text belied Comiskey's assertion.) He also stated that Johnson didn't help him, whatsoever, in the investigation of wrongdoing, and he reminded the judge that Johnson was, in fact, half-owner of the Cleveland Indians, the team that was fighting the White Sox for the pennant. Comiskey's testimony didn't seem to hurt or help his players; instead, it consisted mostly of Johnson bashing.

Giants pitcher Rube Benton's testimony, though, was more damaging; he named Cicotte, Felsch, Gandil, and Williams as coconspirators in the fix right about the same time that the grand jury also heard the names of the eight men whose World Series checks were temporarily withheld by Comiskey. The following day, Cicotte, Felsch, Gandil, McMullin, Risberg, Weaver, Williams, and Jackson were named in the newspapers. When Jackson hit a home run in Cleveland that day, he was soundly booed; he, in turn, thumbed his nose at the fans twice, increasing their ire.[26]

On September 27, Jimmy Isaminger of the *Philadelphia North American* published an interview with gambler Billy Maharg, who named Cicotte as a participant of the scheme. Maharg revealed that the pitcher had accepted a $10,000 payoff for his intentional losses, and stated that White Sox players deliberately lost Games 1, 2, and 8.

After this article appeared, Comiskey realized that he could no longer keep the game-fixing scheme a secret; his next goal, then, was to prevent Johnson from receiving credit for uncovering the scandalous event. He therefore asked Gleason which of the players seemed the most guilt-laden; when the manager named Eddie Cicotte, they convinced the pitcher to go to the grand jury and share what he knew. For more than two hours, Cicotte testified, describing how he'd sewn the payoff money into his jacket lining. He also admitted to purposefully flawed play, including the deflection of Jackson's controversial throw from the outfield, and he named Sleepy Bill Burns and Billy Maharg as the brains behind the financial side of the plan.

"I don't know why I did it," Cicotte told the grand jury, stopping to wipe away tears.[27] "I must have been crazy. Risberg, Gandil, and McMullin were at me for a week before the Series began. They wanted me to go crooked. I don't know. I needed the money. I had the wife and the kids. The wife and the kids don't know about this. I don't know what they'll think. . . . I would have not done that thing for a million dollars. Now I've lost everything, job, reputation, everything. My friends all bet on the Sox. I knew, but I couldn't tell them."[28]

Shortly thereafter, Jackson called the courthouse and asked the judge for advice. He then went for a walk where he saw Risberg who, perhaps sensing that Jackson was at the breaking point, threatened the slugger if he followed suit. "I swear," Risberg told him, "I'll kill you if you squawk."[29] Jackson, who'd already gulped down several drinks, ignored his teammate's words, calling the judge again and then heading to the courthouse. When he arrived, Austrian—who was really looking after Comiskey's best interests—greeted him and advised him to confess everything. He assured Jackson that the judge was really after the gamblers involved, not the players, and he asked the half-intoxicated and fully illiterate Jackson to sign a piece of paper that was, in fact, a waiver of immunity.

Jackson's testimony lasted two hours and in most particulars matched Cicotte's. He had been promised $20,000, Jackson told the judge, but had only received $5,000. He testified that he knew nothing about the financial end of the scheme; besides, he didn't even know Attell, and he hadn't attended any meetings with gamblers. He insisted that he had played to win. His statements sounded credible and, at the end of his testimony, he looked down at the floor and added that he was ashamed of himself for taking money.[30]

After exiting the courthouse, he announced to the waiting crowd that he'd gotten a "big load off my chest! I'm feeling better." He was placed in police custody; he also received a telegram from Comiskey indefinitely suspending him from the team, as did his seven teammates also suspected of involvement. The telegram also promised that, if found "innocent of any wrongdoing," they would be reinstated. Jackson's reaction after hearing that news was to go out and get "polluted."[31]

Legend insists that something else happened, as well. As Jackson exited the courthouse, the story goes, a young boy tugged tearfully at his sleeve, pleading, "Say it ain't so, Joe!" Some say that Jackson actually admitted, sadly, that yes, it was so. Others, including Jackson himself in his 1949 interview with Furman Bisher, swore that the incident never took place. In any case, the anecdote, written by Charley Owens, was printed in the *Chicago Daily News* the following day and spread quickly across the nation. Fullerton's version of the happening was no less poignant. He wrote, "Their idol lay in dust, their faith destroyed. Nothing was true, nothing was honest. There was no Santa Claus. Then, and not until then, did Jackson, hurrying away to escape the sight of the faces of the kids, understand the enormity of the thing he had done."[32]

James T. Farrell, who was nineteen at the time of this grand jury testimony, suggests that another incident, which he himself witnessed, was the true source of the enduring myth. On September 27, 1920, Farrell recalls that a crowd of boys and young men followed Jackson out of Comiskey Park after that day's game had ended.

> A few fans called out to them [Jackson and Felsch], but they gave no acknowledgement to these greetings. They turned and started to walk away. Spontaneously, the crowd followed in a slow, disorderly manner. I went with the crowd and trailed about five feet behind Jackson and Felsch. They walked somewhat slowly. A fan called out, 'It ain't true, Joe.' The two suspected players did not turn back. They walked on, slowly. The crowd took up this cry and more than once, men and boys called out and repeated, 'It ain't true, Joe.' This call followed Jackson and Felsch as they walked all the way under the stands.[33]

Farrell's accounting seems much more likely and considerably less sentimental than the tale of a young boy pleading and tugging on Jackson's sleeve. After all, Comiskey and Austrian had gotten from Jackson the testimony they'd hope for, and it was in their best interests to have Jackson spirited out and hidden away. Comiskey had survived that day's testimony unscathed; the headlines that followed Jackson's confession, and Comiskey's resulting telegram, included "Comiskey Hard Hit By Perfidy of His Players . . . Shock So Great Friends Fear For His Health."[34]

Concurrently, Arnold Rothstein's attorney, William Fallon, was working behind the scenes to prevent derogatory testimony from surfacing about his client. He advised Rothstein—who immediately followed through—that Sport Sullivan deserved an all-expenses-paid jaunt to Mexico, and that Abe Attell ought to visit Canada for a while. Fallon declared it vacation with pay, and Rothstein had the financial resources to provide them with just that.[35]

Meanwhile, all Joe Jackson—who had hired no attorney of his own, believing that Comiskey's attorney, Alfred Austrian, was serving as his legal counsel—could do, as he had done so many times in the past, was sit, wait, and wonder what would come next.

NOTES

1. See http://1919blacksox.com/cicotte4.htm.
2. See http://www.stolaf.edu/depts/cis/wp/malmgren/coursework/philosophyofsport/hughfullerton.html.
3. Frommer, *Shoeless Joe and Ragtime Baseball*, 99.

4. See http://www.stolaf.edu/depts/cis/wp/malmgren/coursework/philosophyofsport/hughfullerton.html.

5. Asinof, *Eight Men Out*, 45.

6. Fleitz, *Shoeless*, 163.

7. See http://www.stolaf.edu/depts/cis/wp/malmgren/coursework/philosophyofsport/hughfullerton.html.

8. Frommer, *Shoeless Joe and Ragtime Baseball*, 115–116.

9. Bill Veeck, with Ed Linn, *The Hustler's Handbook* (New York: Simon and Schuster, 1965), 262.

10. Veeck and Linn's *The Hustler's Handbook* contains a chapter describing the contents of Harry Grabiner's diary. The journal starts out by revealing that, after the first game of the World Series, Monte Tennes, a well-known gambler, approached Charles Comiskey; Tennes told Comiskey that the Series looked fixed (258).

11. Fleitz, *Shoeless*, 195.

12. Ibid., 196.

13. Ibid., 197.

14. Ibid., 198.

15. Ibid., 198.

16. Veeck, with Linn, *The Hustler's Handbook*, 277.

17. Fleitz, *Shoeless*, 199.

18. Ibid., 200.

19. Ibid., 207.

20. Veeck, with Linn, *The Hustler's Handbook*, 266.

21. Fleitz, *Shoeless*, 212.

22. Many decades later, Red Faber said this about some of his 1920 teammates. "Why, the hoodlums had some of the boys in their pocket all through the 1920 season, too, throwing ball games right up to the last week of the pennant. I could feel it out there when I pitched. . . . You want to scream at them but you don't because you can see how scared they are." (Asinof, *Bleeding Between the Lines*, 93–94.) Although Oscar "Happy" Felsch didn't want to talk about his teammates' actions in 1920, he admitted to "playing rotten" himself. His wife said that the gamblers had threatened their six children if he hadn't complied (117).

23. Fleitz, *Shoeless*, 218.

24. Ibid., 214.

25. Harry Grabiner, in his diary, claims that American League President, Ban Johnson, sent all the letters. (Veeck, with Linn, *The Hustler's Handbook*, 269.)

26. Fleitz, *Shoeless*, 222–223.

27. Cicotte's landlord, "the mysterious Mrs. Kelly," also testified at the grand jury, but she presents Cicotte in an entirely different light from the weeping man who worried about his wife and children. According to Mrs. Kelly, she overheard Cicotte tell his brother, "The hell with them. I got mine." (Veeck, with Linn, *The Hustler's Handbook*, 260).

28. See http://1919blacksox.com/transcripts2.htm.

29. Fleitz, *Shoeless*, 224.

30. Newspapers, including the *New York Times*, reported statements that were not made in Jackson's grand jury testimony, including that he admitted striking out or hitting easy balls (meaning that he hit the ball much more softly than he was capable of) when hits would have meant runs. Many newspapers reported Jackson blunders that, when reviewed, simply did not happen. (Evans and Herzog, *The Faith of Fifty Million*, 100–101.)

31. Fleitz, *Shoeless*, 227.

32. Gropman, *Say It Ain't So, Joe!*, 201–202.

33. Farrell, *My Baseball Diary*, 106.

34. Gropman, *Say It Ain't So, Joe!*, 184.

35. According to Eliot Asinof, Arnold Rothstein "was doing the shakes" out of fear when Cicotte testified at the grand jury proceedings, and he therefore gave Attell and Sullivan "a coupla bills to keep you loose" while they were out of the country. Rothstein claimed to be headed out to Europe; instead, he pleaded his innocence in front of the grand jury, telling the jury that, in fact, Attell had been behind the scheme (*Bleeding Between the Lines*, 107).

FROM SQUARE DEAL VERDICT
TO OUTLAW BALL

Baseball is something more than a game to an American boy. It is his training field for life work. Destroy his faith in its squareness and honesty and you have destroyed something more; you have planted suspicion of all things in his heart.
—Kenesaw Mountain Landis[1]

This story is clouded and part of it is locked away in files, in fading and mellowing memories and in the grave.
—James T. Farrell[2]

Baseball fans cringed as newspapers published information about grand jury proceedings. Although rumors had circulated about a World Series fix for months, Eddie Cicotte and Joe Jackson had finally confirmed the awful truth. Lefty Williams then added his own admission of guilt in court, and Happy Felsch granted a damning newspaper interview, verifying that members of the White Sox team had, indeed, conspired with gamblers to lose the Series deliberately in exchange for cash.

While fan disillusionment abounded, club owners were, according to sportswriter Fred Lieb, "running scared; they were thinking of saving the game and their own financial hides."[3] To add to professional baseball's troubles, its leadership structure was also unraveling.

Since 1903, three people—the president of the American League, the president of the National League, and an appointed third party—had officially overseen baseball by a committee known as the National Commission. In theory, whenever the American League president and the National League president dis-

Jackson in about 1922. *National Baseball Hall of Fame Library, Cooperstown, N.Y.*

agreed on an issue, the third member of the committee resolved the conflict by casting the deciding vote. In reality, though, the American League president, Ban Johnson, had ensured that the third party was someone who acquiesced to his wishes. Therefore, Johnson was making all significant decisions for baseball, and had been for nearly two decades. Johnson's influence, though, had recently been declining; he'd made powerful enemies, including several baseball owners.

He also drank heavily and often made an embarrassing spectacle of himself in public.

Furthering baseball's instability was the fact that the "appointed third party," Cincinnati Reds owner Garry Herrmann, had resigned from the National Commission in January 1920, just months before the Black Sox scandal erupted.[4] When he resigned, Herrmann commented that a club owner was not an appropriate choice for the third party of the commission. While owners searched for Herrmann's replacement, Cubs owner Albert Lasker reiterated this viewpoint and suggested that, rather than nominating someone already within baseball leadership, they should replace Herrmann with someone completely outside of baseball. This would provide a more objective viewpoint.[5]

Judge Kenesaw Mountain Landis was quickly recommended as Herrmann's replacement; it's understandable why owners would gravitate towards him. Five years earlier, Landis's inaction on the bench had prevented the Federal League's antitrust suit against established baseball leagues from proceeding. He'd stalled on his findings; had Landis moved more quickly, a court ruling on the monopolistic nature of professional baseball could have jeopardized the entire major league system. Owners naturally felt they owed Landis a debt of gratitude.

Landis wasn't a unanimous choice, though. Johnson felt Landis was too radical and supported, instead, his personal friend, Charles McDonald, who had led the grand jury inquiry into the Black Sox Scandal. Many other candidates were suggested, as well, including former President William Howard Taft. Those opposing Landis were likely concerned about his infamous inconsistencies and arbitrariness. He ruled against those violating Prohibition, fighting against alcohol traffic even before the nineteenth amendment was ratified, and he made stern moralistic pronouncements about matters well outside the purview of federal and state law. He also "swore like a trooper, chewed tobacco, and was fond of bourbon whiskey."[6] He'd faced two impeachment resolutions during his fifteen-year tenure as judge as well.[7]

Throughout the debate over Herrmann's replacement, owners continued to argue about proposed plans to restructure the ruling body of major league baseball. If an owner disagreed about an emerging plan, he might also threaten to remove his team from the league; this atmosphere led to a nearly comical month of projected changes and potential upheavals. By November 8, though, something of a consensus was reached, and eleven owners voted to offer Landis the job.

This news, naturally enough, was quickly leaked to the press; when a reporter asked the judge for a comment, Landis replied that he was deeply honored by the offer, but needed time to mull it over. Within twenty-four hours, a more radical plan was proposed, whereby Landis would serve as the sole administrator of baseball justice, as a "sporting dictatorship."[8] Perhaps this was proposed as a move to block Johnson's ability to continue to control baseball; perhaps the need for dramatic action to "clean up" baseball's gambling-related corruption was the plan's impetus.

Even though that proposal precipitated more vehement arguments, by November 12 the majority of owners agreed with the plan and headed to Landis' courtroom to make a formal offer. While waiting for Landis to finish hearing a case, the owners whispered about specifics of the offer, causing the judge to threaten to clear the courtroom.

After court adjourned, Landis met with the owners in his chambers, and agreed to accept the position if he was guaranteed unfettered powers; he also insisted that he maintain his position as judge. The owners acquiesced, realizing that Landis "projected an image of toughness and integrity at a time when everyone in baseball recognized that the public needed renewed trust in the decency of the game and a diversion from the stench of the Black Sox scandal."[9] Landis promised to dedicate a few days each month, along with the entire period of June through mid-September when the courtroom was adjourned, to his baseball job, for the salary of $50,000.[10]

The negotiating was successful and quite solemn, prompting humorist Will Rogers to offer his own unique and lighthearted twist: "The game needed a touch of class and distinction," Rogers exclaimed, "and somebody said, 'Get that old guy who sits behind first base all the time. He's out here every day, anyway.' So they offered him a season pass and he grabbed it."[11]

It's doubtful that Joe Jackson or any other Black Sox player with knowledge of the fix saw much humor in Rogers' comment. Instead, they must have shuddered over the tough, stern, czar-like man who would now greatly influence their fate.

Throughout the debate over the appointment of Landis, prosecutors in Chicago prepared their case against the suspended players and accused gamblers. The prosecutors quickly discovered, though, that Illinois law did not prohibit fixing the outcome of a ballgame; so the involved players had not committed a crime when they deliberately lost games. Therefore, prosecutors needed to charge them with something else; on October 22, the Cook County Grand Jury indicted Jackson and his tainted teammates on nine counts of fraud and conspiracy.[12]

By this time, Jackson had already returned to Greenville, where he began arranging a series of all-star games. His reception was mixed; on the one hand, the game fixing had repulsed many South Carolina fans. Others, meanwhile, offered "hearty demonstrations of cordiality towards Shoeless Joe."[13] Jackson's baseball play was about to be interrupted, though; after the indictment was announced, he was ordered to return to Chicago to be formally arraigned.

He must have hoped for speedy proceedings. In a startling twist, though, everything stalled when the transcripts containing the confessions and signed waivers of immunities of Cicotte, Jackson, and Williams disappeared. Because of the missing records, the players did not face arraignment proceedings until February 14, 1921; they then took advantage of the absent confessions, denying that they had conspired to lose the World Series. Citing lack of proof, the judge eventually threw the indictments out.[14] Meanwhile, Johnson accused Rothstein of paying $10,000 as a bribe to ensure the disappearance of the papers; Rothstein threatened to sue Johnson for slander, but when the American League president gleefully encouraged such an action so that information could be brought to light, the notorious gambler reconsidered the notion.[15]

The accused players rejoiced at the entire turn of events, perhaps assuming that court action would fail, Comiskey would welcome them back, and they could report to the upcoming spring training; but their celebration was, once again, short lived. On March 12, Landis placed them on baseball's ineligible list, even though they had only been suspended from the White Sox club, not professional baseball as a whole, and even though they had been convicted of no crime. Perhaps Landis felt the pressure of time and thought that he needed to act; after such an alleged crime was committed, only an eighteen-month window existed to indict. Although the courts, not Landis, needed to abide by that stricture, the judge might have feared that the accused would escape all punishment. This would have been an inauspicious beginning for a man noted—and now paid $50,000 by club owners—for his no-nonsense approach.

No matter how tough Landis was in placing the players on baseball's ineligible list, the judge was determined to stay out of the court proceedings. So, perhaps, were it not for Ban Johnson's persistence, the Black Sox scandal would have vanished from the legal docket; but Johnson's hatred for Comiskey was compounded by his sense of having been pushed aside by Landis' appointment. He was not about to accede his position of influence without a parting shot. He therefore hunted down Billy Maharg to offer him immunity if he would arrange a meeting with Sleepy Bill Burns. Not surprisingly, Burns agreed to testify against the players in exchange for his own immunity.[16]

The issue was therefore revived in the court system and, on March 26, seven of the originally indicted players, all except Fred McMullin, were once again indicted on charges of fraud and conspiracy. Specific charges included conspiring to defraud the public; to commit a confidence game; to defraud White Sox catcher Ray Schalk; to injure the business of Charles Comiskey, as well as injure the business of the American League.[17] Moreover, the Internal Revenue Bureau (a forerunner of today's IRS) also announced that they would investigate the possibility that the players had not reported gambler payoffs on their tax returns.[18]

Arnold Rothstein was not named in any indictments, but other gamblers, including Sport Sullivan and Abe Attell, were. Sullivan fled to Canada, while Attell convinced the court, from New York, that although his name was, indeed, "Abe Attell," he was not the same Abe Attell named in the indictment. In reality, then, only seven Black Sox and a handful of minor gamblers, each of whom faced five years of prison and a fine of $2,000, were in the courtroom when proceedings began on June 27. By this time, lead prosecutor and former congressman George Gorman was fed up with the delayed court action and wanted a severe sentence imposed. The defense wanted something quite different and, on July 5, moved to dismiss the case. Judge Hugo Friend refused and, on July 15, jury selection was finally completed.

Although none of the Black Sox had legal representation during the grand jury hearings, they arrived with topnotch attorneys at their trial, a team of legal representation that charged at least two hundred dollars each per day.[19] The appearance of these lawyers created much speculation; the ballplayers clearly could not afford such an expensive defense team, and rumors abounded that Comiskey was paying the legal bill so that he could reunite his talented team, continue winning pennants, and reap the financial rewards. Others hinted that Rothstein was footing the legal bill so that his part in the scheme could remain hidden; those holding this view noted that someone had also convinced four members of the prosecutor's staff to switch over to the defense, and the only person with that type of influence, they reasoned, was Arnold Rothstein.

Early in the trial, Burns testified that Attell served as financial backer of the scheme. Burns also stated that the players, especially Gandil, had played a large role in devising the plan; previously, many had assumed that the gamblers had developed the plot and then enticed participation of players. Significantly, Burns also mentioned that Jackson had not attended the meeting with gamblers.[20]

Oddly enough, defense attorneys asked Kid Gleason and Ray Schalk if they thought the defendants had played to the best of their ability—a strange question for the defense to raise, because both men had previously noted suspicious and erratic play. Even more curious was the prosecution's objection to that particular question each time it came up; the judge always sustained the objections. For some puzzling reason, prosecutors did not want the opinions of these men aired in court, even though the answers may have been favorable to the state's case. Decades later, when Harry Grabiner's diary was found, an explanation surfaced; the diary revealed that Comiskey did know, mere days after the Series ended, that his players had deliberately lost games, but he covered up that fact. Moreover, Gleason was aware that Comiskey knew, and prosecutors wanted to avoid the potential complication of Comiskey's obstruction of justice.

Possibly the most helpful testimony, from a defense perspective, came from

Grabiner, who provided evidence that the players had not, in fact, damaged Comiskey's business. Grabiner noted that 1919 gate receipts equaled $521,175.75, a figure that increased to $910,206.59 in 1920. This significant increase clearly negated at least one of the prosecutor's charges.[21]

On August 2, after hearing Grabiner's testimony, attorneys offered their closing remarks, with the prosecution stating that Jackson, Cicotte, and Williams "sold out the American public for a paltry $20,000," and that the "public, the club owners, even the small boys on the sandlots have been swindled."[22] Jackson's attorney countered that the state was "trying to make goats out of some underpaid ballplayers and penny-ante gamblers,"[23] while Rothstein wasn't indicted, and Attell and Sullivan weren't being tried in the courtroom. He reminded jurors that compared to the revenue of team owners, ballplayers had "nothing left but a chew of tobacco, a glove, and few pairs of worn out socks."[24]

The judge then instructed jurors that, even if a player deliberately lost games, that wasn't enough to be judged guilty. Rather, the player needed to have conspired to defraud someone—Comiskey, the American League, Schalk, or the general public. After hearing those words, the jury left to deliberate, and Jackson was left to sweat and worry. Although much had gone well for the defense and although it would be quite difficult for the prosecution to prove actual conspiracy, the judge had not thrown out Jackson's grand jury testimony, even though the original transcripts—and his signed waiver of immunity—had disappeared. Although it seemed likely that most of the accused would be found not guilty, Jackson, Cicotte, and Williams still had the grand jury testimony hanging over their heads, and were therefore the most likely to be convicted.

The wait must have seemed indeterminably long to Jackson, but the jury actually returned with a verdict in two hours and forty-seven minutes. When the clerk read off a list that contained acquittals for all parties, Jackson breathed a huge sigh of relief. Upon hearing the decision, the courtroom erupted with cheers while papers and hats were gleefully tossed in the air. The verdict also prompted this hard-edged comment from Gandil: "A square deal verdict, and I'm going to give a sailor's farewell to Ban Johnson—good-bye, good luck and to hell with you."[25]

Players celebrated late into the night at a local Italian restaurant, and discussed their return to professional baseball. Jackson had enjoyed an extraordinary year in 1920, racking up seventy-four extra base hits. He'd hit forty-two doubles, twenty triples and twelve home runs for a batting average of .382; his triples led the league. He also had 121 RBIs that year, along with 336 total bases. He still had incredible speed, averaging one triple for every eight games played, and his 1920 statistics highlighted one of the most amazing offensive seasons ever played in major league baseball. So, there was no reason that Jackson couldn't return in 1922 and repeat his performance, especially now that the dead ball era was ending, and a new livelier baseball, more favorable to batters, was being used.[26]

The following day, however, a statement by Landis forever ended those possibilities. "Regardless of the verdicts of juries," he announced, "no player that throws a ball game; no player that undertakes or promises to throw a ball game; no player that sits in a conference with a bunch of crooked players and gamblers where the ways and means of throwing games are planned and discussed and does not promptly tell his club about it will ever play professional baseball. Of course, I don't know that any of these men will apply for reinstatement, but if they do, the above are at least a few of the rules that will be enforced. Just keep in mind, regardless of the verdict of juries, baseball is entirely competent to protect itself against crooks, both inside and outside the game."[27]

The collective disappointment must have been severe, but baseball owners had recently awarded Landis unlimited powers; no one could question his decision, at least not publicly. Landis actually received much praise for his action, overall; he was lauded as the man who was finally "cleaning up" baseball. Jackson, realizing that he couldn't dispute the powerful Landis' word, moved back to Savannah, Georgia without making any public comment.

Privately, though, Landis' verdict must have been devastating. Jackson had been playing organized baseball since he was thirteen, and he didn't want to stop. But, he now faced a serious stumbling block. Even though Landis' jurisdiction didn't technically extend beyond the scope of major and minor league ball, other teams around the country nevertheless feared disputing his declaration that anyone who played on a field with banned Black Sox—even playing *against* them—would never play professional ball.[28] In retrospect, it's hard to imagine one man having the kind of authority that Landis did in the years following the Black Sox scandal, but at the time, the system seemed to be just the right medicine for a sport that was in need of a cure.

Facing the realities of the situation, Jackson began playing baseball under a false name. On June 25, 1922, for example, he attempted one of these deceptions when the New Jersey Hackensack team was slated to play Bogota, and he used the name of "Joe Josephs." Rumors abounded that Josephs was an outstanding ballplayer, and people wanted to see this talent in action. Josephs didn't disappoint them, either, pounding out 4 hits, including a long home run. He also threw out someone at home plate, all the way from deep center field. His skill was extraordinary and Hackensack won the game. Some Bogota fans suspected, though, that Josephs was, in fact, Shoeless Joe Jackson. After all, they reasoned, how many left-handed batters threw with their right arm? And, how many people could hit with that much strength and field with that much accuracy? Besides that, Jackson followed a ritual of drawing lines around the plate with his bat, and Josephs did the same. Once Jackson's identity was confirmed, the Hackensack team was forced to forfeit, and he no longer played on that particular team.

It didn't escape the notice of savvy promoters that many fans still wanted to see Jackson and other banned Black Sox play; perhaps, "outlaw ball," with its forbidden overtones, could be a profitable venture. One promoter formed a league called the "Big League Martyrs," and he asked Jackson to play under his real name. The slugger agreed to participate and, during the games, the promoter handed out cards asking for signatures requesting that Jackson be reinstated to the major leagues. Although the gig only lasted a month, Jackson did earn some money from this publicity-driven endeavor.

Risberg, Cicotte, and Jackson also played together in a league in Louisiana, on the Bastrop team; Cicotte's deadly accurate pitching, Jackson's powerful hitting, and the sharp fielding skills of Jackson and Risberg caused their team to dominate this regional league.[29] Jackson used the name of "Johnson," and Cicotte chose the name of "Moore." During the thirty-five games that he played on this team, Jackson batted over .500 and tagged several long home runs. Their presence caused local controversy, though, and so Jackson moved on, now negotiating with the South Georgia League; officials initially debated whether or not to allow Jackson to play with them. They took a vote and decided 3–2, with one team official abstaining, to accept the former major league player into their ranks. On July 19, 1923, the *Americus Times-Recorder* displayed an ad that read, in part, "You may come expecting to see the famous Joe. . . . Our team has been materially strengthened and with a little BOOSTING instead of knocking from the fans you will be doing your part to help win."[30] Jackson joined the Americus team under his own name and once again demonstrated his incredible prowess. Crowds gathered in great numbers to watch Jackson transform a last-place team into the winners of the championship series. Although he made only $75 per game, he batted over .400.

Americus fans greatly appreciated his presence, and author John Bell writes that Jackson "came to Americus, Georgia in 1923 and helped a struggling, hometown baseball team get back on its feet and win the league title from its chief sports rival. None of the fans really cared what he was accused of or what he did or didn't do. All they knew was that he was the greatest ball player they had ever seen, and for a short time, they could call him their own. When Shoeless Joe Jackson left Americus, he left memories of a hero to a small baseball town—memories of a Shoeless Summer."[31]

After that league ended in August, Jackson switched over to the Million Dollar League in Waycross, Georgia, playing the last two games of their season.

When Jackson first played ball in Waycross he didn't have the proper uniform, so he wore his uniform from the Chicago White Sox.[32]

By this time, newspapers were publishing reports about Jackson's sensational play. Jackson suited up for Waycross again in 1924 and 1925. In August 1924, the *Waycross Journal* reported, "When Joe Jackson hit a 'bullet' to third base Tuesday afternoon, an accident which Jackson regaurds [*sic*] in the light of casualty, the 'Old Hickory' which he has carried through more than nine years of professional baseball and which has been his 'one and only' through major league campaigns too numerous to mention, including world championship games, was cracked from the force of the hit."[33]

Jackson was clearly earning money from semipro ball, and he and Katie were also running a dry cleaning establishment, the Savannah Valet Business, but he still hadn't given up on collecting funds that he believed Comiskey owed him. Grabiner, Jackson believed, had lied about the inclusion of the ten-day clause in his three-year contract; had that clause not been included, Comiskey could not have released him without paying out years two and three of his multi-year contract. Besides, Jackson felt that Comiskey still owed him $700 for his participation in a second-place World Series finish.[34] Jackson had even sent a letter to Johnson in 1922, forwarded to Landis, which had apparently asked for the World Series pay; the request was denied.[35]

Jackson therefore hired Raymond Cannon, an aggressive attorney who had recently sued Comiskey on behalf of Happy Felsch for his World Series pay. Cannon disliked the contractual nature of professional baseball, believing it highly unfair to the ballplayers. He especially despised the ten-day clause, and was forming a union for major league baseball players, the National Baseball Players Association. This made him a natural choice for Jackson when he was challenging the White Sox.

Early in 1923, Jackson filed a lawsuit against Comiskey, requesting $119,000.[36] Jackson arrived at that dollar figure by calculating what sum was outstanding for the two years remaining on his three-year contract: $16,000. Jackson then added $100,000 for slander, along with $1,500 for outstanding 1917 World Series pay and $700 for second-place 1919 World Series pay, and then he rounded up to the nearest thousand.

By the time the trial had begun, though, the amount sued for was reduced to $18,200; Jackson and Cannon had dropped the slander portion of the suit. During the trial, which began on January 28, 1924, Cannon charged that Comiskey's agent, Grabiner, didn't treat Jackson fairly during the last contract negotiation; Grabiner knew that Jackson couldn't read or write and, by refusing to allow Katie to read the contract, he deliberately took advantage of the player. Jackson didn't always appear in the courtroom, though. During those times, Cannon kept him updated through the mail, letting him know that, in one deposition, Lefty Williams had nothing derogatory to say about him. In another letter, the attorney informed him that Buck Weaver signed an affidavit stating that Jackson had nothing to do with the fix.[37]

George Hudnall fought the lawsuit on Comiskey's behalf, denying that any contract trickery took place. He also pointed out that, not only had Jackson admitted to receiving $5,000 from gamblers wishing to fix the results of the 1919 World Series, but Katie had also corroborated that transaction. That action, Hudnall claimed, made the contract with Jackson null and void.

Cannon knew that Jackson stood a much better chance of obtaining a favorable verdict if it appeared that he hadn't taken any funds to throw games, and this is where Jackson began treading on dangerous ground. When he originally testified in front of the grand jury, Comiskey's attorney, Alfred Austrian, reminded Jackson how hazardous it would be to double-cross the gamblers who believed the Southern slugger was involved in the fix. Austrian advised Jackson—who was already bleary-eyed from too much drink—that he shouldn't make any blatant denials that would anger the gamblers. In reality, of course, Austrian was looking out for Comiskey's interests, not the slugger's; Jackson, who was more afraid of the gamblers than he was of jail, attempted to follow that glib advice as best he could.

But now Jackson was in a different situation, with his own attorney advising him to slant his testimony in another direction entirely. In this court appearance, Cannon advised Jackson to emphasize the fact that his teammates had used his name without permission because the gamblers wanted reassurance that the star of the White Sox, Shoeless Joe Jackson, was going to assist in throwing games. This, of course, was highly plausible.[38] Cannon went one step further, though, and had his client testify that Williams hadn't offered him any money until after the Series ended. That way, Cannon assured Jackson, he couldn't have truly known about the fix until after the Series ended—too late for Jackson to have effected any change. Therefore, he hadn't done anything wrong, and Comiskey owed him the money. Jackson followed his attorney's advice, and directly contradicted his grand jury testimony where he'd testified that he'd received $5,000 after the fourth game, and where he'd added that this sum was significantly less than the $20,000 originally anticipated.

This was a risky strategy to begin with, and the situation dramatically worsened when, with a flourish, Hudnall produced Jackson's original confession, a document that had been missing since 1920. While that unsettled Jackson, Comiskey also had reason to panic over the events occurring in the courtroom, and he visibly paled when his attorney produced the stolen document, thereby uncovering another layer of the behind-the-scenes machinations and maneuvering. Comiskey's attorney, Austrian, had also represented Arnold Rothstein in legal matters; it's entirely possible that Comiskey and Rothstein had colluded in an effort to steal the grand jury confessions. Comiskey had desperately wanted to cover up his early knowledge of the game-fixing, while Rothstein wished to distance himself from the financial backing of the scheme.[39] But now Hudnall, who was representing Comiskey in this lawsuit, had decided to produce the document to protect his employer against a potential judgment of $18,200.

Of more immediate concern, at least to Jackson, was whether or not the grand jury testimony would be admissible in court. The judge ruled that it was, indeed, admissible, and he ordered Jackson arrested under charges of "perjury, rank perjury."[40] Shoeless Joe was therefore arrested and he sat in jail for several hours before raising $5,000 in bail.

The next day, ironically enough, the jury found in favor of Jackson, awarding him the sum of $16,711.04. The judge, appalled that someone could benefit from perjured testimony, regardless of which rendering was the most true, set aside the verdict. Cannon's credibility was also damaged by his participation in this lawsuit; most major league ballplayers withdrew their support of Cannon's player's union after the court debacle ended, and the entire operation crumbled.

Comiskey eventually offered Jackson a small settlement to quiet the matter of back pay, which the ballplayer accepted, just as quietly; in many ways, though, neither man ever recovered from the lawsuit. Comiskey could never adequately explain the disappearance and sudden re-appearance of the purloined document, and his reputation was damaged; seven years later, he died, without ever justifying his actions. As for Jackson, he had just suffered through a dismal and humiliating appearance in court—and briefly, in jail—and he never again challenged the authority of anyone connected with major league baseball.

NOTES

1. Evans and Herzog, *The Faith of Fifty Million*, 105.
2. Farrell, *My Baseball Diary*, 99.
3. Lieb, *Baseball As I Have Known It*, 116.
4. Pietrusza, *Judge and Jury*, 160–161.
5. Veeck, with Linn, *The Hustler's Handbook*, 267.
6. Lieb, *Baseball As I Have Known It*, 116.
7. Fleitz, *Shoeless*, 236.
8. Pietrusza, *Judge and Jury*, 161.
9. Lieb, *Baseball As I Have Known It*, 116.
10. Pietrusza, *Judge and Jury*, 170.

11. See http://www.inficad.com/~ksup/landis.html.

12. Fleitz, *Shoeless*, 231–232.

13. Perry, *Textile League Baseball*, 31.

14. Fleitz, *Shoeless*, 236.

15. Pietrusza, *Judge and Jury*, 186.

16. Fleitz, *Shoeless*, 237.

17. Asinof, *Eight Men Out*, 240.

18. Fleitz, *Shoeless*, 240.

19. Asinof, *Eight Men Out*, 227.

20. Fleitz, *Shoeless*, 240.

21. Eliot Asinof, *1919: America's Loss of Innocence* (New York: Donald J. Fine, 1990), 338.

22. Asinof, *Eight Men Out*, 266.

23. Fleitz, *Shoeless*, 242.

24. Ibid.

25. See http://www.1919blacksox.com/trial.htm.

26. See http://www.baseball-reference.com/j/jacksjo01.shtml.

27. Pietrusza, *Judge and Jury*, 187.

28. In one of the most ironic twists of this entire scandal, the commissioner even banned Dickie Kerr, the only White Sox pitcher not involved in the fix, for playing against banned Black Sox players in a Texas semipro league in 1922. (Fleitz, *Shoeless*, 248–249.)

29. After one heated game, Risberg and Cicotte got into a brawl over money, and Risberg knocked out two of Cicotte's teeth. (Frommer, *Shoeless Joe and Ragtime Baseball*, 173.)

30. John Bell, *Shoeless Summer: The Summer of 1923 When Shoeless Joe Jackson Played Baseball in Americus, Georgia* (Carrollton, GA: Vabella Publishing, 2001), 30.

31. Ibid., 84.

32. See http://www.blackbetsy.com/jjinwaycrossnumber3.htm.

33. See http://www.reallegends.com/auctions/joe_history/page5.html.

34. Fleitz, *Shoeless*, 250.

35. To read the letters sent in response to Jackson's request, see Gropman, *Say It Ain't So, Joe!*, 286–287.

36. Another astonishing notion is also possible. According to Gene Carney (http://www.baseball1.com/carney), J. G. Taylor Spink, the editor of the *Sporting News* throughout the Black Sox scandal, made a startling claim in his now-hard-to-find book, *Judge Landis and Twenty-Five Years of Baseball* (St. Louis: The Sporting News Publishing Company, 1974). According to Spink, not only did Jackson sue Comiskey for back pay, he and Happy Felsch also brought damage suits against the White Sox owner and "unknown persons" charging a "conspiracy against them." (Spink suspects that Landis was one of the unknowns.)

Carney speculates that the court combined the two suits, adding, "You almost wish that the players forgot about the back pay, and pursued the conspiracy in the courts."

Spink also writes that, "Judge John J. Gregory at first ruled against Comiskey, but later the court ordered amended petitions filed in the cases described." If, indeed, these events transpired the way that Spink—the respected editor of the "Bible of Baseball"—described, our understanding of the dynamics between Jackson and Comiskey, and possibly with Landis, as well, would change dramatically.

37. Fleitz, *Shoeless*, 252, 254.

38. In Gropman, *Say It Ain't So, Joe!* (226), Lefty Williams' grand jury testimony states that Jackson's name was used with the gamblers, without Jackson's knowledge or permission.

39. Eliot Asinof interviewed Hugo Friend, who confided his belief that Arnold Rothstein's attorney, William Fallon, engineered the disappearance of the confessions, adding that Comiskey was well aware of what was transpiring (*Bleeding Between the Lines*, 111).

40. Fleitz, *Shoeless*, 255.

SHADOWED BY PARADOXES

*Jackson's fall from grace is one of the real tragedies of baseball. I always thought
he was more sinned against than sinning.*
                                                            —Connie Mack[1]

According to legend, after Kenesaw Mountain Landis dealt firmly with the corrupt White Sox players, no other gambling-related baseball scandal occurred
during his lifetime. In reality, though, whereas Landis' tough stance certainly
discouraged future collaborations between gamblers and players, other instances
of previous collusion ultimately surfaced. Indeed, the Black Sox Scandal was
hardly an isolated instance.

In fact, Landis had to deal with two separate incidents in 1926, one periph-
erally involving Jackson. Late that year, former Tigers player Hubert "Dutch"
Leonard accused the player-manager of the Cleveland Indians, Tris Speaker, and
the player-manager of the Detroit Tigers, Ty Cobb, of organizing a gambling
scheme several years earlier. Leonard claimed that the two men, assisted by former pitcher "Smoky" Joe Wood, created a plan whereby Speaker would deliberately cause his team to lose on September 25, 1919, so that Cobb's team could
secure third place in the American League. Moreover, Speaker and Cobb, according to Leonard, bet on the outcome of the game, figuring the fix was in.
American League president, Ban Johnson, banned both from professional baseball after receiving Leonard's information.

Shortly afterwards, Chicago's former shortstop, Swede Risberg, stated in a
newspaper interview that the Detroit Tigers had deliberately lost two games to

the White Sox on September 2 and 3, 1917, for the sum of $1,100, given to pitcher Bill James. Two years later, Risberg added, the White Sox purposely lost two games to the Detroit Tigers to help them clinch third place in the 1919 season. Landis, infuriated by such charges, requested that Joe Jackson, among other banished Black Sox players, appear at a hearing. The banished slugger was comfortable in Georgia, though, and did not want to become involved in another scandal.

Jackson declined to attend, telling Landis that business concerns wouldn't permit his absence, and then later commenting, "I owed nothing to baseball. I had given them my word once and they wouldn't take it."[2] Eddie Cicotte didn't even bother to respond to Landis's request; Chick Gandil reacted quite differently, traveling from Arizona for a chance to confirm Risberg's story. Nothing of substance occurred because of Risberg's charges, and Landis overruled Johnson's ban on Speaker and Cobb.[3] The duo resigned as managers, but continued to play, albeit for different teams: Speaker went to the Washington Senators and Cobb traveled to Philadelphia and played for the Athletics. Meanwhile, Jackson continued to play semipro ball and work at his dry cleaning business.

In 1929, Jackson's mother Martha became ill and needed constant attention, so he and Katie returned to Greenville where they opened a restaurant, "Joe Jackson's Barbecue Cabin." Once Prohibition was repealed, they also opened the liquor store that they operated for the rest of Jackson's life. This did not go over well in his temperance-minded hometown. Some of the same people who welcomed him back in spite of his role in the Black Sox scandal were horrified when Shoeless Joe started peddling liquor. Eventually, he and Katie resigned from the Brandon Methodist Church when the minister refused their donation of a pipe organ because the funds came from the sale of liquor; undaunted in their philanthropy, they gave the organ to the Brandon Baptist Church.[4]

After Jackson's refusal to provide testimony about Risberg's accusations, he never communicated directly with Landis again. Two years later, any chance of further remuneration or communication from Charles Comiskey also ended; on October 26, 1931, the "Old Roman" died of a heart attack at the age of seventy-two and was buried in the Calvary Catholic Cemetery in Cook County. Comiskey was certainly wealthy when he died, but the Black Sox scandal had significantly lessened the amount of his estate. The priest who delivered his funeral sermon attributed his death to a broken heart, while Comiskey's obituary in the *New York Times* suggested that he had symbolically died along with his now-notorious team. Perhaps an anonymous poem about Comiskey, published in the *Chicago Times* in 1919, sums up his death better than any accounting of the actual event:

The unsettling dust
Settles in the throat of all men
There are not enough beers
In all the bars
In all the worlds
To flush out the stale bitterness
Of too many afternoons
In too many suns.[5]

One year later, the *New York Sun* published a retrospective of Comiskey's life, and included updates about the Black Sox players; by this time, the other banned men had apparently quit semipro ball, with "only Jackson still playing with his black bat, clear eyed, ruddy-faced, big-bellied, slow moving, soft spoken. . . . A home run on a sand lot before a bunch of South Carolina farmers gives him as much of a thrill as a wallop over the roof of a big league stadium."[6]

In fact, Joe Jackson continued to play ball in South Carolina well into his forties; in 1932, at the age of forty-four, he signed with the Greenville Spinners, earning one hundred dollars per game, a decent sum during the Great Depression. According to the *Greenville News*, on August 1, "Joe will don his baseball harness again Wednesday to give the home folks an eyeful of the modern Joe Jackson. He will play in his old position, center field, for the Greenville Spinners. . . . Joe has his famous bat 'Black Betsy' with him, and he will use the bludgeon in the game."[7]

In Greenville, Jackson also served as mentor for many mill team players, including Murphy Grumbles and Pelham Ballenger, the second of whom played three games for the Washington Senators. He offered advice to younger ballplayers, as well, stressing the importance of a man's honor.

Greenville resident Joe Thompson personally recalls many instances of Jackson's kindness toward children. "Joe would come outside," Thompson writes, "and talk baseball with the kids who gathered around him. There were many times when Katie had to come forth to rescue Joe, by shooing the kids away from him." He would often treat the children to ice cream cones and Coca-Colas, as well; when a youth particularly needed money, Jackson would suddenly remember that he could pay someone to sweep the floor of his restaurant.[8]

Although Jackson and Katie never had children of their own, after their return to Greenville they helped raise McDavid, the son of Joe's brother, David, and they talked about adopting him. David struggled with health issues, and McDavid lived a tragic life as well, finally committing suicide on Christmas Eve in 1947, several years after his wife had died giving birth to their first baby, who also died. (In a 1949 interview, Jackson averred that a gun McDavid was cleaning had accidentally gone off, but official reports indicate that his death was a result of suicide.) Shortly after McDavid's death, Jackson suffered the first of a series of heart attacks.[9]

Jackson and Katie also continued to nurse his loyal and protective mother until she died on August 25, 1932. The family buried her in Graceland Cemetery in West Greenville, South Carolina, next to her husband, George. She was 68 years old. The following year, on January 2, 1933, Jackson's former manager, William "Kid" Gleason, died of a heart ailment. He'd always considered the 1919 White Sox team the best he'd ever seen, and he died while still mourning over the scandalous taint the team had carried while under his management.

In 1933, Jackson attempted his own hand at baseball management when a group of Greenville businessmen put together a new Class D team. Unfortunately, even such a lowly category was under the auspices of "organized baseball," which meant that Jackson needed Landis' approval to participate. The investors applied to Landis for permission on Jackson's behalf; in January 1934, they received a negative answer. They didn't pursue the matter any further; instead, Jackson began supervising umpires for the Western Carolina Semi-Pro League and he spent the next few years serving as manager of a semipro team located in Winnsboro, South Carolina. Both of these jobs were apparently outside Landis' influence.

Not everyone connected to the Greenville team, though, accepted Landis's intransigence, insofar as Joe Jackson was concerned, quietly. Many had hoped Jackson's presence on the newly formed team would draw spectators and bring in revenue. Greenville's mayor, John Mauldin, was furious; he'd collected over 5,000 signatures from people who had requested Jackson's reinstatement to professional baseball, then mailed the petition to Landis. Some sportswriters attempted to get major league–level comment about the groundswell effort, but only one man—Ed Barrow, the New York Yankees business manager—"had the gumption and the human sympathy to come out in favor of the reinstatement of Joe Jackson."[10]

Barrow's portrayal of the post scandal Jackson was misleading, though. He was quoted in the *New York World Telegram* on December 21, saying that Jackson was "starving down there, eking out a bare and brutal living pressing pants."[11] At that time, Jackson and Katie actually employed over twenty people between two dry cleaning stores and, while they were by no means wealthy, the Jacksons owned a $10,000 home and two automobiles. Jackson cheerfully admitted that giving money to frugal Katie was as good as putting it in the bank.

Shortly after the Barrow quotes appeared, syndicated columnist Westbrook Pegler reacted to the call for reinstatement, denigrating those who believed Jackson deserved a chance at redemption. Pegler believed that, in fact, banishment from major league baseball hadn't been severe enough punishment; he advocated jail time for the Black Sox Eight. Even in retirement, it seems, Shoeless Joe Jackson could rile up the sportswriters.

By the time the Depression ended, so had Jackson's baseball career, other than the odd exhibition game or two; the "Carolina Confection" could still hit and throw the ball with extraordinary strength, but his ability to run had greatly diminished. The people of Greenville, though, still valued him, and city officials hosted a special event to honor his career in 1942, when the slugger was 53, naming it "Joe Jackson Appreciation Night."

The event was held at the ballfield in Brandon where Jackson hit his mill team "Saturday Specials." Although the field looked somewhat different—center field was now where home plate used to be, and a concrete grandstand covered what used to be the center field dump—one thing remained the same: to pay homage to Jackson's amazing swing, fans passed a hat around the field, tossing in coins.

That summer, Jackson also granted an extensive interview to Carter "Scoop" Latimer, the sports editor of the *Greenville News* and the man who originally coined the nickname "Shoeless Joe" several decades earlier. In this interview, Jackson denied any wrongdoing and spoke of having no regrets. The article was accompanied with down-home photos of Jackson cooking eggs, working at his liquor store, and swinging a bat. It appeared in the widely-read *Sporting News*, a fact that displeased Landis immensely.[12]

Ironically, on November 25, 1944, right about the time that Jackson finally retired from baseball for good, Kenesaw Mountain Landis, a man who had retained his stronghold over Organized Baseball throughout his lifetime, died of a heart attack and complications from respiratory problems. In accordance with his wishes, no funeral service was held, although the Baseball Hall of Fame did honor the fierce commissioner two weeks later by a special induction ceremony.

Although his impact on the game was profound, Landis' status in baseball's history was mixed; those who admired him would probably agree with David Pietrusza's assessment that he "may have been arbitrary, capricious, old-fashioned, vindictive, and more than occasionally profane, but no one could deny Kenesaw Mountain Landis had accomplished what he had been hired to do."[13] Those who strongly disliked him became fond of pointing out that within three years of his death, the first black man appeared on a major league roster, implying that Landis was at least a partial cause of blocking Negro League players from entering the ranks of major league baseball. Baseball owners, who appreciated much of what Landis did, but also regretted granting him all-encompassing powers, seemed to learn from their experience of having an all-powerful and totally autonomous commissioner. They voted to limit the scope and authority of his replacement and also began permitting court challenges to future commissioner rulings.[14]

As for Jackson, he shared thoughts about his relationship with Landis in a 1949 interview with Furman Bisher, an on-the-record conversation that Eliot Asinof labeled a "concoction of depressing distortions . . . the confusions of a life he could never understand."[15] In that interview, Jackson asserted:

> If I had been the kind of fellow who brooded when things went wrong, I probably would have gone out of my mind when Judge Landis ruled me out of baseball. I would have lived in regret. I would have been bitter and resentful because I felt I had been wronged.
>
> But I haven't been resentful at all. I thought when my trial was over that Judge Landis might have restored me to good standing. But he never did. And until he died I had never gone before him, sent a representative before him, or placed before him any written matter pleading my case. I gave baseball my best and if the game didn't care enough to see me get a square deal, then I wouldn't go out of my way to get back in it.
>
> Baseball failed to keep faith with me.[16]

If Jackson was correctly quoted in this interview, then he obviously chose to deny knowledge of the Greenville businessmen's request for him to manage their team in 1933. Furthermore, in Landis' April 6, 1922 response to a Jackson letter, the commissioner writes, "Neither can any club in organized baseball that had entered into a contract with you be permitted to carry out the contract."[17] Although Jackson's actual request has been lost, that response certainly implies an appeal for reinstatement. In any case, although the major league system had, indeed, condemned Jackson, he was living out his postbaseball years in a forgiving environment; so perhaps Jackson should be forgiven, as well, for wanting to present himself in a good light. Certainly most of Greenville saw him that way. According to Thomas Perry, "For the folks on the mill hill, the hero had returned. He may have been bloodied, his armor dented by a vindictive commissioner of baseball and a selfish owner, but Jackson was home, and village citizens looked after their own."[18]

There was also at least one major league ballplayer, besides Lajoie, who did not forget Joe Jackson—the ever-contrary and unpredictable Ty Cobb. During the 1940s, Cobb walked into Jackson's liquor store. Jackson didn't particularly react to Cobb's presence, one way or the other, prompting the Georgia Peach to say, "Don't you know me, you old so-and-so?" Jackson responded, "Sure I do, but I didn't think you knew me after all these years. I didn't want to embarrass you or nothing." At that point, Cobb told Jackson, "I'll tell you how well I remember you. When I got the idea I was a good hitter, I'd stop and take a good look at you. Then I knew I could stand some improvement."[19]

This account of the encounter seems to be more or less accurate, as both Jackson and Cobb recalled the incident; so did Grant Riceland, the sportswriter who accompanied Cobb on this trip and later wrote about the conversation.[20] Some Greenville residents still remember the tour of his hometown that Jackson gave Cobb, as well. Other retellings of this incident, though, then have Cobb asking Jackson for an autographed ball, which doesn't seem likely. Surely Cobb knew that Jackson, a lifelong illiterate, struggled to write his name, and Cobb's visit seemed motivated by camaraderie, not spite.[21] His admiration of Jackson as a ballplayer seemed genuine, as well; in 1945, when Cobb was asked to name the greatest baseball players of all time, he chose Jackson, without hesitation or reservation, as his choice for left fielder.[22]

By the time 1949 rolled around, Joe Jackson was a 61-year-old man who was ready to reminisce about those great years of baseball. That year, he granted a lengthy interview to Furman Bisher, a reporter from Atlanta; the article appeared in the October 1949 edition of *Sport* magazine. In this interview, Jackson claimed that a "fellow" propositioned him to throw ballgames in 1919; the request, he said, was made in front of two other players and their wives. His response, Jackson told Bisher, was, "Why you cheap so-and-so! Either me or you—one of us is going out that window."

Jackson said that he then went to Comiskey and begged to be benched for the Series, saying, "Tell the newspapers you just suspended me for being drunk, or anything, but leave me out of the Series and then there can be no question." Journalist Hugh Fullerton, according to Jackson's account, overheard the entire conversation with Comiskey and offered to testify in Chicago on his behalf. Because Fullerton had died in 1946, there was no way for that statement to be verified or contested, but if it was true, the question has to rise why Jackson kept it to himself for so long.

In the interview, Jackson also talked about the frequent and public mocking of his intelligence, saying, "All the big sportswriters seemed to enjoy writing about me as an ignorant cotton-mill boy with nothing but lint where my brains ought to be. That was all right with me. I was able to fool a lot of pitchers and managers and club owners I wouldn't have been able to fool if they'd thought I was smarter."[23]

This article once again revived interest in Joe Jackson; on February 27, 1951, both bodies of South Carolina's legislature passed a formal resolution asking for Jackson's reinstatement into professional baseball. This resolution states, in part, that, "fact and fancy have been so confused that today it still is not known what actually took place . . . thirty-two years is too long for any man to be penalized for an act as to which strong evidence exists that it was never committed by him."[24]

Bisher, the sportswriter who had published Jackson's side of the story in 1949, also supported this resolution. He said that Jackson "was a man who had been brought up to know sin when he saw it, and this [the World Series fix] was sin in capital letters."[25] These pleas did not, however, change the mind of Ford Frick, the commissioner of baseball at the time.[26]

Also in 1951, the Cleveland Indians founded the Cleveland Baseball Hall of Fame. Jackson was not listed on the initial ballot, but a grassroots effort to include him succeeded and he received the third most votes, overall. So, although Jackson was banned from professional baseball, the Cleveland Baseball Hall of Fame elected him, along with baseball greats such as Tris Speaker, Cy Young, and Napoleon Lajoie, as one of their ten original members. Jackson was invited to attend the induction ceremony, but numerous health problems involving his liver and heart, compounded by diabetes, prevented him from doing so. The Cleveland Indians inscribed a gold clock in his name, but decided to wait for another ceremony to present the gift to him.

The honor, joined with the South Carolina legislature's resolution to reinstate him into professional baseball, brought Jackson's name even further into the news of the nation; another opportunity to give him the clock soon presented itself. Jackson was invited to appear on the nationally televised variety program, *Toast of the Town*, later renamed *The Ed Sullivan Show*. On the program, it was proposed that Tris Speaker present the gold clock to Jackson; because of his declining health, Katie and a physician planned to accompany him, and sportswriter Latimer also intended to travel with them.

Unfortunately, eleven days before he was to appear on the show, Jackson complained of feeling ill while working at his liquor store. He had suffered two more heart attacks earlier that year, and was therefore immediately taken home to rest. He fell into an exhausted sleep, and the following evening, he complained of chest pains and was clearly in the throes of yet another heart attack. Katie quickly contacted both his doctor and his brother David.

David arrived in time to hold Joe's hand, but the doctor did not. Jackson reportedly squeezed David's hand and said, "Goodbye, good buddy. This is it," before falling unconscious for the last time.

Shoeless Joe Jackson—mill town worker, baseball player, mentor, subject of scandal, brother and husband—died just after 10:00 P.M. on December 5, 1951. He was sixty-three years old, and he had died only days before he had a chance to present his side of the story on national television. At first glance, that seems like extraordinarily bad luck. Perhaps, though, when thinking about the ups and downs that occurred throughout his entire life, that wasn't so surprising, after all. "In retrospect," writes author Thomas Perry, "his whole life was shadowed by such paradoxes."[27]

Simple funeral services were conducted at the Brandon Baptist Church in Greenville in accordance with Jackson's wishes. Survived by all seven of his younger siblings—brothers David, Jerry, Earl, Ernest, and Luther, and sisters Gertrude and Lula—and his wife, hundreds of former mill workers and ballplayers also attended his funeral. Flowers abounded at the funeral home, and blossoms were heaped upon his grave.

Jackson, the first of the eight Black Sox to die, also received wired condolences from the grandson of Charles Comiskey.[28] His death certificate, dated December 9, 1951, lists the cause of death as coronary thrombosis caused by arteriosclerosis and cirrhosis of the liver. He was buried in Woodlawn Memorial Park in Greenville, South Carolina, plot 333 of Section V, where his beloved Katie would join him in April 1959.

At last, one of the most controversial and sensational athletes of the twentieth century was at rest. His life and accomplishments speak, in large part, for themselves.

NOTES

1. Frommer, *Shoeless Joe and Ragtime Baseball*, unnumbered front matter page 3.

2. Gropman, *Say It Ain't So, Joe!*, 229.

3. Speaker's involvement was never corroborated. As for Cobb, it might be inferred from a letter written by him that he was guilty of charges made, but that is nowhere near conclusive.

4. Thompson, *Growing Up with Shoeless Joe*, 122.

5. See http://www.baseball-almanac.com/poetry/po_1919.shtml.

6. Frommer, *Shoeless Joe and Ragtime Baseball*, 175.

7. See http://www.reallegends.com/auctions/joe_history/page5.html#, Greenville News, August 1, 1932.

8. Thompson, *Growing Up with Shoeless Joe*, 92.

9. Fleitz, *Shoeless*, 268.

10. Gropman, *Say It Ain't So, Joe!*, 231.

11. Ibid.

12. J. G. Taylor Spink, the editor of the *Sporting News* throughout the Black Sox scandal, wrote that "Jackson was one of the few players that I got to know well and I always felt that he was unwittingly taken into the alleged Black Sox ring." He also recalls how angry Landis was at the publication of the *Sporting News* article. (See http://www.baseball1.com/carney.)

13. Pietrusza, *Judge and Jury*, 452.

14. See http://mlb.mlb.com/NASApp/mlb/mlb/history/mlb_history_people_story.jsp?story=com.

15. Asinof, *Bleeding Between the Lines*, 99.

16. Furman Bisher, "This Is the Truth, The Story of the 1919 World Series as Told by Shoeless Joe Jackson," *Sport*, October 1949, 12–14, 83, 84.

17. Gropman, *Say It Ain't So, Joe!*, 287.

18. Perry, *Textile League Baseball*, 32.

19. Ty Cobb, with Al Stump, *My Life in Baseball: The True Record.* Reprint ed. (Lincoln, NE: University of Nebraska Press, 1993), 266.

20. Grantland Rice wrote about this in *The Tumult and the Shouting: My Life in Sport* (New York: Rigby, 1977).

21. Given Cobb's own turbulent career, his admiration for Jackson's "Black Sox" designation may have also been sympathetic. Cobb had been castigated, sued, and threatened throughout his own years as a major league star; for years he was unable to appear in Ohio for fear of being arrested on an open warrant for murder, and he was haunted by scandalous stories involving his investments and his vitriolic family. That both men came from the anonymous south to rise to such heights of fame in professional baseball also gave them much in common, and set them into a class of players that remains, even today, unique in the annals of the sport.

22. In fact, Cobb ended his friendship with Ted Williams, the "Splendid Splinter" of baseball, after a quarrel that ensued after Williams suggested that Joe DiMaggio may have been a better hitter than Jackson. (See Al Stump, *Cobb: The Life and Times of the Meanest Man Who Ever Played Baseball: A Biography* [Chapel Hill, NC: Algonquin Books of Chapel Hill, 1994, 25].) Ironically, Williams became a driving force behind the request for Jackson's reinstatement to professional baseball.

23. Bisher, "This Is the Truth," 1949.

24. Gropman, *Say It Ain't So, Joe!*, 242.

25. Frommer, *Shoeless Joe and Ragtime Baseball*, 180.

26. In between the tenures of Landis and Frick, Senator Albert "Happy" Chandler also served as commissioner of baseball; he also refused to reopen the case of the Black Sox suspensions.

27. Perry, *Textile League Baseball,* 32.

28. Asinof, *Eight Men Out*, 293.

EPILOGUE: MAKING OF A LEGEND

Shoeless Joe Jackson, your pain is healed. Heaven is baseball in an Iowa corn field.

—Billy Goerdt[1]

Joseph Jefferson Wofford Jackson

As a thirteen-year-old, Joe Jackson earned a position on the Brandon Mill Team. He possessed a talent so uncommon that legends grew from his deeds. His home runs were known as "Saturday Specials," his line drives "blue darters," his glove "a place where triples die." Shoeless Joe was the greatest natural hitter ever to grace the diamond, and was such an inspiration that Babe Ruth chose to copy his swing. He was banished from baseball for his complicity in the 1919 Black Sox scandal, yet his memory still moves across the conscience of America. Shoeless Joe Jackson never had to say it wasn't so, for the people who knew him best never questioned his integrity.

Textile Baseball

The industrial cotton mills were chiefly responsible for the south's recovery from the Civil War. Collectively, the mills brought the "true grit" American working class together. The timeless competitive spirit of work and play, from scratch to scrap teams, evolved into a baseball era of unyielding desire, aspiration, and anticipation to excel. Textile baseball produced many great legendary ball players. Mill workers by the thousands once swarmed out of drudgery when the whistles blew on Saturday af-

Post-baseball, Jackson was an entrepreneur, owning pool halls, dry cleaning establishments, and this liquor store, where Ty Cobb stopped by to visit. *Bettmann/Corbis and Cleveland Public Library.*

ternoons, to their village ballparks to enjoy the thrill of America's favorite pastime—baseball.[2]

So reads the inscription on the bronze statue that was dedicated to Shoeless Joe Jackson on July 13, 2002, in Greenville, South Carolina. The statue, crafted by Douglas R. Young in the lobby of Greenville's city hall, developed in the public eye. Visitors could chat with Young as he sculpted his edifice; clay samples rested on the tables in the lobby so that people could touch the base material used to create the memorial and some applied clay on the emerging statue for Young to mold. Many of them also expressed a wish to see Jackson restored postmortem to professional baseball; for them, this statue serves as a symbol of the resurgence of goodwill towards Greenville's hometown hero.

That Joe Jackson wanted to be reinstated during his lifetime so that he could play professional baseball again is unquestioned. However, to Jackson's supporters, reinstatement more than fifty years after his death means something else entirely. To them, the clearing of Jackson's name means he can potentially be inducted into the National Baseball Hall of Fame and Museum in Cooperstown, New York. Founded in 1936 and officially dedicated on June 12, 1939, the Hall of Fame is a "not-for-profit educational institution dedicated to fostering an appreciation of the historical development of the game and its impact on our culture by collecting, preserving, exhibiting and interpreting its collections for a global audience, as well as honoring those who have made outstanding contributions to our National Pastime."[3] To have one's name included on the wall along with the greatest players who ever stepped between the foul lines, as well as the most sensational managers and owners who influenced the sport, is the ultimate achievement of a professional career.

Each year, qualifying sportswriters vote on whose performance they believe contributed significantly to the game of baseball; candidates must have played ten years of professional baseball and must have been retired for at least five years. Whenever 75 percent of the writers vote affirmatively for the same qualified ballplayer, he is honored as a member of the Hall of Fame. Currently, sportswriters must base their votes upon the "player's record, playing ability, integrity, sportsmanship, character, and contribution to the team(s) on which the player played."[4] In the Hall of Fame's initial year, 1936, writers selected Ty Cobb, Babe Ruth, Honus Wagner, Christy Mathewson, and Walter Johnson. In 1939, electees from 1936–1939 were honored at a ceremony; included in their numbers were Charles Comiskey; Ban Johnson; Jackson's former Cleveland teammate, Nap Lajoie; and White Sox second baseman, Eddie Collins. On the day of the actual ceremony, Jackson worked at his store in Greenville. If he so much as mentioned Cooperstown, no one recalled it.

Analysis of the electees over that four-year time span reveals that only Ty Cobb had a higher career batting average than Jackson; only Cobb, George Sisler, and Lajoic ever out-batted Jackson in a single season, and none matched Jackson's accomplishment of batting over .400 in his rookie season.[5] Even today, Jackson's all-time batting average of .356 is the third highest in major league baseball, and no other rookie has broken the .400 barrier. Jackson still holds the record for the most triples in a season (26 in 1912) and is tied for the most hits for a World Series (12 in 1919). He also played on a World Series–winning team in 1917.

It's safe to assume, then, that the Black Sox Scandal—rather than any lack of playing ability or proven performance—was the reason why Jackson only received two Hall of Fame votes in 1936.[6] It is also reasonable to assume that anyone who publicly campaigned for Jackson—or perhaps merely voted for him—during that era would have faced the wrath of Commissioner Kenesaw Mountain Landis and risked his own reputation and status in the sport.

Sportswriters did, however, theoretically have the option of inducting Joe Jackson into the Hall of Fame, at least until 1991. That year, Hall of Fame officials adopted Rule 3-e stating, "Any player on baseball's ineligible list shall not be an eligible candidate." This rule precluded Jackson's possible inclusion in future elections.[7]

Many who support Jackson's reinstatement to professional baseball status believe that he was innocent of the charges made against him. Others believe that he was not given a fair chance to state his case, which makes judgment preliminary and unfounded; still others believe that his punishment, even if he was guilty to some degree, was too severe and should be mitigated.

The list of those who have either proclaimed or alluded to his innocence in book form include Joe Thompson, author of *Growing Up with Shoeless Joe*; Harvey Frommer, author of *Shoeless Joe and Ragtime Baseball*; and Donald Gropman, author of *Say It Ain't So, Joe!: The True Story of Shoeless Joe Jackson*. Thompson presents an often-forgotten side of Joe Jackson: that of a man who loved his hometown and was loved by Greenville, South Carolina, residents in return. This book reveals the hitter as a mischievous young boy crossing a dangerous railroad trestle to impress his friends, as well as a caring man in his fifties who was gently mentoring young and impressionable ballplayers. Thompson is fiercely pro-Jackson and, as an author, creates a contextual description of the place that Shoeless Joe called home.

Frommer juxtaposes events in Jackson's life next to defining moments of popular culture, often related to music, as well as pertinent demographic material. He employs a telegraphic writing style, publishing quotes from Jackson's contemporaries next to quotes attributed to the ballplayer; and he allows those quotes to provide illumination for events just described. The author provides the complete grand jury testimony of Joe Jackson as an appendix; he is also pro-Jackson in his interpretation of the events of 1919.

Gropman's book was originally published in 1979, and much of the 2001 edition remains the same as the original. Gropman has, however, added information-rich appendices that contain the text of several Jackson-related documents uncovered after 1979. This author is unapologetically pro-Jackson and uses much of this book to attempt to persuade readers that Jackson should be reinstated to professional baseball.

An introduction to Gropman's book by Harvard Law Professor Alan Dershowitz is thought provoking and supplements the text. While the previously mentioned three authors proclaim Jackson's innocence, either subtly or openly, Dershowitz argues a second point: that the ballplayer was not given a fair chance to state his case. In his introduction to Gropman's book, Dershowitz suggests that Jackson was caught up in a maelstrom of conspiracy, and should not be faulted for his inability to escape that snare. "Jackson received shoddy treatment, but this probably would not happen today," he writes. "A modern-day Jackson would have his own lawyer from the very beginning. Nor would the shenanigans employed by Comiskey's lawyer be tolerated by the bar today. Most important, an honest prosecutor today generally seeks to follow the criminal trail to the top of the mountain."[8]

Lawrence Ritter, author of *The 100 Greatest Baseball Players of All Time*, includes Jackson on his list of stellar players; he is among those who believe that Jackson's banishment should end, regardless of its origin. "Whatever Joe did or did not do, it's a long time past now, time for a game which denied Blacks entrance until 1946 to end its pose of total purity. The Hall of Fame should induct Joe Jackson, shoes and all."[9] Or, as Stephen Jay Gould eloquently stated in his introduction to Eliot Asinof's *Eight Men Out: The Black Sox and the 1919 World Series*, "His sin is so old, the beauty of his play so enduring."[10]

Yet another faction of Jackson supporters insists that if Pete Rose, a former Cincinnati Reds player made ineligible because of gambling allegations, becomes reinstated into professional baseball,[11] then Shoeless Joe's redemption should be automatic. Jackson also received backing from a baseball legend and Hall-of-Famer, the late Ted Williams. Until shortly before his death on July 5, 2002, Williams, who had the eighth highest career batting average, and who was the last player to hit .400 or better,[12] was a vocal supporter. When asked to list the greatest hitters of all time, Williams placed Jackson eighth on his list, ahead of such notables as Tris Speaker, Hank Aaron, Willie Mays, and Mickey Mantle.[13] Although Williams never saw Jackson play, Eddie Collins had mentored the "Splendid Splinter," and Williams once asked Collins to tell him about Jackson. The former second baseman "closed his eyes and dropped his head, and he kind of looked skyward, and he said, 'Boy what a player he was.'"[14] In January 1998, Williams joined forces with former Cleveland Indians pitcher Bob Feller, also a member of the Hall of Fame; jointly, they filed a petition asking the commissioner of baseball to remove Joe Jackson from baseball's ineligible list.

In this petition, they spoke as "spiritual teammates in a flannel-clad fraternity who have stepped across the chalk lines and played their allotted innings." Williams and Feller argued that Jackson has not been a "person" since 1951; therefore, he cannot be on baseball's "current ineligible list." Keeping him on this list, they conclude, is an attempt to punish a player on the "other side of the grass." Moreover, Jackson ceased being a person four full decades before Rule 3-e—the section that prohibits players declared ineligible from obtaining Hall of Fame status—came into effect. Williams and Feller therefore asked that the commissioner put aside the ineligible status; Gropman included the entire original petition in his book, along with a significant number of footnotes analyzing the contents, and an amended memorandum.[15]

For Jackson to achieve Hall of Fame status, several steps must occur. First, his estate—the only entity that can officially apply for reinstatement—must petition the commissioner of baseball (currently Allen "Bud" Selig) to overturn the 1920 decision of baseball's first commissioner, Kensesaw Mountain Landis, thereby removing Jackson from the list of ineligible players. At this point, the current commissioner can grant or refuse the plea for reinstatement. To date, Jackson's estate has not formally applied; previous requests have come from other interested parties, and all have been rejected.[16]

Assuming that a commissioner of baseball eventually does agree to lift the ban, this does not guarantee further movement towards Hall of Fame induction. The next action must come from the Committee on Baseball Veterans of the National Baseball Hall of Fame and Museum, the committee that determines the Hall of Fame potential of pre-1946 major league players who participated in at least ten seasons and have been retired for twenty-one years or more. If Jackson becomes reinstated, then committee members would have the option of reviewing Jackson's baseball performance in the same manner that they might appraise any other qualified candidate; but they are not required to take any action whatsoever. If, however, they review Jackson's records and decide to consider him as a candidate, then 75 percent of the qualified committee members must vote affirmatively for him to achieve Hall of Fame induction.[17]

Of course, some people oppose Jackson's reinstatement and potential induction. Although their views currently appear to be in the minority, they are no less passionate and no less outspoken in their beliefs. Rob Neyer, in his article for ESPN.com, "Say it ain't so . . . for Joe and the Hall," lists several reasons why Jackson does not belong in the Hall of Fame, including his "guilty knowledge" and the fact that, "when he agreed to throw the Series, he almost certainly emboldened his teammates to do the same." Moreover, Neyer contends, it doesn't "make sense to confer this highest honor upon a man who committed a terrible crime against the very essence of sport," especially because "Jackson and his cohorts committed a truly evil crime, compromising the integrity of their profession and violating the trust of their fans."[18]

David Fleitz author of *Shoeless: The Life and Times of Joe Jackson*, agrees, saying, "Joe Jackson profited from the fix, nearly doubling his admittedly meager salary, and actively participated in the throwing of games in 1919 and (possibly) 1920. This should be enough to bar his entry to the Hall of Fame."[19] Although Jackson supporters in general do not agree with Fleitz's conclusions, his interpretation is not so easily dismissed. Fleitz's biography is logically written and comprehensive in scope, providing a more objective point of view throughout the majority of the text and then challenging pro-Jackson assertions in its conclusion. Fleitz's attention to detail lends credibility to his speculations, and his citations will be appreciated by anyone wishing to track down original sources.

Bill James, author of *The Politics of Glory: How Baseball's Hall of Fame Really Works*, is even more blunt in his anti-Jackson assessment than Fleitz: "My own opinion is that the people who want to put Joe Jackson in the Hall of Fame are baseball's answer to those women who show up at murder trials wanting to marry the cute murderer."[20]

The debate over Jackson's Hall of Fame eligibility, then, rages on; meanwhile, the southern slugger continues to receive postmortem honors and inductions. In 1969, he was inducted into the South Carolina Athletic Hall of Fame; in 1980, Jackson became a member of the Ohio Baseball Hall of Fame and, in 1995, the Pennsylvania Baseball Sports Hall of Fame welcomed his presence.[21]

Further attention was focused on Joe Jackson in the 1990s when the American Cancer Society and the American Heart Association sued the State of South Carolina for possession of his signed will. After Katie, who inherited Jackson's entire estate, died of cancer, she left her estate to these two charities. However, nobody attempted to gain possession of Jackson's will until one of his six known autographs sold for $23,100 at a Sotheby's auction. After the auction, however, the beneficiary organizations wanted his will, and they hoped to auction it off in excess of $100,000 to benefit their charities. If that happened, one newspaper reporter noted, Jackson's rare scrawl would be "worth more than the signatures of Beethoven and Babe Ruth combined."[22]

The South Carolina Supreme Court ruled that Jackson's will was public record and could not be given to the charities. Although the ruling appears firm, one friend of Jackson's, Joe Wade Anders, believes that the slugger would have opposed the results. "Knowing Joe, knowing how generous and caring a person he was, I think he would have wanted that will to be sold and the money to go to the charities. Joe was that kind of person, always wanting to help somebody."[23] Meanwhile, court officials must work hard to protect the will itself. The original is locked up, but people are allowed to purchase photocopies made from microfiche. The problem is that the microfiche has already been stolen numerous times and it's unlikely that this nefarious practice will abate any time soon.

In another court-related matter, the transcript of Jackson's grand jury testimony that disappeared in 1921 and then resurfaced at his 1924 lawsuit against Comiskey, was displayed at the Chicago Historical Society Museum in 1989. The document was loaned to the museum by the "descendant firm of Alfred Austrian's old firm." Attached to that document was this disclaimer, written by a partner of the current firm: "As is true today, an employer's lawyer was not required by the rules of legal ethics to provide a Miranda-type warning to an employee suspected of dishonesty." This disclaimer was most likely attached in response to modern-day criticism about Austrian; people, including Dershowitz, have been pointing out the unjustness of having Comiskey's attorney advise Jackson before the player was going on the stand. The law firm must have felt a need to justify their stance.[24]

As the criticism of Austrian and Comiskey rises, honors, for Jackson, increase. On December 7, 1993, KM Fabrics, Inc. donated Old Brandon Mill Ball Field, the "field on which Joe learned to play the game he truly loved,"[25] to the Greenville County Recreation District. On October 27, 1994, the recreation district held a groundbreaking ceremony in the field where Joe first hit his "Saturday Specials"; on Saturday, March 30, 1996, this park was renamed the "Shoeless Joe Jackson Memorial Park," in honor of the boy who brought glory and excitement to their mill team games. In spite of bad weather, more than a thousand people attended the dedication ceremony, including seven former major league players.

In 1996, the South Carolina Legislature passed legislation to rename a portion of United States Highway 123 in Greenville County to "Shoeless Joe Jackson Memorial Highway"; this section is near Brandon Mill and Shoeless Joe Jackson Memorial Park. In February 1998, the legislature also asked the commissioner of baseball to reinstate Jackson into professional baseball status (Bill 993). Jackson, understandably enough, also receives a significant amount of support from residents of Greenville; in 1998, Mayor Knox White declared July to be "Shoeless Joe Jackson Month."[26]

While ardent fans continue to honor him and push for reinstatement, baseball collectors continue to value his former possessions. On November 3, 1998, Christie's auction house sold several items from Jackson's estate, including a set of letters exchanged among Jackson, Ban Johnson, and Landis that discussed the player's desire for reinstatement. Paired with two letters from Landis refusing the request, this collection sold for $19,550. Another group of letters sold for $9,775, and a collection of Jackson's photographs netted $7,475. One single letter referencing Jackson's lawsuit against Comiskey brought in $11,500, while

Jackson's endorsed mortgage note sold for $20,700. His signed driver's license netted another $14,950.[27]

On September 2, 1999, the Hall of Fame opened the Barry Halper Gallery, which was named after one of baseball's most prolific memorabilia collectors. Ironically, even though Shoeless Joe Jackson is banned from entering the Hall of Fame, the initial exhibit, which remained on display through summer 2001, contained one of Jackson's gloves, a pocket watch, his entire 1919 White Sox uniform, and Black Betsy.

Also in 1999, fans voted Jackson into major league baseball's "All Century Team"; he received the twelfth most votes. In 2000, the Chicago White Sox announced their twenty-seven-player "Team of the Century"; Jackson received the second highest number of votes and was honored at Comiskey Park for this accomplishment on September 30.[28] The National American Legion Baseball Tournament, held in Dyersville, Iowa, was renamed "The Shoeless Joe Jackson National Baseball Tournament," and Jackson supporters used this sporting event to rally further support for his cause.

The United States Congress raised the pressure for reinstatement in November 1999 with a bill sponsored by Tom Harkin, Fritz Hollings, and Strom Thurmond in the Senate and Jim DeMint in the House of Representatives. These bipartisan resolutions asked major league baseball to remove Jackson from the ineligible list, again to clear a path for Hall of Fame induction. Jackson's "athletic abilities on the diamond," Harkin wrote, "were unmatched, and the dignity he brought to the game was vital to baseball's growing popularity."[29] The famous South Carolinian Dixiecrat Thurmond wrote, "I have been contacted by many constituents who believe that it is a profound injustice to continue punishment of an innocent man."[30]

Two years later, Jackson's famous bat, Black Betsy, reemerged in the news when Jackson's cousin, Lester Erwin, offered the famous stick for sale. After the bat was analyzed by a leading sport authentication service, it was displayed in a variety of public venues. Dubbed the "Holy Grail of Baseball"[31] by memorabilia collectors, this bat appeared on an eBay auction in August 2001, and its sale price—$577,610—was almost double the price of any bat ever sold.[32] This is an extraordinary sum for a piece of hickory wood gifted to an illiterate mill town boy in Greenville, South Carolina.

In all, nearly fifty items of Jackson's have been sold on eBay, including another bat that bore his signature. Other items included trading cards, baseball photos of Jackson, letters of support from senators, a 1917 World Series program, his war bond folder, and several baseball-related newspaper clippings from the 1910s. Quirkier objects included a 1914 framed tobacco blanket, a Comiskey Park stadium seat, and a Jackson comic book.[33]

As Jackson items were selling on the Web, the slugger's Internet presence continued to grow, with the following Web sites being among the best and most informative:

- "Shoeless Joe Jackson's Virtual Hall of Fame," created and maintained by Mike Nola, www.blackbetsy.com; this site has a vast amount of Jackson resources, from photos to the 1949 Jackson interview, from historical data to regular updates about potential reinstatement. Nola is unabashedly pro-Jackson; he is also easily accessible by email.
- "Notes from the Shadow of Cooperstown," by Gene Carney, http://www.baseball1.com/carney; this writer e-publishes a regular baseball column, and a significant number of them focus on the Black Sox Scandal. Carney delights in deep analyses of source documents, and his columns are thought provoking. By reading the columns in chronological order, one can glimpse the trial-and-error processes of a dedicated researcher.
- The Chicago Historical Society, http://www.chicagohs.org/history/black sox.html, provides information about the scandal and includes photos and other links.
- The official Web site of "Shoeless" Joe Jackson, http://www.shoelessjoejack son.com, provides information about the slugger, as well as describing the application procedure to use Jackson's image or name in a business venture.
- Greenville South, http://www.greenvillesouth.com/joe1.html; if you intend to visit Greenville, South Carolina to see sites associated with Jackson, consult this Web site before traveling.

This last Web site also details the creation of the Douglas Young statue of Jackson; in 2002, Greenville residents hosted its unveiling, the statue now moved outside to its permanent location, the "Shoeless Joe Jackson Plaza." House Representatives Jim DeMint and Lindsey Graham participated in the ceremonies. Featured speaker Tommy Lasorda, the manager who led the Dodgers to two World Series championships and who managed the 2000 United States Olympic team to its first gold medal in baseball, received the Shoeless Joe Jackson Society Award for "outstanding contributions to the game, humanity and the American way of life."[34] Lasorda was the first person to receive this award since Ted Williams in 1998.

On July 28, 2002, Jackson was inducted into the Shrine of the Eternals in Los Angeles. The Shrine of the Eternals, according to its mission statement, considers induction factors beyond quality of play, including "uniqueness of character and personality . . . as an arena for the human imagination."[35]

Although it is hard to say with certainty what caused this remarkable resurgence of interest in and support for Jackson, it is reasonable to assume that, while most early-twentieth-century Americans must have heard of Shoeless Joe Jackson during the era of the Black Sox Scandal, those of a later generation most likely learned about him in 1963, when Eliot Asinof published his now well-known book, *Eight Men Out: The Black Sox and the 1919 World Series*. Often described as the "groundbreaking" or "definitive" book about the Black Sox Scandal, Asinof wrote his story in a novel-like fashion. He attempted to interview many involved parties, including Abe Attell, Happy Felsch, Swede Risberg, and Ray Schalk. The first two cooperated; the second two didn't. Subsequent authors have quoted and relied heavily upon Asinof's work; he did not include any endnotes or citations. For more information about the creation of this book, see *Bleeding Between the Lines*, also by Asinof, and *1919: America's Loss of Innocence*, another Asinof book that dedicates over fifty pages to the Black Sox events. Shortly after the publication of *Eight Men Out*, in 1966, Victor Luhrs countered with *The Great Baseball Mystery: The 1919 World Series*, where he argued that, for the most part, the White Sox played to win.[36]

In 1988, a movie version of *Eight Men Out* reached theaters, furthering the general public's knowledge of Jackson. But perhaps the most significant impetus to the slugger's revitalization occurred in 1989 when Hollywood released the movie, *Field of Dreams*, starring Kevin Costner and featuring Ray Liotta as Jackson.

Producers based the movie on W. P. Kinsella's award-winning novel, *Shoeless Joe*, published in 1982; this novel is actually an expanded version of one of Kinsella's short stories published in the 1980 collection entitled *Shoeless Joe Jackson Comes to Iowa*. In the movie, a struggling Iowa corn farmer named Ray Kinsella hears a mysterious voice whispering to him, "If you build it, he will come." Although the murmurs initially confuse him, Ray remains open-minded and eventually realizes that, even though his farm is laden with debt, he needs to convert part of his valuable acreage into a baseball diamond because an underlying reason exists for this transformation.

The fictional Kinsella's act of faith is rewarded when a ghostly Shoeless Joe Jackson, the psychologically wounded hero of Ray's deceased father, shows up to hit a few balls. Although the plot and theme of the book—and movie—are far more complex and have more to do with Ray's relationship with his father than with baseball, the storyline suggests that this ballfield exists for the purpose of salvation. "It is a place where dreams die and subsequent redemption occurs."[37] For those of us who have made questionable choices in life, and for those of us whose days didn't progress as planned, the "field of dreams" offers up a second chance for healing, for deliverance, and for an act of clean conscience. Who better, then, to symbolize the regrets of life and its unfulfilled longings than Shoeless Joe Jackson?[38]

Without a doubt, pundits, scholars, and baseball fans will continue to argue Jackson's now-legendary life. They will challenge and predict, analyze and wish, debate and try to regulate. The uncertainty over what Jackson thought and did—and the intense curiosity over his motivations—fuels the ongoing interest in his life; perhaps if Jackson had actually had the opportunity to appear on "Toast of the Town," he might have effectively cleared his name and would have been quietly forgotten along with the other seven men who were punished with him. It is the eternal wondering, it seems, about what really happened, what Jackson did or didn't do, what he knew or didn't know, that adds the intrigue to the usually heated—and often wistful—arguments about Jackson's life and memory.

Christopher H. Evans and William R. Herzog II offer another spin on this notion in *The Faith of Fifty Million: Baseball, Religion, and American Culture*, as they analyze the tendency of Americans to label baseball players as either saints or sinners. Reality isn't always that clear, and Jackson was a living, breathing example of the misty lines fogging the two concepts. "No one illustrates this ambiguity better than Shoeless Joe Jackson," the authors write, "who was, during his lifetime, vilified by the baseball establishment for his presumed role in the Black Sox scandal but has, in more recent times, been exonerated and seen as a scapegoat sacrificed to protect the interests of the owners and gamblers. Joe Jackson's strange journey stands as a reminder that, in baseball as in every other area of life, there is often a 'cover story' and a 'real story' underneath it."[39]

Their analysis is intriguing, and segues nicely into the final voice of closure, which should be granted to Jackson himself, a man who was born to a family strapped of cash, who worked 12-hour days in the grimy and often dangerous cotton mills of South Carolina, and whose pure love of baseball transformed his life and determined its direction.

Although much of what Jackson said about his role in the Black Sox Scandal concealed rather than revealed, and though whatever Jackson did or did not do during the 1919 World Series remains a mystery, the fact remains that the former millhand was caught up in a tangled scheme of epic proportions, while men of wealth and power stood at cross purposes, using and then discarding others, ruthlessly and selfishly. There is one statement, though, that cannot be disputed; it was made by Jackson in 1949, while he was ending reminiscences about his tumultuous years of baseball with Furman Bisher.

"Well," Jackson concluded, "that's my story. I repeat what I said when I started out—that I have no axe to grind, that I'm not asking anybody for anything. It's all water over the dam as far as I am concerned. I can say that my conscience is clear and that I'll stand on my record in that World Series. I'm not what you call a good Christian, but I believe in the Good Book, particularly where it says, 'what you sow, so shall you reap.' I have asked the Lord for guidance before, and I am sure He gave it to me. I'm willing to let the Lord be my judge."[40]

Somehow, on balance, it seems to be a certainty that a celestial judge did not hesitate to forgive Joe Jackson whatever transgressions fell to his life, and that, regardless of the storms that rage around his name now, so long after all took place, the man in question can finally rest in peace.

Requiescat in pace, Shoeless Joe Jackson. Rest in peace.

NOTES

1. This is a line from "Ballad of Shoeless Joe," written by Billy Goerdt. Used with permission.

2. See http://www.greenvillesouth.com/joe1.html.

3. See http://www.baseballhalloffame.org/about/mission.htm.

4. See http://www.baseballhalloffame.org/hofers_and_honorees/rules.htm.

5. Fleitz, *Shoeless*, 265.

6. He received two more votes in 1946. See http://www.baseballhalloffame.org/history/hof_voting/alpha/J.htm.

7. This has been nicknamed the "Pete Rose Rule" because it was instituted the year before Rose would have been eligible for induction. Rose was accused of gambling on sports and banned from professional baseball; he denied the allegations for fourteen years, including in writing in his 1989 biography, *Pete Rose: My Story* (with Roger Kahn, New York: Macmillan Publishing Company). He confessed, however, in his 2004 biography *My Prison Without Bars*, written with Rick Hill (Emmaus, PA: Rodale). A significant irony should be noted. Because of the Black Sox Scandal, Kenesaw Landis Mountain banned players from betting on baseball (Fleitz, *Shoeless*, 257), which led to Pete Rose's banishment from professional baseball. Rule 3-e of the National Hall of Fame and Museum, which prohibits banned players—including Joe Jackson—from being eligible for induction, was instituted because of the allegations against Pete Rose. The two men, who played baseball many decades apart, have been intricately tied together because of these connections.

8. Introduction to Gropman's *Say It Ain't So, Joe!*, xx.

9. Lawrence Ritter and Donald Honig, *The 100 Greatest Players of All Time* (New York: Crown Publishers, 1986), 204.

10. Introduction to Asinof's *Eight Men Out*, xvii.

11. See note 7.

12. Frank Fitzpatrick, "Baseball's Ted Williams, Last to Hit .400, Dies at 83," *Philadelphia Inquirer*, July 5, 2002. See http://www.thedesertsun.com/news/stories/obituaries/1025916936.shtml.

13. Dave Kindred, "Ted Williams Could Spin a Tale with the Same Skill that He

Could Hit a Fastball." *Sporting News* online archive, 2002. See http://www.sportingnews.com/archives/williams/kindred.html.

14. Bill Porter, "'Splendid Splinter' Goes to Bat for Shoeless Joe," *New Bedford Standard-Times*, 1998.

15. Gropman, *Say It Ain't So, Joe!*, 315–372.

16. Quoted directly from the Hall of Fame Web site: "In order for Jackson to be eligible for the Hall of Fame, the following criteria must be met: Since he is deceased, a party acting on behalf of Jackson's estate must apply to the Office of the Commissioner for reinstatement to Major League Baseball; should Jackson's estate apply for reinstatement and his eligibility is regained, he would then be a viable candidate for consideration by the Baseball Hall of Fame Committee on Baseball Veterans. Once Jackson's name is on the ballot for the Committee on Baseball Veterans, Jackson would have to receive votes on at least seventy-five percent (75%) of the ballots to be elected to membership in the National Baseball Hall of Fame." For more information, see http://www.baseballhalloffame.org/hofers_and_honorees/rules.htm and http://www.baseballhalloffame.org/hofers_and_honorees/veterans/index.htm.

17. See http://www.baseballhalloffame.org/hofers_and_honorees/veterans/rules.htm.

18. Rob Neyer, "Say It Ain't So . . . For Joe and the Hall." ESPN.com, August 2, 2003. See http://espn.go.com/classic/s/2001/0730/1232950.html.

19. Fleitz, *Shoeless*, 284.

20. See http://www.baseball1.com/carney/index.php?storyid=180; James's book was published by Macmillan Publishing Co. in 1994.

21. Mike Nola regularly updates Jackson's awards at his Web site: http://www.blackbetsy.com.

22. Jonathan Dube, "Shoeless Joe's Will, Valuable Name on It Not for Sale, Court Says," *Charlotte Observer*, September 3, 1997. See http://www.jondube.com/resume/charlotte/shoeless.html; Katie Jackson's will can be found in Gropman's book, *Say It Ain't So, Joe!*, 312–314.

23. Ibid.

24. Gropman, *Say It Ain't So, Joe!*, 275.

25. This text is part of South Carolina legislation to rename Highway 123 "Shoeless Joe Jackson Memorial Highway."

26. Jackson was born on July 16 and was married on July 19.

27. See http://www.blackbetsy.com/joenews98.htm.

28. Also chosen were Buck Weaver, Eddie Cicotte, Eddie Collins, Red Faber, and Ray Schalk. See http://www.blackbetsy.com for the complete listing.

29. Dave Kindred, "A Shoeless, Clueless Schmo," *Sporting News*, April 12, 1999. Ironically, this quote is found in an article opposing Jackson's reinstatement.

30. See http://www.blackbetsy.com/stromlet.htm.

31. See http://www.reallegends.com/auctions/joe_history/.

32. Collectors Universe, "Joe Jackson's *Black Betsy* Bat Smashes Price Record with $577,610 Bid," August 15, 2001; see http://www.collectors.com/articles/article_view.chtml?artid=3124.

33. See http://www.reallegends.com/auctions/joe_history/page6.html.

34. See http://www.blackbetsy.com.

35. See http://www.baseballreliquary.org/shrine.htm.

36. Another version of this point of view was reintroduced in 2001 when William A. Cook, an openly avid fan of the Cincinnati Reds, presents a book-length argument that the 1919 Reds were, in fact, a stronger team than the White Sox of that year, and that they would have won the World Series with or without a fix. In *The 1919 World Series*, he provides play-by-play analyses that differ from what is usually presented and he is adamant about his beliefs.

37. Evans and Herzog, *The Faith of Fifty Million*, 46.

38. There are a significant amount of other Jackson-related books and movies, both fiction and nonfiction. For more information, see the Bibliography in this volume.

39. Evans and Herzog, *The Faith of Fifty Million*, 8.

40. Bisher, Furman, "This Is the Truth, The Story of the 1919 World Series as Told by Shoeless Joe Jackson," 12–14, 83, 84.

APPENDIX: JOE JACKSON'S CAREER AND WORLD SERIES STATISTICS

CAREER STATISTICS

Year	Club	League	G	AB	R	H	2B	3B	HR	RBI	BA	PO	A	E	FA
1908	Phil. Athletics	AL	5	23	0	3	0	0	0	3	.130	6	1	1	.875
1909	Phil. Athletics	AL	5	17	3	3	0	0	0	3	.176	10	0	2	.833
1910	Cleve. Naps	AL	20	75	15	29	2	5	1	11	.387	40	2	1	.977
1911	Cleve. Naps	AL	147	571	126	233	45	19	7	83	.408	242	32	12	.958
1912	Cleve. Naps	AL	154	572	121	226	44	26	3	90	.395	273	30	16	.950
1913	Cleve. Naps	AL	148	528	109	197	39	17	7	71	.373	211	28	18	.930
1914	Cleve. Naps	AL	122	453	61	153	22	13	3	53	.338	195	13	7	.967
1915	Cleve. Indians	AL	83	303	42	99	16	9	3	45	.327	352	21	10	.961
	Chicago W.S.	AL	45	158	21	43	4	5	2	36	.272	84	6	5	.947
	1915 Totals		128	461	63	142	20	14	5	81	.308	436	27	15	.953
1916	Chicago W.S.	AL	155	592	91	202	40	21	3	78	.341	290	17	8	.975
1917	Chicago W.S.	AL	146	538	91	162	20	17	5	75	.301	341	18	6	.984
1918	Chicago W.S.	AL	17	65	9	23	2	2	1	20	.354	36	1	0	1.000
1919	Chicago W.S.	AL	139	516	79	181	31	14	7	96	.351	252	15	9	.967
1920	Chicago W.S.	AL	146	570	105	218	42	20	12	121	.382	314	14	12	.965
Major League Totals (13 seasons)			1332	4981	873	1772	307	168	54	785	.356	2646	198	107	.964

WORLD SERIES RECORD

Year	Club	G	AB	R	H	2B	3B	HR	RBI	BA
1917	Chicago W.S.	6	23	4	7	0	0	0	2	.304
1919	Chicago W.S.	8	32	5	12	3	0	1	6	.375

A = assists; AB = at-bats; BA = batting average; E = errors; FA = fielding average; G = games; H = hits; HR = home runs; PO = put-outs; R = runs; RBI = runs batted in; 2B = doubles; 3B-triples

SELECTED BIBLIOGRAPHY

BIOGRAPHIES OF JOE JACKSON

Fleitz, David L. *Shoeless: The Life and Times of Joe Jackson*. Jefferson, NC: McFarland and Company, 2001.

Frommer, Harvey. *Shoeless Joe and Ragtime Baseball*. Lanham, MD: Taylor Trade Publishing, 1992.

Gropman, Donald. *Say It Ain't So, Joe! The True Story of Shoeless Joe Jackson*. New York: Citadel Press, Kensington Publishing Corp., 2001.

Kavanagh, Jack. *Shoeless Joe Jackson*. New York: Chelsea Publishing House, 1995. A children's biography intended for ages 9–12.

Thompson, Joe. *Growing Up With Shoeless Joe: The Greatest Natural Player in Baseball History*. Laurel Fork, VA: JTI Publishing, 1998.

NONFICTION BOOKS ON THE BLACK SOX SCANDAL

Many of these volumes on the 1919 World Series contain biographical material on Jackson.

Asinof, Eliot. *Eight Men Out: The Black Sox and the 1919 World Series*. New York: Henry Holt and Company, 1963.

Cook, William A. *1919 World Series: What Really Happened?* Jefferson, NC: McFarland and Company, 2001.

Ginsburg, Daniel E. *The Fix Is In: A History of Baseball Gambling and Game Fixing Scandals*. Jefferson, NC: McFarland and Company, 1995.

Luhrs, Victor. *The Great Baseball Mystery: The 1919 World Series.* South Brunswick, NJ: A. S. Barnes and Co., 1966.
Nathan, Daniel A. *Saying It's So: A Cultural History of the Black Sox Scandal.* Urbana and Chicago: University of Illinois Press, 2003.
Veeck, Bill, with Ed Linn. *The Hustler's Handbook.* New York: Simon and Schuster, 1965.

OTHER NONFICTION BOOKS OF INTEREST

Bell, John. *Shoeless Summer: The Summer of 1923 When Shoeless Joe Jackson Played Baseball in Americus, Georgia.* Carollton, GA: Vabella Publishing, 2001.
Perry, Thomas K. *Textile League Baseball: South Carolina's Mill Teams, 1880–1955.* Jefferson, NC: McFarland and Company, 1993.
Pietrusza, David. *Judge and Jury: The Life and Times of Judge Kenesaw Mountain Landis.* South Bend, IN: Diamond Communications, 1998.

NOVELS ON THE BLACK SOX SCANDAL

Boyd, Brendon. *Blue Ruin: A Novel of the 1919 World Series.* New York: W.W. Norton and Company, 1991.
Kinsella, W. P. *Shoeless Joe.* New York: Houghton Mifflin Company, 1982.
Stein, Harry. *Hoopla.* New York: Knopf, 1983.

WEB SITES

Carney, Gene. "Notes From the Shadow of Cooperstown." Web site: http://www.baseball1.com/carney.
The Chicago Historical Society. Web site: http://www.chicagohs.org/history/blacksox.html.
Nola, Mike. "Shoeless Jackson's Virtual Hall of Fame." Web site: http://www.blackbetsy.com.
"Shoeless Joe Jackson Memorial Ball Park." GreenvilleSouth.com Web site: http://www.greenvillesouth.com/joe1.html.
"'Shoeless'" Joe Jackson: The Official Web Site." http://www.shoelessjoejackson.com.

MAGAZINE ARTICLES

Bisher, Furman. "This Is the Truth, The Story of the 1919 World Series as Told by Shoeless Joe Jackson." *Sport*, October 1949, 12–14, 83, 84. Full text is available online at www.blackbetsy.com.

Lardner, John, "Remember the Black Sox." *Saturday Evening Post*, April 30, 1938, 14–15, 85. Text will be made available online at www.blackbetsy.com.

Latimer, Carter "Scoop." "Joe Jackson, Contented Carolinian at 54, Forgets Bitter Dose in His Cup and Glories in His 12 Hits in '19 Series." *Sporting News*, September 24, 1942, 1, 8. Text will be made available online at www.blackbetsy.com.

MOVIES

Eight Men Out (1988). Directed by John Sayles, this PG film was released by Orion Pictures. D. B. Sweeney plays the role of Joe Jackson, Charlie Sheen is "Happy" Felsch, and Studs Terkel portrays Hugh Fullerton. A DVD is available.

Field of Dreams (1989). Directed by Phil Alden Robison, this PG film was released by Universal Studios. The movie stars Kevin Costner as Ray Kinsella and Ray Liotta as Joe Jackson, while James Earl Jones and Burt Lancaster play a reclusive novelist and thwarted baseball player, respectively. The movie was an Academy Award nominee for "Best Picture of the Year," and a DVD was released in 2003 that contains behind-the-scenes footage and interviews with many involved with the project.

INDEX

legal representation of, 136; origin of nickname, 67, 99; update of, 147

Black Sox Scandal: baseball and gambling, 91; commissioner selection and grand jury, 133–135; Jackson's participation in, 114; later analyses of, 165–166; lessened Comiskey's estate, 146, 155; prevented Jackson's induction, 158; public outcry about, 125

Blue darter, 7, 101, 155

Blues, Cleveland, 29

Boston: American League formation, 24; 75, White Sox trashing hotel in, 80–81. *See also* Red Sox, Boston

Brandon Mill: compared and contrasted to Cleveland, 28; dedicate ball field and highway in, 162; settling in town, mill life and baseball, 1, 3–8; tribute in, 155

Broncos, Cleveland, 29

Brotherhood of Professional Base Ball Players, 47

Burns, "Sleepy" Bill: Cicotte's grand jury testimony about, 126; financing and double crosses, 93–99, 101–103, 114; grand jury, 135–136; involvement in fix, 86–87

Cannon, Raymond, filed lawsuit against Comiskey, 140–142

Chalmers: automobile company prize, 32; Chalmers Most Valuable Player Award, 35

Chase, Hal, baseball and gambling, 88

Chicago: American League formation, 24; celebrated 1917 World Series win, 73; Comiskey to pay Jackson's expenses to, for investigation, 121; criticism of Jackson's wartime decision, 75; gambler Nat Evan's arrival to, 98; Jackson ordered to return to, for grand jury investigation, 134; Jackson's trade to, and Opening Day in, 59–61; 1919

World Series played in, 103. *See also under* White Sox, Chicago

Chicago Colts, game-fixing accusations, 90

Chicago Daily News, published "Say It Ain't So, Joe!" anecdote, 127

Chicago Herald and Examiner, published rumors of fix, 125

Chicago Record-Herald, Standard Oil fine, 56

Chicago Times, published poem about Comiskey, 146

Chicago Tribune: criticizing Jackson's wartime decision, 75, 82; published letter demanding investigation, 125

Christie's auction, 162

Cicotte, Eddie: contract negotiations, 121, 123–124; Game 4, 108–109; game 7 and post-series analyses, 111–115, 119; landlady's testimony, 129n27; missing confession, 135; 1917 season and World Series play, 70–72; persuaded to fix games, 81–82, 84, 86–87, 93; post–Black Sox, 139, 146; scandal revealed and grand jury testimony, 126–127, 131; shine ball controversy, 61–63; specifics of fix and Game 1, 97–101; trial, 137

Civil War, 1–3, 18, 56, 155

Class D Carolina Association, 9

Clayton Anti-Trust Act, 1914, 49

Cleveland: demographics, and baseball history, 27–31; first Sunday game in, 35; formation of American league, and Jackson's trade to, 23–24. *See also* Indians, Cleveland; Naps, Cleveland

Cleveland Baseball Hall of Fame, 152

Cleveland Plain Dealer, 27, 39, 41–43, 49, 51–52, 57–59, 109

Cobb, Ty: batting races, friendship and comparisons with Jackson, 17–18, 21, 31–36, 42–45; charges made, 153n3, 154n21, 154n22; Federal League, 49;

About the Author

KELLY BOYER SAGERT is a freelance writer who has published biographical material with Gale, Scribner, Oxford, and Indiana University Press, focusing on athletes and historical figures. She is the author of *Bout Boomerangs: America's Silent Sport*, which has been published in twenty-one different countries.